The Complete Dialectical Behavior Therapy Workbook:

(3-Books-In-1)

Proven DBT Skills For Mental Wellness, Trauma Recovery & Lasting Transformation

Conquer BPD, PTSD & Emotional Eating for Men & Women

By Barrett Huang

https://barretthuang.com/

© Copyright 2024 by Barrett Huang. All rights reserved.

This book contains information that is as accurate and reliable as possible. Regardless, purchasing this book constitutes an agreement that both the publisher and the author are in no way experts on the topics discussed and that any comments or suggestions made herein are solely for educational purposes. The information provided is not a substitute for professional medical advice, diagnosis, or treatment. Always consult a professional before taking any action advised herein.

This declaration is deemed fair and valid by both the American Bar Association and the Committee of Publishers Association and is legally binding throughout the United States.

Furthermore, the transmission, duplication, or reproduction of any of the following work, including specific information, will be considered illegal, whether done electronically or in print. This extends to creating a secondary or tertiary copy of the work or a recorded copy and is only allowed with express written consent from the publisher. All additional rights reserved.

The information in the following pages is broadly considered a truthful and accurate account of facts. Any inattention, use, or misuse of the information in question by the reader will render any resulting actions solely under their purview. There are no scenarios in which the publisher or author of this work can be deemed liable for any hardship or damages that may occur after undertaking the information described herein.

Additionally, the information in the following pages is intended only for informational purposes. It should thus be thought of as universal. It is presented without assurance regarding its prolonged validity or interim quality as befitting its nature. Trademarks mentioned are done without written consent and should not be considered an endorsement from the trademark holder.

Contents

FREE Guide: Mastering DBT Essentials 11
Introduction 15
    Who Should Read This Book 21
    Goals of This Book 22
    How to Use This Book 22
    Content Warning 22
    Safety 22
    About Me 24
    You Can Feel Better. You Can Be Happy. 24
Chapter 1: What is Borderline Personality Disorder? 25
    What Causes BPD? 26
    What are the Symptoms of BPD? 27
    What are the Different Subtypes of BPD? 29
    Borderline Personality Disorder vs Bipolar Disorder 31
    BPD Recommended Treatments 33
        Cognitive Behavioral Therapy (CBT) 33
        34
        Schema-Focused Therapy 34
        Mentalization-based Therapy (MBT) 35
        Dialectical Behavior Therapy (DBT) 35
Chapter 2: Living with Borderline Personality Disorder 37
    BPD and Your Brain 38
        What is the Amygdala? 39
        What is the Anterior Cingulate Cortex? 39
        What is the Prefrontal Cortex? 39
    BPD Triggers 40
Chapter 3: What is Dialectical Behavioral Therapy? 42
    A Brief History of DBT 42
    DBT Core Concepts: Acceptance and Change 43

    Radical Acceptance 45

    Desire to Change 47

  DBT Core Skills 55

    Mindfulness 55

    Distress Tolerance 64

    Emotion Regulation 71

    Interpersonal Effectiveness 82

Chapter 4: Dialectical Behavior Therapy for Borderline Personality Disorder (DBT for BPD) 88

  Worksheet: Radical Acceptance of Triggers 90

  Worksheet: Turning the Mind to Cope 91

  Worksheet: Desire to Change 92

  Mindfulness 93

    Worksheet: One-Mindfully 94

    Worksheet: Mindfulness Using Your Five Senses 96

    Worksheet: Mindful Body Scan (Self-Observation) 98

    Worksheet: 4-7-8 Breathing 99

  Distress Tolerance Skills for BPD 100

    Worksheet: Grounding Activities 101

    Worksheet: TIPP 102

    Worksheet: ACCEPTS 104

    Worksheet: IMPROVE 108

    Worksheet: PROs and CONs 112

  Emotion Regulation Skills for BPD 114

  Interpersonal Effectiveness Skills for BPD 130

  Self-Harm 138

    The Vicious Cycle of Self-harm 138

    Top 6 Tips to Stop Yourself from Engaging in Self-Harm 140

Conclusion 142

Appendix A – BPD Self-Assessment 143

  McLean Screening Instrument for BPD 143

  How to Convey Your BPD to Others 145

How to Deal with Stigma	148
Appendix B – Trigger Journal	150
Review Request	152
Further Reading	153
FREE Guide: Mastering DBT Essentials	155
Introduction	158
Who Should Read This Book	162
Goals of This Book	162
How to Use This Book	163
Content Warning	163
Safety	163
About Me	165
You Can Feel Better	165
Chapter 1: What is PTSD?	166
What Causes PTSD?	168
What are the Symptoms of PTSD?	173
What are the Different Types of PTSD?	176
PTSD Treatments	177
Cognitive Behavioral Therapy (CBT)	177
Prolonged Exposure Therapy (PET)	178
Eye Movement Desensitization and Reprocessing Therapy (EMDR)	178
Dialectical Behavior Therapy (DBT)	179
Chapter 2: Living with PTSD	181
How PTSD Affects Your Brain	182
Amygdala – Your Alarm System	182
Hippocampus – Your Memory Center	183
Prefrontal Cortex – Your Learning Center	183
How PTSD Affects Your Life	184
Chapter 3: What is Dialectical Behavior Therapy?	188
DBT History	188
DBT Concepts: Radical Acceptance and Desire to Change	190
DBT Worksheets in this Book	193

  DBT Core Skills 198

    Mindfulness 198

    Distress Tolerance 207

    Emotion Regulation 211

    Interpersonal Effectiveness 228

Chapter 4: DBT for PTSD 234

  Why DBT for PTSD? 234

    Avoidance and Radical Acceptance 235

    Desire to Change 239

    Mindfulness Skills for PTSD 240

    Distress Tolerance Skills for PTSD 248

    Emotion Regulation Skills for PTSD 262

    Interpersonal Effectiveness Skills for PTSD 272

Chapter 5: Continuing the Road to Coping and Healing 285

Chapter 6: Conclusion 290

Appendix A – Trauma Resiliency 291

Appendix B – PTSD Self-Evaluation 293

Appendix C – Establishing a Sleep Routine 297

  Top 3 Tips to Set a Sleep Routine 298

Review Request 303

Further Reading 304

FREE Guide: Mastering DBT Essentials 306

Introduction 311

  Who Should Read This Book 315

  Goals of This Book 315

  Be Patient and Kind to Yourself 315

Chapter 1: Understanding Emotional Eating 316

  What is Emotional Eating? 316

  Emotional Eating vs. Stress Eating vs. Binge Eating 317

  Emotional Hunger vs. Physical Hunger 318

  It's NOT About Food 319

  It's NOT All About Willpower 321

    Emotional Eating: Causes and Triggers 322

    Impact of Emotional Eating on Your Mental and Physical Health 324

        Mental Health 324

        Physical Health 325

Chapter 2: Dialectical Behavior Therapy 101 328

    What is DBT? 328

    How DBT Can Be Used to Treat Emotional Eating 328

    DBT Primary Concepts: Acceptance and Change 329

        Radical Acceptance 329

        Worksheet: Radical Acceptance 331

        Desire to Change 332

        Worksheet: Desire to Change 333

        Worksheet: Radical Acceptance + Desire to Change 334

    DBT Primary Skills: Mindfulness, Distress Tolerance, Emotion Regulation, Interpersonal Effectiveness 335

Chapter 3: Mindfulness Skills for Emotional Eating 337

    Introduction to Mindfulness 337

        Worksheet: Belly Breathing 338

        Worksheet: Take 5 339

        Worksheet: 4-7-8 Breathing 340

    Mindful Eating 341

        Principles of Mindful Eating 341

        Benefits of Mindful Eating 343

        Worksheet: Mindful Eating 345

        Worksheet: TASTE 348

        Worksheet: Wise Mind 349

Chapter 4: Distress Tolerance Skills for Emotional Eating 352

    Introduction to Distress Tolerance 352

    Stress and Emotional Eating 352

    Stress vs. Distress 352

    Importance of Distress Tolerance Skills for Emotional Eating 353

        Worksheet: Self-Soothe Using Your Five Senses 355

    Worksheet: The Grounding Grid 357

    Worksheet: STOP 359

    Worksheet: TIPP 362

Chapter 5: Emotion-Regulating Skills for Emotional Eating 364

  Introduction to Emotion Regulation 364

  Practicing Self-Compassion, Self-Forgiveness, and Self-Validation 365

    Worksheet: Self-Compassion 367

    Worksheet: Self-Forgiveness 369

    Worksheet: Self-Validation 371

  Identifying the Emotions That Trigger Your Emotional Eating 373

    Worksheet: Identifying Your Emotional Triggers 374

    Worksheet: The Happiness Habit 378

    Worksheet: Opposite Action 381

    Worksheet: PLEASE 386

Chapter 6: Interpersonal Effectiveness Skills for Emotional Eating 388

  Introduction to Interpersonal Effectiveness 388

  Importance of Healthy Relationships in Recovering from Emotional Eating 389

    Worksheet: Communicating Boundaries 391

    Worksheet: DEARMAN 394

    Worksheet: GIVE 397

    Worksheet: FAST 399

Chapter 7: Developing Healthy Habits 402

  Top 10 Healthy Food and Eating Habits 402

  Quick Guide to Meal Planning and Prepping 405

    What is Meal Planning? 406

    What is Meal Prepping? 407

  Incorporate Physical Activity into Your Routine 408

  Manage Daily Stress through Healthy Coping Mechanisms 410

Chapter 8: Building a Support System 413

  Cultivate a Supportive Inner Voice (Self) 413

    Self-Sabotage – What You May Be THINKING 413

    Self-Sabotage – What You May Be DOING 414

- Build Your Support Circle (Others) 415
- Chapter 9: Dealing with Setbacks and Relapses 418
  - How to Prevent Setbacks 418
  - How to Recover from a Setback 421
- Chapter 10: Maintaining Long-Term Success 424
  - Top 10 Strategies for Maintaining Healthy Eating Habits 424
  - Celebrate Progress and Achievements with Non-Food Related Rewards 426
  - Reflection and Gratitude Practice 428
    - Worksheet: Reflection and Gratitude 429
- Conclusion 432
- Appendix 434
  - Emotional Eating Self-Assessment Quiz 434
  - The Clean Your Plate Syndrome 438
    - Top 10 Tips to Stop Cleaning Your Plate 438
  - How to Establish a Sleep Routine 440
  - How to Support an Emotional Eater 442
- Review Request 445
- Further Reading 446
- About the Author 447
- Index 448
- References 452

DBT Workbook For BPD

Powerful Dialectical Behavior Therapy Strategies for Treating Borderline Personality Disorder in Men & Women

Manage BPD with a Science-Backed Action Plan for Emotional Wellbeing

By Barrett Huang
https://barretthuang.com/

FREE Guide: Mastering DBT Essentials

FREE DOWNLOAD ALERT!

Master Dialectical Behavior Therapy Skills in 5 Simple Steps with my Free DBT Quick Guide. Access the 'Mastering DBT Essentials' quick guide at:

https://barretthuang.com/dbt-quick-guide/

Or scan the code below:

Contents

FREE Guide: Mastering DBT Essentials 11
Introduction 15
    Who Should Read This Book 21
    Goals of This Book 22
    How to Use This Book 22
    Content Warning 22
    Safety 22
    About Me 24
    You Can Feel Better. You Can Be Happy. 24

Chapter 1: What is Borderline Personality Disorder? 25
    What Causes BPD? 26
    What are the Symptoms of BPD? 27
    What are the Different Subtypes of BPD? 29
    Borderline Personality Disorder vs Bipolar Disorder 31
    BPD Recommended Treatments 33
        Cognitive Behavioral Therapy (CBT) 33
        34
        Schema-Focused Therapy 34
        Mentalization-based Therapy (MBT) 35
        Dialectical Behavior Therapy (DBT) 35

Chapter 2: Living with Borderline Personality Disorder 37
    BPD and Your Brain 38
        What is the Amygdala? 39
        What is the Anterior Cingulate Cortex? 39
        What is the Prefrontal Cortex? 39
    BPD Triggers 40

Chapter 3: What is Dialectical Behavioral Therapy? 42
    A Brief History of DBT 42
    DBT Core Concepts: Acceptance and Change 43

  Radical Acceptance...45

  Desire to Change..47

 DBT Core Skills..55

  Mindfulness...55

  Distress Tolerance...64

  Emotion Regulation...71

  Interpersonal Effectiveness...82

Chapter 4: Dialectical Behavior Therapy for Borderline Personality Disorder (DBT for BPD) 88

 Worksheet: Radical Acceptance of Triggers...90

 Worksheet: Turning the Mind to Cope..91

 Worksheet: Desire to Change..92

 Mindfulness..93

  Worksheet: One-Mindfully...94

  Worksheet: Mindfulness Using Your Five Senses................................96

  Worksheet: Mindful Body Scan (Self-Observation).............................98

  Worksheet: 4-7-8 Breathing...99

 Distress Tolerance Skills for BPD...100

  Worksheet: Grounding Activities..101

  Worksheet: TIPP...102

  Worksheet: ACCEPTS...104

  Worksheet: IMPROVE..108

  Worksheet: PROs and CONs..112

 Emotion Regulation Skills for BPD...114

 Interpersonal Effectiveness Skills for BPD...130

 Self-Harm..138

  The Vicious Cycle of Self-harm...138

  Top 6 Tips to Stop Yourself from Engaging in Self-Harm.................140

Conclusion..142

Appendix A – BPD Self-Assessment...143

 McLean Screening Instrument for BPD..143

 How to Convey Your BPD to Others...145

    How to Deal with Stigma 148
Appendix B – Trigger Journal 150
Review Request 152
Further Reading 153

Introduction

"I would say what others have said: It gets better.
One day, you'll find your tribe. You just have to trust that people are out there waiting to love you and celebrate you for who you are. In the meantime, the reality is you might have to be your own tribe. You might have to be your own best friend. That's not something they're going to teach you in school.
So start the work of loving yourself."
— Wentworth Miller

It's been 20 years since I started my journey to mental healing. Before that, I was a very lonely, troubled, and depressed teen. Here's my story...

My parents emigrated from China to Canada in the 1980s. The move was to provide a better future for the family, but I guess my parents underestimated the severe psychological effects of being "different."

For the record, I was born in Toronto, and English is my first language, so there was no "language barrier" for me to overcome. I also attended a multicultural school, so it's not like I was the only Asian on campus. However, I still felt like I didn't belong. Why? Because for most of my teen life, I was alone.

I spent most of my time eating alone and sleeping in the library during lunchtime. After school, I would usually go straight to an arcade or internet café, alone, of course. In a school of 5,000 students... I didn't have a single friend. This went on for the duration of my high school years.

Even today, I find it very difficult to discuss my severe loneliness back then. When no one sees you and cares even to say "Hi," it's easy to believe there's something wrong with you.

Unfortunately, that's not all that was going on. I wouldn't say I liked school, but I didn't like going home either.

My father was a hoarder who had undiagnosed Obsessive-Compulsive Disorder (OCD). Everything had to be in its rightful place and arranged or positioned the way he wanted. If they weren't, he would get upset, and the whole family would have to walk on eggshells. Imagine living in a home where you were always afraid to touch something and could not put it back precisely where it should be.

On the other hand, my mother suffered from undiagnosed General Anxiety Disorder (GAD). She was constantly worrying and anticipating a tragedy. For example, even though we lived in a safe and secure neighborhood, she was always concerned that someone would break into our home. My mother also had a victim mindset. Whenever things went wrong or a situation did not go her way, she would never take any responsibility for her part in it and start blaming others. Imagine living in a house where you were constantly warned that something disastrous would happen at any moment.

I'm not sharing these about my parents because I blame them. I know they love my sister and me; I never doubted that. But I wish they realized they had mental health problems and sought help (or someone had suggested or offered help). If they had, perhaps they would have led happier lives.

However, the reality is this: there was a lot of chaos, confusion, anxiety, and instability in our home. This was my daily life; this was my "normal." When you combine this setting with the isolation and loneliness I felt as a teen at school, it's no surprise I was diagnosed with OCD and GAD as an adult.

Obsessions, compulsions, and that constant feeling of dread, like something terrible, is about to happen at any moment, are wired deeply into my psyche. And while I wasn't formally diagnosed, I was aware that I suffered from depression too. (I will share more stories about my struggles with these mental health conditions throughout the book.)

After high school, I was in a really bad way. I remember lying in bed one day—completely unmotivated, tired, and angry—and thinking, is this how the rest of my life will be? Is it not possible to be happier? Can't life be better?

I eventually left home for college. This was the first time I was in a different environment and the first time I had experienced "coming home" to a place that was not filled with anger, confusion, and instability. I established a routine for myself and began to see a psychologist. (I already wanted to talk to someone and get help in my teens. I knew my obsessions, compulsions, and constant worrying was holding me back. Yet, it still took some time to meet a mental health professional.)

Sadly, I only saw the psychologist a couple of times. I wasn't comfortable talking about my issues with him and didn't know what was happening, so I stopped seeing him. I then started to read self-help books, which gave me a better understanding of what I was going through. Once I understood myself better, I contacted a mental health professional again. This time, I was more prepared—and open—about the whole process. I was eventually officially diagnosed and prescribed anti-anxiety medication, which helped me deal with daily life better. But this was only the beginning of my journey.

I attempted many forms of therapy. But the one I found most effective in helping me cope with my many co-existing mental health disorders is the one I'm sharing in this book—**Dialectical Behavior Therapy (DBT)**.

During one of our group DBT therapy sessions, I met Margot* and learned about her ordeal with Borderline Personality Disorder.

Content Warning: the following story contains distressing material.

---

* *Name changed for privacy.*

"Everyone was downstairs having birthday cake, MY birthday cake. I had turned 15. I didn't want a party. What for? I'm just going to get stuff I don't like or deserve. But my mother wanted one for me, so there you go.

I hated it when everyone sang "Happy Birthday" because I felt everyone's eyes on me. I couldn't help but feel they were just being polite and didn't really want to be there. After I blew out the candles, the cake was served. Each time someone greeted me, I felt increasingly uncomfortable because I didn't feel I deserved any "well wishes." And then, one of my uncles took a slice of cake and passed me. He didn't greet me! And just like that, I felt invisible, absolutely worthless.

As quietly as I could, I went upstairs to the bathroom. I turned the faucet on, ensured the water ran "loud," and cut myself.

I had started cutting myself the year before.

I was at school, got a B+ on a test, and got depressed. I hated myself, and when a friend asked at the cafeteria why I was looking all "Miss Doom and Gloom," I ran to the bathroom, curled into a ball, and cried.

Then, I felt so embarrassed running out like that that I started thinking my friend probably didn't want to be with me anymore. Who wants to be friends with a "Drama Queen," right?

I didn't talk to anyone for the rest of the day. When I got home, I went straight to my bedroom and locked the door. I took a razor blade I had been secretly keeping between the pages of a book and cut myself for the first time. I wasn't even afraid. I just wanted to stop hurting inside.

I don't know how to describe the years that followed, except that every single day was a struggle. Most of the time, I felt like I was being swallowed whole by my emotions. I still feel like this at times.

I stayed home until my late 20s. I tried to live by myself, but I couldn't cope with people and everyday life. Some catastrophe would happen, and I'd return to my parents. My two younger siblings hated me. To them, I'm just a spoiled, lazy drama queen, and the only thing I could do was behave badly, create a scene, and manipulate our parents. Ironically, my youngest brother, Ray, was the one who ended up helping me.

I left home (again) when I was 25 and moved in with my girlfriend. That first weekend together, I proclaimed I'd never been so happy! On Monday, my girlfriend was running late for work and forgot the lunch I had packed for her, and I spent the whole day crying in bed.

After two short months, we broke up, and the pain and emptiness were more intense than I'd ever felt. I don't know how many days have passed. I lived in a fog until I decided I didn't want to be in a fog anymore. I tried to take my own life. I woke up in the psychiatric ward of a hospital. Ray, who was dating the daughter of a psychologist at the time, looked at me and said quietly, "I think you should talk to someone."

I cried and cried. I didn't want to talk to anyone. I didn't want to let anyone know just how pathetic and worthless a human being I was. But I was just so broken. So broken, tired, and empty. So I agreed to talk to a psychiatrist at the hospital.

I was diagnosed with Borderline Personality Disorder (BPD) at 26. I moved out of my parent's house when I was 28 years and 151 days old, and I haven't been back since. I'm now 32.

I am, though, by no means "cured." I still have BPD. I no longer cut my arms, and I've even managed to meet and keep a few friends, but I still have my mood swings and go through periods of paranoia and depression. So, yes, I still have BPD episodes. But I'm better at coping with them now. And although I know that recovery is still a long way off, I believe with all my heart that it can happen to me."

When I had a chance to speak with Margot, I asked her about one of the turning points in her life. She said, *"I think I was lucky to get an appointment with a psychiatrist who gave me my BPD diagnosis."*

That may sound a bit weird, but I completely understand her. When I was officially diagnosed with OCD and GAD, part of me was relieved. Finally, there was some explanation about me; I wasn't just some weird, unlovable person no one cared about. There might even be something I could do to get better!

Margot also told me that as she learned more about her diagnosis, she realized that the stigma surrounding BPD made it hard for many people to get a diagnosis in the first place. As BPD is considered one of the most difficult personality disorders to treat, many therapists don't want to diagnose it. People with BPD are often (incorrectly) thought to be "difficult," "overreactive," and "manipulative," so many health professionals avoid them. This both saddens and enrages Margot. *"I just can't imagine my life if I hadn't been diagnosed then. And it makes me so sad and angry to know that others are struggling and can't get the right help."*

I didn't get the right help because (1) I didn't understand what was going on to begin with, and (2) I didn't know what to do to get help!

Even though there was love in my family, there was also a lot of chaos and instability, which I thought was normal. So, when I was young, I never really understood that I needed help. I just knew that I was terribly unhappy. As I got older, I became more and more unhappy. Each day felt more miserable than the last, and I struggled to get through them. When I left home, that was the first time I had thought of seeking help and getting better.

So, some "awareness" was there, but I was clueless about how to get help. So when I had the chance to meet a psychologist, I took it. Even though my first attempt was unsuccessful, I didn't give up and stopped trying. I took the necessary steps to lead a happier and better life.

I sincerely hope this book helps you in your journey. I hope it provides some relief, helps you understand yourself more, enables you to cope with your struggles, and puts you on the right track to mental healing.

But I'll be honest with you. You deserve nothing less. Healing from a mental illness is not linear; your journey will have many ups and downs. Addressing a mental health disorder can take a lot from you mentally, emotionally, and physically. Believe me, I've been there, and I genuinely get it. However, I promise that you'll always be going forward if you stick with it. Things WILL get better.

So, before you start your journey in the following pages, I encourage you to begin with empathy for yourself. **Be kind, compassionate, and patient with yourself**.

Who Should Read This Book

This book is for anyone who is showing symptoms of BPD or has already been diagnosed with it. You may want to use this book to get some clarity about BPD, or perhaps you're already undergoing therapy and want to use this book and its exercises as part of your healing journey.

This book is also for anyone with a spouse, friend, or family member showing symptoms or receiving a BPD diagnosis. Understanding is one of the first actions we can take to assist and support someone suffering from this illness, and educating yourself about BPD will help your relationship.

Goals of This Book

This book aims to teach Dialectical Behavior Therapy (DBT) skills and how to use them to deal with BPD. However, it's not all "theory." Plenty of exercises follow each DBT concept and skill so that you can effectively adopt DBT in your life.

How to Use This Book

The first section of this book discusses BPD (i.e., what it is, its causes, symptoms, treatments, etc.). BPD is one of the most misunderstood mental illnesses. So, the first part of your journey is to understand it.

The second section of this book discusses DBT (i.e., its history, concepts, how you can apply it in your life, and so on). You'll also understand what distinguishes DBT from other types of treatment and why it's an effective way of addressing BPD.

The final section of this book is about how to apply DBT skills to help you live a happy and abundant life with BPD. You'll be presented with various exercises and worksheets in this section. Many of these exercises are adapted from the *DBT Skills Training Manual*[1], while the rest are ones I've found helpful when practicing DBT skills.

Content Warning

This book contains content that may be upsetting or disturbing. Some stories, topics, and instances may prompt or trigger you. Content may include but is not limited to abandonment, rejection, depression, trauma, self-harm, emotional abuse, problematic relationships, and emotional invalidation. Please be aware of these and other topics that upset you. Most importantly, please reach out and ask for help or seek professional advice when you feel overwhelmed.

Safety

This book will discuss many BPD-related things, some of which may be upsetting or triggering. As such, staying safe and feeling safe while reading this book is essential.

But what does it mean to be safe? What does *safety* feel or look like to you? You know how to answer this question best, but here are some ideas:

- Set up or identify a **Safe Space**. This can be any place or location where you feel most safe and comfortable. Remember, besides what you'll be reading, plenty of exercises and worksheets are in the coming pages. So, you must be as safe and relaxed as possible while doing them.
- Write or record a **"feel good" story**. Think about times when you felt happy and safe, and write about those times as much as possible. If you don't feel like writing, you can voice record. The purpose is to have something to turn to whenever you have a negative feeling or reaction to any material here. Allow the memory and sense of safety to wash over you before proceeding.
- Create an actionable "**Plan B**." Make a list of things you should do if you feel unsafe. Here are a few suggestions:
    - Call _____.
    - Hug your pet.
    - Look at a picture of _____.
    - Stop and go to _____.
    - Stop and listen to _____.
    - Others:

    _____
    _____
    _____

About Me

*"I'm not saying I will heal you.
But I am sharing what healed me." – Barrett Huang*

My mental health journey made me want to know more about the mind and its workings. So I got my bachelor's degree in psychology and completed Dr. Marsha Linehan's DBT Skills certificate program. I have also taken Dr. Linehan's advice to "live a life worth living" to heart. I've spent years learning more about happiness, philosophy, and how to improve myself.

I want to stress that this book is based mainly on my experiences with mental health disorders and on the experiences of people I know who were kind enough to let me tell their stories. DBT has dramatically helped us cope with our mental health problems and live happy, productive lives, so the least we can do is pay it forward.

You Can Feel Better. You Can Be Happy.

Suffering from a mental health disorder is difficult with a capital "D." Life was a constant struggle when I suffered from mental health problems. I was stuck, and I didn't know how to move on. I didn't feel like I had any control over anything, including myself.

So I understand what you're going through. I've been there, and honestly, I'm still "there" at times—I just cope better today. And you can, too!

I'm proof that you can feel better while having a mental illness and be happy. All you need to do is to invest in your own healing. So, please turn the page, start your journey, and keep going until you feel better.

Chapter 1: What is Borderline Personality Disorder?

*"I don't know what it's like to not have deep emotions,
even when I feel nothing, I feel it completely."*
— A.R. Asher

Borderline Personality Disorder (BPD) is a mental health condition characterized by intense and unstable emotions, impulsive behavior, distorted self-identity, and unstable relationships with others.

The term "borderline" was first used to describe a group of patients in psychiatric hospitals nearly 3000 years ago.[2] However, it wasn't until the 1930s that Hungarian-American psychoanalyst Adolph Stern categorized and identified the illness. But since there was so much confusion about the condition, it would remain an undiagnosable disorder until 1980, when it was included in the Diagnostic and Statistical Manual for Mental Disorders, Third Edition (DSM-III).

People with BPD have difficulty regulating emotions, resulting in extreme mood swings and often-changing behaviors. They also have trouble with how they think and feel about themselves and others, making it very hard to get close to people and trust them. And since they are constantly doubtful, they have an intense fear of abandonment, and when they are abandoned, the feeling of rejection they experience is severe.

These extreme ups and downs always happen and can last a few hours or several days. During these times, their distress over the situation and volatile feelings can make them act impulsively. For example, they might drive recklessly, cut themselves, engage in risky sexual behavior, use drugs, and even try to take their own lives.

All of the above points to a complete lack of stability inside and outside people suffering from BPD. For this reason, this mental illness is also known as Emotionally Unstable Personality Disorder (EUPD).

What Causes BPD?

BPD is a complex and multifaceted personality disorder that can be influenced by various factors, including:

1) **Genetics**: Studies have shown a strong link between BPD and genetics.[3,4] Individuals with a family history of the disorder are more likely to develop it themselves. However, please note that genetics alone is not enough to cause BPD, as environmental factors and life experiences also play a role in the development of the disorder.

2) **Brain structure and function**: Abnormalities in the structure and function of some brain regions, such as the amygdala and prefrontal cortex, have been linked to BPD.

3) **Childhood experiences**: Trauma, abuse, neglect, and abandonment during childhood can increase the risk of developing BPD. A recent 2022 paper also suggests that *emotional invalidation* by parents or caregivers may also significantly contribute to the development of BPD.[5]

    Emotional invalidation is when someone dismisses, ignores, or belittles another person's emotions or feelings. This can make the other person feel like their emotions are not important or valid and can cause them to feel frustrated, angry, sad, or hurt.

    A child who doesn't feel believed can grow up with low self-esteem because they don't know what it's like to be believed. As adults, it can be difficult for them to express themselves and trust others.

4) **Interpersonal relationships**: Difficult and unstable relationships with family, friends and romantic partners can contribute to the development of BPD.

5) **Environmental factors**: Exposure to ongoing stress, such as financial or housing insecurity, can increase the risk of BPD.

6) **Substance abuse**: Substance abuse and addiction can contribute to the development and severity of BPD symptoms.

It's important to note that **no single factor causes BPD**. It's usually a complex combination of biological, psychological, and social factors that cause BPD.

What are the Symptoms of BPD?

As mentioned, BPD is characterized by a *persistent pattern* of instability in emotions, relationships, self-image, and impulsiveness. The Diagnostic and Statistical Manual of Mental Disorders, 5th edition (DSM-5) outlines the following nine (9) classic symptoms of BPD:

1) **Fear of being left alone:** Individuals with BPD may do anything to avoid being alone or having other people leave them. Persons with BPD get very angry or scared when they feel like they are being ignored or left alone. So, they might keep track of where their loved ones are all the time or make plans to make sure they don't get left behind. To avoid being left alone, they might try to ruin a relationship so the other person won't get too close.

2) **Relationships that are unstable and changeable:** Individuals with BPD find it hard to maintain good relationships because their views on others change quickly and significantly. They can quickly switch from treating others concerning treating them with disrespect, and the other way around. "Splitting" is another word for this trait.

For example, a person with BPD who is splitting might look up to a friend or partner one moment and think they are perfect and wonderful. The next moment, they might see them as completely bad or intolerable and think they are terrible and can do nothing right. As you might guess, this can lead to very up-and-down relationships.

3) **A pattern of unstable self-perception:** Persons with BPD often have a distorted or confusing sense of themselves and frequently feel guilty, ashamed, and empty. They often think they are "bad" or "insufficient." They can also change a lot about how they see themselves by quickly shifting goals, beliefs, jobs, and even the people they hang out with. They may also obstruct their own advancement. For example, they may try to get fired on purpose because they think they don't deserve to work there, because of the atmosphere at work, or for other reasons.

4) **Emotional instability:** Persons with BPD may experience abrupt fluctuations in their self-esteem and how they see others and the world. Anger, fear, concern, hatred, grief, and love are all irrational emotions that shift swiftly and frequently. These abrupt mood changes usually last a few hours and never more than a few days.

5) **Impulsive and risky behavior:** Individuals with BPD often use drugs, get violent, overeat, gamble, engage in risky sexual behavior, and do other things that aren't responsible. This is because they can't keep their (emotional) urges in check. For example, let's say that a person with BPD feels lonely and sad. So they don't have to be alone, they might do risky sexual things with a stranger.

6) **Frequent self-harm and suicidal ideation:** Individuals with BPD often hurt themselves by cutting, burning, or hitting themselves. People often do these things to calm down strong emotions, but they can cause serious harm or even death. People with BPD may also think about killing themselves or try to kill themselves often. Most of the time, these acts of self-harm are caused by rejection, likely betrayal, or frustration from people they care about and love.

7) **Habitual feelings of worthlessness or emptiness:** Individuals with BPD often feel unhappy, bored, unfulfilled, or "empty." Many people believe they are useless and despise themselves.

8) **Outbursts of anger that are out of proportion:** Persons with BPD often have anger management issues. They might lash out with sarcasm, anger, or violent outbursts. Most of the time, these outbursts are followed by embarrassment and regret.

9) **Stress-related paranoid thoughts or severe dissociative symptoms**: People with BPD may go through short periods of paranoia or dissociation, which is when they feel disconnected from themselves. A fear of being left alone often causes this.

Please remember that not everybody with BPD has all the symptoms listed above. The gravity, regularity, and length of the symptoms differ for each person. But for a person to be officially diagnosed with BPD, they must meet at least five (5) of the nine (9) above criteria, and their symptoms must cause them a lot of pain or trouble in daily life.

What are the Different Subtypes of BPD?

BPD is a complex condition; not a single type applies to all individuals with the disorder. However, Theodore Millon[6], an American psychologist and personality theorist, defined four *subtypes* of BPD in the 1980s and 1990s. These subtypes are each characterized by a particular pattern of symptoms and behaviors: **Impulsive**, **Self-destructive**, **Depressive**, and **Aggravated**.

However, in recent years, some researchers and clinicians have proposed that there may be FIVE BPD subtypes. This revised categorization of BPD subtypes includes the four original subtypes identified by Millon and a fifth subtype: **Lethargic**.

Here's a more detailed description of each of these subtypes.

1. **Impulsive BPD**: This subtype is characterized by **impulsive and risky behaviors** (e.g., substance abuse, binge eating, reckless driving, overspending, etc.). People with this subtype have difficulty controlling their impulses and indulge in these actions without thinking about the consequences.

2. **Self-Destructive BPD**: This subtype is characterized by **self-harm behaviors**, such as cutting, burning, or hitting oneself. People with this subtype may struggle with intense emotions and may use self-harm behaviors as a means of regulating their emotions or relieving psychological pain.

3. **Depressive BPD**: This subtype is characterized by feelings of **hopelessness, helplessness**, and chronic feelings of **emptiness**. People with this subtype may struggle with a distorted self-image and struggle to form and maintain relationships.

4. **Aggravated BPD**: This subtype is characterized by **intense and explosive anger** and difficulty controlling anger and aggression. Individuals with this subtype may engage in verbal and physical outbursts and struggle with interpersonal relationships due to their angry and hostile behavior.

5. **Lethargic BPD**: This subtype is characterized by a **passive, apathetic, and withdrawn pattern of behavior**, as well as a lack of energy and motivation. Individuals with this subtype may experience a persistent feeling of emptiness and boredom. They may struggle with initiating and sustaining social and personal relationships. This subtype is also considered distinct from the other subtypes of BPD, which tend to involve more impulsive, unstable, and intense emotions and behaviors.

While these subtypes can help understand the symptoms of BPD, they are not official diagnostic categories. They serve as a guide to further understanding BPD symptoms.

Also, it's not uncommon for individuals with BPD to experience symptoms from more than one subtype, and some may not fit into any of these subtypes at all. In my opinion, it's vital to have an understanding of our mental illness. But we DO NOT need to be "put in a box."

Further, as proven by adding a *fifth* subtype in recent years, the mental health field is constantly changing and evolving. So it's okay if you don't fit into the abovementioned subtypes. Perhaps what you feel has not been thoroughly studied or recognized yet.

Borderline Personality Disorder vs Bipolar Disorder

BPD is often confused with Bipolar Disorder (BD) because many symptoms are similar. However, there are some key differences.

Symptoms: Both BPD and BD are characterized by mood swings and instability. However, the nature of these mood swings is different. In BPD, mood swings are more frequent and may be triggered by minor events or interactions, but they are typically less severe than in BD.

In BD, the mood swings are more intense, last longer, and may involve episodes of mania or hypomania (an elevated or irritable mood) alternating with bouts of depression.

Impulsive Behavior: Impulsive behavior is another common symptom in both BPD and BD. However, the *type* of impulsive behavior can differ between the two conditions. In BPD, impulsive behavior may be more likely to include self-harm, binge eating, or substance abuse. In BD, impulsive behavior may be more likely expressed as spending sprees, risky sexual behavior, or other reckless behavior.

Relationships: BPD and BD impact a person's ability to form and maintain healthy relationships. However, in BPD, relationship problems are often characterized by intense and unstable relationships, fear of abandonment, and frequent conflicts. In BD, relationship problems are usually caused by how manic or depressive episodes affect the person's behavior and ability to keep stable relationships.

Treatment: The treatment for both disorders may entail a combination of psychotherapy and medication, but the specific types of treatment may differ between the two conditions. BPD is often treated with therapy, while BD is typically treated with mood stabilizers such as lithium and antipsychotics.

The following is a quick infographic adapted from recent research.[7]

Borderline Personality Disorder	Overlapping Features	Bipolar Disorder
• fear of abandonment • unstable self-image • unstable relationships • feelings of emptiness • mood often shaped by interpersonal conflicts • sudden and short-lived mood shifts	Disproportionate anger Suicidal thoughts Risky behaviors Impulsivity Delusions	• sleep disturbance • distinct euphoric and depressive states • mood often stable between episodes • sustained mood shifts lasting days or weeks

Common Question: Does this mean you cannot have BPD and BD simultaneously? No. In fact, BPD-BD comorbidity is common, with about one in five people diagnosed with both.[8] Following is a list of the most common co-occurring disorders with BPD:

1. Major Depressive Disorder (MDD)
2. Generalized Anxiety Disorder (GAD)
3. Post-Traumatic Stress Disorder (PTSD)
4. Substance Use Disorders
5. Eating Disorders
6. Obsessive-Compulsive Disorder (OCD)
7. Attention-Deficit/Hyperactivity Disorder (ADHD)

BPD Recommended Treatments

I tried various types of treatments and therapy to deal with my various mental health disorders, so I don't think there's a single solution to mental health problems that works for everyone.

I went through Cognitive Behavioral Therapy when I had OCD and GAD. I was given anti-anxiety medication during this time, which jumpstarted my healing. I improved to the point that I felt I no longer needed to take medicine. However, I was still having many problems with my mental health. At this stage, I knew CBT was no longer what I needed. In my quest to live a happier and better life, I discovered Dialectical Behavior Therapy (DBT). With DBT, I could finally break free from the mental health problems holding me back from the life I wanted to live.

So, I guess I'm saying that looking for and getting treatment is a journey. Getting better takes time, so my advice to you is to: **have an open mind**, **be curious**, **be kind to yourself**, and **give yourself time to heal**.

Following are some of the known treatments for BPD today.

Cognitive Behavioral Therapy (CBT)

Cognitive Behavioral Therapy (CBT) is a form of psychotherapy that helps individuals with BPD identify and change negative patterns of thought and behaviors that contribute to their symptoms.

For example, say a person with BPD has this persistent negative thought, "I am worthless." The next step is to challenge this negative thought. This may involve questioning the evidence for the thought, looking for alternative explanations, and considering the thought's impact on emotions and behavior. Next is to replace this negative thought with a positive one (e.g., "I am valuable and have unique strengths and talents.")

In addition to changing negative thoughts, CBT for BPD also involves modifying behavior. This may include learning new coping skills, such as stress management techniques, or engaging in behaviors inconsistent with their negative thoughts and beliefs.

In summary: CBT for BPD usually involves helping the individual identify and challenge negative thoughts, replace them with positive and realistic ones, and modify their behavior through coping skills and other techniques.

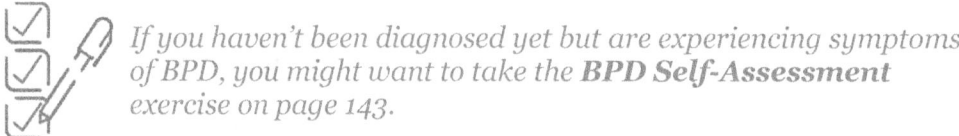

*If you haven't been diagnosed yet but are experiencing symptoms of BPD, you might want to take the **BPD Self-Assessment** exercise on page 143.*

Schema-Focused Therapy

Schema-focused therapy concentrates on an individual's underlying schemas (core beliefs) about themselves, others, and the world. The next step is to change these schemas to reduce BPD symptoms.

For example, say a person with BPD has this core belief, "I am worthless." The next step is to explore WHY this person has this thought. This could mean discussing past experiences, looking at relationships from childhood, and figuring out how this schema (core belief) affects how the person thinks, feels, and acts now.

The next step is to challenge and change the negative schema. This may involve using various therapeutic techniques (e.g., role-playing, visualization, reframing, etc.) to help the individual see things differently and develop new, more positive schemas.

A technique often used in schema-focused therapy is "re-parenting." Many of our core beliefs stem from our experiences at home. Re-parenting may involve the therapist acting as a supportive and nurturing parent figure, helping the individual feel loved, accepted, and valued. This way, the person with BPD can heal from past negative emotional experiences.

<u>In summary</u>: Schema-focused therapy for BPD involves identifying and exploring negative schemas, challenging and changing them, using techniques such as "re-parenting" to heal from past emotional experiences, and practicing and maintaining changes made in therapy.

Mentalization-based Therapy (MBT)

Mentalization-based Therapy (MBT) helps individuals with BPD understand their own thoughts and emotions, as well as the thoughts and feelings of others.

For example, say a person with BPD has this prevailing thought, "I am worthless." The next step is to understand how this thought is affecting their behavior. For instance, this person may constantly expect to fail or do the wrong things.

The following step is to practice "mentalizing." This is imagining in your mind the possible thoughts and feelings of others. This may involve exploring the perspectives of others, learning to read body language and nonverbal cues, and practicing empathy and understanding.

Now that a person better understands their own and other people's thoughts and feelings, therapy may shift to teaching how to communicate and cope with stress to strengthen relationships.

<u>In summary</u>: MBT helps individuals with BPD become aware of their thoughts and feelings and to understand how these affect their behavior. It also helps them "mentalize" (think or imagine in their own minds) the thoughts and feelings of others so they can understand how other people behave. Finally, it teaches good communication and coping skills to help improve their relationships with other people.

Dialectical Behavior Therapy (DBT)

Dialectical Behavior Therapy (DBT) is a type of psychotherapy developed explicitly for individuals with BPD by someone who suffered from BPD herself. It is widely recognized as an evidence-based treatment for BPD and is considered one of the most effective interventions available. We will discuss DBT in great detail in [Chapter 3](#).

A note about medication: While there are no specific medications for BPD, some individuals may benefit from taking medications for symptoms such as anxiety, depression, or impulsive behavior. However, suppose you're not showing signs, or you're not suffering from these particular mental illnesses, my advice is to focus on psychotherapy. Still, when in doubt, please consult a doctor regarding your best option.

Chapter Highlights:

- Borderline personality disorder (BPD) is a type of personality disorder that is marked by intense and unstable emotions, impulsive behavior, a distorted sense of self-identity, and unstable relationships with other people.
- BPD Causes: Genetics; brain structure and function abnormalities; negative childhood experiences, difficult and unstable interpersonal relationships, high-stress environmental factors; substance abuse.
- BPD Symptoms: Fear of abandonment; pattern of unstable, intense relationships; pattern of unstable sense of self; emotional instability; impulsive and dangerous behavior; recurrent self-harm or suicidal behavior; chronic feelings of emptiness; disproportionate outbursts of anger; and transient, stress-related paranoid ideation or severe dissociative symptoms.
- BPD Subtypes: Impulsive-BPD, Self-destructive-BPD, Depressive-BPD, Aggravated-BPD, and Lethargic-BPD.
- BPD Recommended Treatments: Cognitive Behavioral Therapy (CBT), Schema-focused Therapy, Mentalization-Based Therapy (MBT), and Dialectical Behavior Therapy (DBT).

Chapter 2: Living with Borderline Personality Disorder

"People with BPD are like people with third-degree burns over 90% of their bodies. Lacking emotional skin, they feel agony at the slightest touch or movement."
— *Dr. Marsha M. Linehan*

BPD is one of the most misdiagnosed mental health disorders today. It's estimated that approximately 1-2% of the world's population has BPD. Still, it's widely accepted that **BPD often goes undetected**[9], so that number is likely much higher.

Part of the problem is that there are many myths associated with BPD. For instance, there's the myth that women are more likely to develop BPD than men. The truth is, when it comes to mental health, women are more likely to *seek* treatment than men, making "BPD in men" seem rare. Also, men with BPD symptoms are more likely to be misdiagnosed with another disorder, such as post-traumatic stress disorder (PTSD) or major depressive disorder (MDD, clinical depression).

But perhaps one of the most damaging myths about BPD is that it's not a real disorder and that the people who suffer from it are just "manipulative" and "attention-seeking." This is incorrect. People with BPD often struggle with intense and unstable emotions, which can cause them to act impulsively. This can be mistaken as manipulation or attention-seeking by others, yet these behaviors are actually symptoms of BPD.

Another challenge is that BPD symptoms are broad and look like other mental health problems. Its comorbid (co-existing) nature with other mental health conditions also makes diagnosis—and appropriate treatment—difficult.

You may be wondering why I'm even mentioning this whole misdiagnosis situation.

Looking back at the start of my healing journey, I couldn't get proper help because of all the confusion surrounding my co-existing mental health disorders (OCD + GAD + Depression). Luckily, today, there's much more information concerning mental health, so my advice is to advocate yourself.

The fact that you have this book in your hands means you're actively helping yourself. Great! But if you seek professional help and encounter confusion, stigma, a mismatch between your struggles and what the professional identifies, etc., then know that YOU ARE NOT ALONE.

Someone is going through precisely the same thing you're going through somewhere, so just keep going and find what works for you.

BPD and Your Brain

The brain during a BPD episode can show nonstandard activity in areas associated with emotional regulation, such as the **amygdala**, the **anterior cingulate cortex**, and the **prefrontal cortex**. These irregular activities can result in intense emotions, impulsive behavior, and distorted perceptions of situations and relationships.

This diagram[10] shows a cross-section of the parts of the brain discussed below.

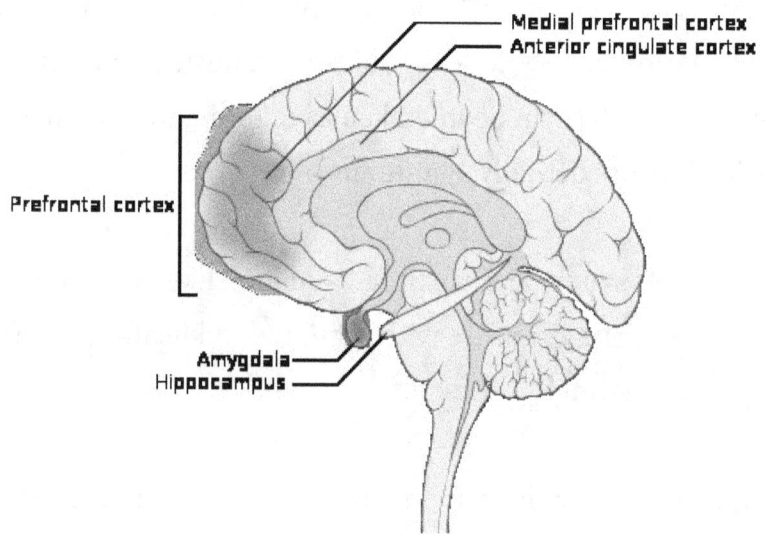

What is the Amygdala?

The amygdala is a small, almond-shaped brain structure involved in processing emotions and generating the body's stress response. It plays a crucial role in fear and anxiety and helps to direct our attention to potential threats. The amygdala also influences other areas of the brain, including the hippocampus and prefrontal cortex, which regulate emotions, form memories, and make decisions.

Research has shown that the amygdala is *hyperactive* in people with BPD[11,12,13], leading to heightened emotional reactivity and increased stress responses.

What is the Anterior Cingulate Cortex?

The anterior cingulate cortex (ACC) is a brain region in the frontal lobe near the brain's center. It is involved in various functions, including executive control, attention, emotion regulation, and pain processing. The ACC is also assumed to be involved in conflict experience, decision-making, error detection, social cognition, and empathy.

Research suggests that individuals with BPD show irregular activity in the ACC during emotional processing tasks, which may contribute to experiencing intense, unstable emotions.[14,15]

What is the Prefrontal Cortex?

The prefrontal cortex is a part of the brain involved in many higher-level cognitive processes, such as decision-making, impulse control, and emotion regulation. Some evidence suggests that the prefrontal cortex may not function optimally in people with BPD.

For example, some studies that used functional magnetic resonance imaging (fMRI) have shown that when people with BPD do tasks that make them feel strong emotions, their prefrontal cortex tends to be less active than healthy controls.[16,17] This *hypoactivity* could make it harder for people with BPD to control their emotions and stop acting on emotional impulses, two of the most classic symptoms of this disorder.

What does this all mean? The areas of the brain that control emotion and behavior DO NOT communicate effectively in people with BPD. So, it's not that people with BPD *choose* to experience intense emotions and act impulsively because of these feelings. Their brain structure makes it hard to manage their emotions and behavior. However, having said that, it is possible to achieve this. We will explore how in Chapter 3.

BPD Triggers

A trigger is an event, internal or external, that causes a significant worsening of BPD symptoms. Triggers vary from person to person, but the following are some of the most common ones:

Relationship triggers. As discussed, fear of abandonment is one of the most common symptoms of BPD. So anything less than perfect in a relationship may trigger a BPD episode.

For instance, individuals with BPD who send an e-mail or text to someone and don't get a reply right away may conclude that the other person doesn't care about them. And it doesn't stop there. Their thoughts can quickly spiral out of control from *"They don't care"* to *"They've abandoned me"* to *"No one has or ever will love me."* These intense and rapid thoughts and emotions may then lead to self-harm.

Other examples of relationship triggers are:
- Lack of attention.
- Seeing a negative facial expression on someone.
- Being ignored, talked over, or overlooked.
- Being misunderstood.

Trauma triggers. Recollections of trauma can trigger a BPD episode. When a person with this illness thinks about or sees something that reminds them of a traumatic event (e.g., a specific person, place, sound, etc.), their symptoms can worsen, and their emotions can quickly spiral out of control.

Criticism or judgment triggers. Since a person with BPD has an unstable sense of self, they can be extremely sensitive to criticism. They find it difficult to distinguish between positive and negative feedback, and they don't experience the criticism as a single event but rather an attack on their character. This then leads to feelings of rejection, which sets BPD in motion.

The first step to avoiding a trigger is identifying which specific events bring on a BPD episode the most. We all have our own sensitivities, and identifying them allows us to prevent them more effectively. How do you do this? One helpful strategy is starting a "Trigger Journal" (page 150).

Chapter Highlights:

- BPD is one of the most undiagnosed mental disorders. Stigma and myths surrounding the disorder contribute greatly to this.
- BPD and the brain. Studies show that parts of the brain responsible for *emotional regulation* behave in a nonstandard way in people with BPD. This explains why their feelings and thoughts can quickly spiral out of control, pushing them to behave in ways that are not beneficial for them (and others).
- BPD triggers. It's important to know what triggers a BPD episode so that steps can be taken to avoid it.

Chapter 3: What is Dialectical Behavioral Therapy?

"The goal of DBT is to help people find the path to getting out of hell." — Dr. Marsha Linehan

A Brief History of DBT

Dialectical Behavior Therapy, or **DBT**, was developed by Dr. Marsha Linehan[18], Ph.D., in the late 1980s and early 1990s. It was initially meant to treat people with BPD who had difficulty managing their emotions and engaging in healthy relationships. Traditional therapies at the time had limited effectiveness for people with BPD, and Dr. Linehan saw the need for a new approach. She combined CBT with Eastern mindfulness practices and the philosophy of dialectics (*opposite ideas*) to create a new **form of therapy specifically designed to help individuals with BPD**.

But before we discuss DBT, let's look at Dr. Linehan's affinity with BPD. [19]

Dr. Linehan was admitted into the *Institute of Living*, a psychiatric facility, for her "extreme social withdrawal" when she was 17. At the clinic, she engaged in self-harming activities such as cutting her arms and burning her wrists using cigarettes. She also considered taking her own life, so she was isolated for safety.

In the 1960s, BPD was not an officially diagnosable disorder yet.[†] So although Dr. Linehan exhibited classic BPD symptoms, she was instead misdiagnosed with *schizophrenia*, for which she was heavily medicated with anti-psychotic drugs. She was also subjected to electroconvulsive therapy or ECT for this illness. Of course, since she did not have schizophrenia, none of these treatments worked.

[†] First mentions of the term *borderline personality* occurred in the 1930s. However, it would be 50 years later, in the 1980s, when it would be an official mental health disorder.

Dr. Linehan was eventually released from the clinic after two years. But that doesn't mean she was better. She continued to struggle with her mental health problems for years. In her own words, she has described her experiences as a "hellish" period of her life, characterized by intense emotional pain and a sense of hopelessness. She has also expressed her journey to recovery as slow and difficult, involving several different therapeutic approaches and medications.

Still, despite these challenges, Dr. Linehan was eventually able to turn her own experiences into a positive force for change by developing DBT, a therapy that has helped countless individuals with BPD and related conditions to find relief from their symptoms and improve their lives.

DBT Core Concepts: Acceptance and Change

Dr. Linehan was raised in a religious family, and one of her coping ways whenever she was struggling was to pray. She recalls one night in 1967 when she had an epiphany. She realized that she had made many attempts to take her own life because the gap between who she was and the person she wanted to be was so huge that she often felt hopeless and desperate for a life she would never know.

WHO SHE WAS   WHO SHE WANTED TO BE

Dr. Linehan then realized that the first step she must take to move toward who she wanted to be was to **ACCEPT** her current situation. This was the start of the concept she would later call *Radical Acceptance*.

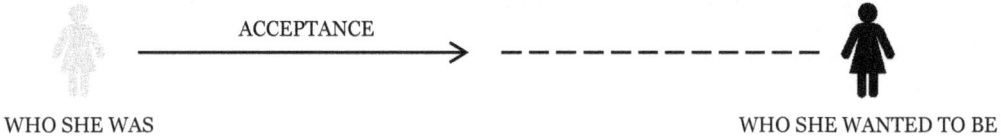

WHO SHE WAS   WHO SHE WANTED TO BE

However, accepting reality does not magically improve one's situation. To achieve what one wants, one must learn and adopt new ways. This is the **CHANGE** phase in DBT.

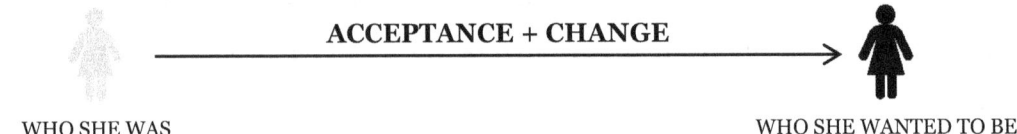

At first, it might seem hard to understand. How can one Accept AND Change at the same time? But you see, we're not accepting and changing the same thing.

We're only accepting the truth or reality of our current situation, including feelings, experiences, and circumstances that may be difficult to accept. What we're changing is how we usually handle these kinds of situations.

> Content Warning: the following story contains distressing material.

This is what Cheryl[‡], a reader, had to say: *"Whenever people ask me about living with BPD, I say that, for me, it's like living with a deep pain in my heart every single day. Many simple, everyday things confuse and hurt me, and what others find "trivial" can devastate me. While others would isolate or suffer in silence, I would do the opposite; I would get furious and lash out.*

One time, I got so mad at my dad for being five minutes late from picking me up from the train station that when he got there, I grabbed his mobile phone and threw it at his head as violently as I could. The phone hit my dad on the side of his right eyebrow, and when I saw it slightly bleeding, I burst into tears, fearing that he would leave me right there and then and I would never see him again.

[‡] *Name changed for privacy.*

When we got home, my dad tried to downplay everything to my mom and brothers, which made me seethe inside for reasons I couldn't understand or control. We were in the kitchen then, and my eyes kept going to the set of knives hanging on the kitchen wall. Whether I meant them harm or myself, I honestly don't know. Whatever it was, it was my wake-up call. Somewhere deep inside, I knew I needed help.

I went through various forms of therapy before someone recommended DBT to me. For me, Radical Acceptance was incredibly freeing; it was like someone opened a door I didn't know was closed. The second phase, Change, was where things really started to improve for the people around me and me. Don't get me wrong, it's a lot of work! But I'm happy to say I don't lash out as much as I used to. Thanks to DBT, anger is no longer my "go-to" move. I've learned other, better ways to cope."

Radical Acceptance

Radical Acceptance is the process of fully accepting and embracing reality. The idea is that instead of trying to ignore, resist or change painful emotions and experiences, we should learn to accept them AS IS. By doing so, we reduce the distress they cause.

RADICAL ACCEPTANCE = IT IS WHAT IT IS

Often, if we don't accept a negative or unpleasant situation, we ruminate or think about it over and over (e.g.,. *Why is this happening?, Why is this happening to me?, Why is everything so wrong?, This isn't fair!* etc.) However, we stay in that negative state of mind by doing this. This, in turn, may lead us to an emotional (rather than logical) reaction that may make the situation worse.

I'll be the first to admit that Radical Acceptance is not easy. When I first came across this concept, I thought, *"What?! I'm supposed just to be okay with all of this?"* Of course, the more I understood the idea, the more I realized how healing it could be for my mental health. I believe one of the best ways to "accept" Radical Acceptance is to understand what it's NOT.

Radical Acceptance (RA) is NOT:

1. **Denial**: RA isn't about denying or minimizing the reality of a situation. It's about acknowledging what is happening, even if it's painful or difficult to accept.
2. **Approval**: RA doesn't mean you approve of what's happening. It simply means that you are willing to acknowledge and accept the reality of the situation.
3. **Resignation**: RA isn't about giving up or resigning yourself to a situation. It is about accepting what is happening in the present moment and working towards change.
4. **Passivity**: RA doesn't mean that you are passive or that you cannot take action. In fact, accepting reality can often lead to greater clarity and motivation to take steps toward positive change.
5. **Forgiveness**: RA isn't the same as forgiveness. Forgiveness involves letting go of anger and resentment towards another person. In contrast, RA involves accepting the reality of a situation, regardless of whether it involves another person or not.
6. **For Others**: RA isn't for the benefit of other people. It's for you. It's a means to minimize the pain and suffering you feel from unpleasant situations.

When I was younger, I was very angry with my parents. I was mad at my father for being a hoarder and for the chaos he brought into our lives. I was also angry at my mother for her constant worrying and the resulting atmosphere of anxiety that she created.

I've since learned to accept them for who they are; I cannot change them. I've also learned to accept the reality of my childhood; I cannot go back and relive those years. And finally, I learned to accept the reality of my situation at the start of my journey. I was an adult suffering from OCD, GAD, and depression.

Radical Acceptance didn't happen overnight. I had to work at it. But in the end, accepting reality is what started to heal me.

Desire to Change

In DBT, change or the desire to change means having the motivation and willingness to make *positive changes* in one's thoughts, emotions, behaviors, and relationships. Why? Because you're NOW is not working for you.

CHANGE = LEARNING NEW BEHAVIORS TO FEEL BETTER

Just like radical acceptance, change is not easy. One of the reasons for this is that our brains actually don't like change.[20] We often see change as a "problem" or "challenge" rather than an opportunity for learning and growth. I was like this too. However, DBT taught me that **change is not something to be afraid of but something to be a friend of**.

To stop suffering from my mental health problems, I must befriend and embrace change in my life. Only by learning new behaviors and skills will I be able to live the life I want to live.

"Your life doesn't get better by chance. It gets better by change."
—Jim Rohn

Worksheet: Radical Acceptance

Although Radical Acceptance might not seem easy to do, it's actually a straightforward concept. It's the practice of accepting things as they are.

For this exercise, please write inside the circle what your reality is right now. Don't evaluate or judge your thoughts; write whatever comes to mind.

Examples: (1) I'm scared. (2) I don't want to be alone. (3) People confuse me. (4) I hate myself. (5) I'm not lovable.

Worksheet: Desire to Change

This exercise is to help you welcome change in your life. There's no need to plan anything here. Just be kind to yourself and think about how change could help you. Write whatever comes to mind in the circle below.

Examples: (1) I want to try "new." (2) I'm ready for "better." (3) I want to be happier. (4) It's time for "more." (5) I want to heal.

Worksheet: Radical Acceptance + Desire to Change

Now, let's put the two DBT concepts together. Copy what you wrote in the previous exercises in the Radical Acceptance and Desire to Change circles below. By doing this, you're accepting your today and stating your desire to change for tomorrow. Next, write a Healing Statement for yourself in the middle of the circles.

Here's an example for you.

RADICAL ACCEPTANCE

I'm scared.

I DON'T WANT TO BE ALONE.

People confuse me.

I hate myself.

I'm not lovable.

HEALING STATEMENT:

"I accept who I am today. I'm like this for a reason even though I don't fully understand why. What I do know is that I don't feel happy or fulfilled living this way. This is not my best life. So I'm opening myself to learning new things to increase my happiness."

DESIRE TO CHANGE:

I want to try "new."

I'M READY FOR "BETTER."

I want to be happier.

I WANT TO HEAL.

It's time for "more."

Now, it's your turn! Do the same exercise on the next page.

RADICAL ACCEPTANCE: Write statements acknowledging your circumstances at the moment.

DESIRE TO CHANGE: Write statements that affirm your openness and willingness to change for the better.

HEALING STATEMENT: State your acceptance of today and desire for a better life tomorrow.

RADICAL ACCEPTANCE:	HEALING STATEMENT:	DESIRE TO CHANGE:

Worksheet: Turning the Mind

Acceptance takes practice, especially if we're in a situation where we're not happy or not getting our way. In such instances, we're more likely to reject the situation than to accept it. We don't realize, however, that by dismissing the issue, we are merely prolonging our misery over it.

Turning the Mind is an exercise about repeatedly trying to move toward acceptance. There are three critical steps to this exercise: (1) noticing when you're not accepting something, (2) making a promise to yourself to accept reality as it is, and (3) doing Steps 1 and 2 over and over again until you genuinely and fully accept the situation.

Here's an example: Say you texted someone, and you can see that they've read your message. However, they're not texting back, and this is upsetting you. How can you *turn your mind* to accept the situation?

(1) **Notice that you're not accepting something.** (What are you thinking, saying, or doing that's rejecting the situation?)
I keep checking my phone for their message.

(2) **Make a promise to yourself to accept reality as it is.**
"I don't control other people, and I can't make someone reply to my message. So I accept this as is."

(3) **Repeat steps 1 and 2 until you fully accept what's happening.**

(1) **Notice that you're not accepting something.** (What are you thinking, saying, or doing that's rejecting the situation?)
I'm thinking about what this person has done to me before.

(2) **Make a promise to yourself to accept reality as it is.**
"I don't need to dredge up my whole past with this person. This has nothing to do with my message. So I'm going to accept this as is."

(3) **Do you accept the situation now? If not, repeat steps 1 and 2 until you fully accept what's happening.**

(1) Notice that you're not accepting something. (What are you thinking, saying, or doing that's rejecting the situation?)

I think that this person doesn't like me and probably never has. That's why they're not responding to my message.

(2) Make a promise to yourself to accept reality as it is.

"I don't have the power to read minds. I'm going to accept this as is."

(3) Do you accept the situation now? If not, repeat steps 1 and 2 until you fully accept what's happening.

It's your turn now...

Upsetting Situation: Write a situation that's making you upset. (You can make this a *reflective exercise* and refer to a situation that happened in the past.)

_____
_____
_____
_____

(1) **Notice HOW you're not accepting the situation.** (Notice your *thoughts*, *feelings*, or physical reactions regarding the situation.)

_____
_____
_____
_____

(2) **Make a promise to yourself to accept reality as it is.** (Turn your thoughts to what you KNOW (not what you think you know), and then make an internal commitment to accept things as is.)

_____
_____
_____
_____

(3) Do you accept the situation now? If not, repeat steps 1 and 2 until you fully accept what's happening.

DBT Core Skills

Implementing **Acceptance** and **Change** requires learning and continuously practicing four core skills: **Mindfulness, Distress Tolerance, Emotion Regulation**, and **Interpersonal Effectiveness**.

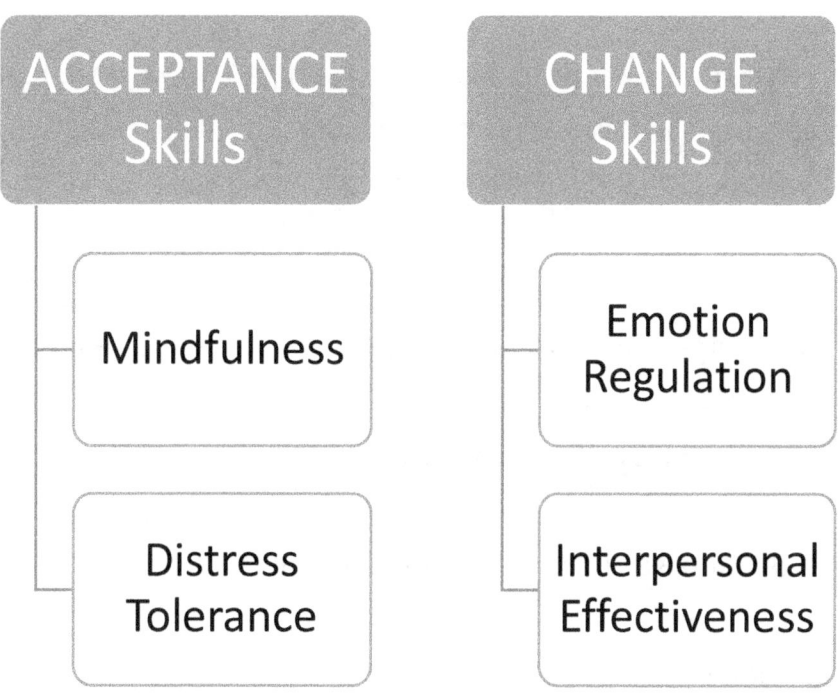

As illustrated above, **Acceptance** happens if we adopt **Mindfulness** and **Distress Tolerance** skills. **Change** happens when we learn how to manage our emotions (Emotion Regulation) better and build better relationships (**Interpersonal Effectiveness**).

Mindfulness

> *"Mindfulness is the aware, balanced acceptance of the present experience. It isn't more complicated than that. It is opening to or receiving the present moment, pleasant or unpleasant, just as it is."* - Sylvia Boorstein

Mindfulness is a state of awareness. It's deliberately placing your attention in the present moment and calmly noticing and accepting your feelings, thoughts, and body sensations without judgment. Numerous studies have shown that practicing mindfulness can improve mental health by lowering symptoms of anxiety and depression, improving mood, and increasing general well-being.[21,22,23,24,25]

Mindfulness makes us more aware of our thoughts and feelings, and we learn to observe them without getting caught up in them or reacting to them. This helps us develop a greater sense of control over our thoughts and emotions, reducing our experiences of unpleasant emotions.

Additionally, mindfulness helps us cultivate a more positive and compassionate attitude toward ourselves and others. By observing our thoughts and feelings *without judgment*, we become more accepting of ourselves, other people, and life in general.

In DBT, **Mindfulness** is composed of WHAT and HOW skills.

Mindfulness WHAT Skills

These skills are about <u>what you should do</u> to be more mindful.

1. **Observe**: Place your attention on what's happening in and around you. Please note them and your reactions to them, but DO NOT process, evaluate, hold on to, or dismiss anything. Just watch and observe.
2. **Describe**: Put words on what you observe but stick to the facts. Don't apply any opinions or try to interpret what you're observing.
3. **Participate**: Engage completely at the moment. You may not notice it, but you multitask constantly. For example, you're brushing your teeth for bed, but you're also (1) thinking about what to eat tomorrow while (2) planning your schedule so you don't get backed up, while (3) worrying if your partner will remember your birthday next week. STOP! Just brush your teeth. Stay in the moment and do just that one thing.

Mindfulness HOW Skills

These skills are all about how to be more mindful every day.

1. **Non-Judgmentally**: Be aware but don't label or judge anything. It just IS. And even though some situations may indeed be helpful or harmful, safe or dangerous, etc., acknowledge that fact and that fact alone. Don't evaluate or judge it further.
2. **One-Mindfully**: Pay FULL ATTENTION. Do one thing and one thing only. Don't let yourself be distracted, not even by your own intruding thoughts.
3. **Effectively**: Focus on what works for you and act based on your situation (not the situation you wish you were in).

If this all seems too much to take in, please STOP THINKING. Just embrace it for a while and see how it goes.

Worksheet: Box Breathing

One of the best ways to be "at the moment" is to start paying attention to how you breathe.

1. Lie on your bed or mat, or find a comfortable seated position.
2. Close your eyes and take a few deep breaths to relax your body.
3. **Inhale** through your nose for four counts. Imagine drawing the air all the way into your belly.
4. **Hold** your breath for four counts.
5. **Exhale** gently and completely through your mouth for four counts, releasing all the air from your lungs.
6. **Hold** your breath for four counts before starting the next inhale.

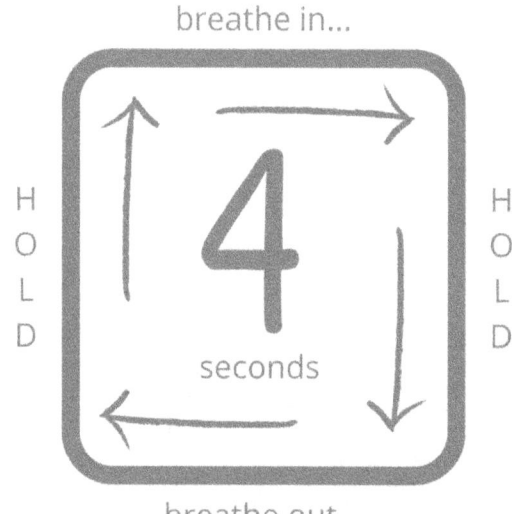

Repeat this pattern for several minutes, gradually increasing the duration of each breath and holding as you become more comfortable with the technique. The goal is to create a slow, steady breathing rhythm that helps calm your mind and body.

Worksheet: Belly Breathing

Belly breathing (a.k.a. diaphragmatic breathing) is a breathing technique that helps promote relaxation and reduce stress. Here are the steps to perform belly breathing:

1. Sit down comfortably or lie down on your bed.
2. Put one hand on your belly and the other on your chest.
3. Inhale gently through your nose, allowing your belly to expand like a balloon. (Your chest should remain relatively still.)
4. Exhale slowly through your mouth, letting your belly deflate like a balloon. (Try to let all the air out of your lungs.)
5. Continue to breathe this way, focusing on the sensation of your belly rising and falling like gentle ocean waves with each breath.

Ensure that you're breathing deeply from your diaphragm rather than shallowly from your chest. You can also practice this technique with closed eyes, visualizing a peaceful scene, or repeating a calming mantra to enhance relaxation. Gradually increase the duration of your belly breaths as you become more comfortable with the technique.

Wise Mind

Wise Mind is our inner wisdom. It's the synthesis of our emotional and rational sides. Often, when we're in the middle of an unpleasant situation, our emotions take over.[26] However, acting based purely on negative feelings doesn't always bring out the best in us or lead to the best situations. Basing decisions or actions purely on logic is not good either. This is because it means ignoring your own or someone else's feelings.

So, the best way to move forward is to consult both the **Emotional Mind** and the **Reasonable Mind**. The good news is that we do not need to "create" Wise Mind. We all have it already. Think of it as a muscle that we need to exercise more frequently. With consistent effort, relying on Wise Mind will become second nature.

EMOTIONAL MIND:
- feelings
- stress
- anger
- fear
- **acting based solely on emotions**
- judgmental
- opinionated
- reactive or defensive

WISE MIND

Wise Mind is the balance between emotions and reason.

It honors feelings, but it also considers reason or logic *before* acting or reacting to a situation.

REASONABLE MIND:
- data
- statistics
- facts
- **acting/reacting based solely on logic**
- focused
- organized
- based on past experience
- non-judgmental

Worksheet: Wise Mind

1. Write down a thought, person, or situation that may be upsetting you right now or has upset you in the past. *Example: I'm having this thought, "I don't belong here."*
   _____
   _____

2. Under **Emotional Mind**, please write down your mood or feelings about it. *Example: I feel sad, lonely, drained, empty, etc.*

3. Under **Reasonable Mind**, write down facts about the situation. (What do you KNOW for sure?) *Example: I deserve a place on earth. I've experienced happiness before.*

4. Under **Wise Mind,** write down any conclusions you reach after combining emotions and reasoning. *Example: I'm struggling now. That's okay; my feelings are valid. But I've been happy before, so I can be happy again.*

EMOTIONAL MIND   **REASONABLE MIND**

WISE MIND

Mindfulness is NOT for Me

Do you find yourself *rejecting* mindfulness? If you are, you're not alone. When I started my journey to mental healing, I was so desperate to get better that I was open to trying anything. So, I welcomed mindfulness. But I've also come across A LOT of people with mental illnesses who refuse to try mindfulness. At first, I was baffled, but I soon narrowed it down to a few reasons why.

1. **Misconceptions**: Some people think that mindfulness is a religious practice or that it requires them to engage in countless minutes of mind-numbing meditation. They may also believe it's too complicated or must be in a particular state of mind to practice it.
2. **Lack of Understanding**: Others may not fully understand mindfulness and how it can benefit them. They may not realize that mindfulness is a simple practice that can be done anywhere and anytime.
3. **Discomfort with Being Present:** Some people may feel uncomfortable and find it challenging to focus on the present moment without getting distracted by their thoughts or surroundings.
4. **Time Constraints:** People may feel they don't have enough time to practice mindfulness, especially if they have a busy schedule or a demanding job.
5. **Fear of Change**: Lastly, some may fear that practicing mindfulness will lead to changes in their lives for which they're not ready. It may also mean challenging their current beliefs and values.

Although I welcomed mindfulness into my life, I had a problem with #3 above. I wasn't uncomfortable being present but amazed at how difficult it was! I wasn't aware of how frantic my thoughts were until I attempted mindfulness. But, remembering Radical Acceptance + Change, I thought, *"I accept that I'm not as present as I want to be now. But I want to be, so I'll keep trying."*

I've also realized that mindfulness is not something you're just born with. True, it may come easier to others, but it's a skill anyone can learn given time, patience, and practice.

So I urge you to imagine mindfulness as an acorn seed. It's small, and it's hard to imagine what it would be like fully grown or what benefits you can get from it, but plant it anyway! Nurture it; keep at it and just let it grow and grow and grow. One day, you'll wake up, and there's an oak tree. It's strong; it's magnificent; it's powerful.

Distress Tolerance

> *"Stress is not what happens to us. It's our response to what happens. And RESPONSE is something we can choose."*
> — Maureen Killoran

Stress is a natural reaction to anything unpleasant. When a person is stressed, their body releases hormones like adrenaline and cortisol to help them respond to the perceived threat (a.k.a. the "fight or flight" response). Stress can be experienced in response to both positive and negative events, and it can be beneficial in small doses. For example, if you have a report due soon at work, stress can motivate you to think clearer and work faster. However, when stress becomes *distressing*, it's no longer helpful.

Distress is defined as excessive or continuous stress that negatively affects a person's well-being. It can cause physical and emotional symptoms, such as headaches, muscle tension, anger, depression, etc. When chronic or long-term distress can interfere with a person's ability to function in daily life and lead to long-term health problems.

Distress is stress that's crippling. It makes you perceive unpleasant situations as a "threat" and may make you incapable of coping. But distress isn't always paralyzing. **It can also make you behave in ways that make the situation worse.**

> Content Warning: the following story contains distressing material.

This is what Lucas[§], a reader, had to say: *"My girlfriend, Geri, went on a Ladies Only Weekend. She knows about my BPD, so she told me about her plans ahead of time. I knew where she would be staying, who she would be with, and what their plans were; we even made a calling and texting schedule. All was well, and I was genuinely okay with everything until the day she actually left.*

I saw her to her Uber, but as the car was driving away from me, I felt a sudden bolt of loneliness and resentment simultaneously. I went back inside, grabbed my phone, and deleted her phone number. I couldn't help it.

I was then filled with fear that I won't be able to communicate with her and that she won't ever return, so I frantically went through my address book and added her phone number again. I managed to wait until her plane touched down, and then I started to text her repeatedly, over and over. I knew I was being needy, but again, I couldn't help it.

When Geri didn't reply for three hours, I lost it. I was switching between anger and hatred, so I went out; one thing led to another, and I ended up cheating on her. I later found out that Geri's flight was delayed landing, and there was so much chaos with one of their luggage getting lost that she didn't hear my text messages. She eventually found out about my cheating, and we broke up.

As you can see from Lucas' story, if only he had given himself time and could tolerate his distress rather than behaving according to it, maybe he and Geri would still be together.

Now, you might be wondering, why do we lash out? Why can't we help but behave in ways that will probably worsen things? It's because we want relief from our distress. With Lucas' story, he wanted to be reassured *right away*. When that didn't happen, he tried to escape

---

[§] *Name changed for privacy.*

his distress by doing something impulsive. He didn't stop to think things through and consider the consequences.

This is what **Distress Tolerance** is all about. It's about learning ways to effectively cope with high-stress emotions and situations... so we don't worsen them.

Worksheet: Self-Soothe Using Your Five Senses

Grounding techniques connect you to the present to disconnect from your distress. For this grounding exercise, you'll use your five senses—sight, smell, sound, touch, and taste— to help you stay centered and focused and to lessen feelings of anxiety or overwhelm.

List FIVE (5) things you can see right now.

Example: coffee mug, water bottle, keys, notepad, alcohol gel

1.
2.
3.
4.
5.

List FOUR (4) things you can touch right now.

Example: keyboard, mouse, candy, tissue

1.
2.
3.
4.

List THREE (3) things you can hear right now.

Example: neighbor, passing car, howling wind

1.
2.
3.

List TWO (2) things you can smell right now.

Example: coffee, my hand lotion

1.
2.

List ONE (1) thing you can taste right now.

Example: dark chocolate

1.

If you're still distressed, repeat this exercise or write down as many things as possible per sense.

Worksheet: STOP

This **STOP** exercise will help you gain control of your emotions and avoid acting on them.

		STOP *Prevent Yourself from Reacting Based on your Distress*
S	Stop	Stop! Freeze and remain motionless. Don't even twitch a muscle. By entirely and physically freezing in your tracks, you prevent yourself from doing what your emotions want you to do.
T	Take a step back	Take a physical step back from the distressing situation. Take deep breaths or Box Breathe (page 58) for as long as you need to until you regain control of your feelings. Do not let your emotions dictate your behavior. We rarely need to make split-second decisions about anything, so give yourself time before deciding on anything. (**Tip**: Consult Wise Mind, page 60.)
O	Observe	Pay attention to what's happening inside you and around you. Make observations as if you're making a list. *Examples of observing something inside yourself:* *I'm mad.* *I'm freaking out right now.* *Examples of observing your surroundings:* *It's windy outside.* *My neighbors' kids are playing tag outside.* **What are you observing?** _____ _____ _____ _____ _____

STOP
Prevent Yourself from Reacting Based on your Distress

| P | Proceed mindfully. | Take a deep, relaxing breath and ask yourself, *"What can I do to improve this situation?"*

Example: I'm having self-harming thoughts. I'm going to call a hotline right now to talk to someone.

What do you want to do to proceed mindfully?
_____
_____
_____
_____ |

Emotion Regulation

> *"You do control the thoughts that follow an emotion, and you have a great deal of say in how you react to an emotion*
> *—as long as you are aware of it."*
> *– Travis Bradberry*

Emotions are an important component of the human experience, and they play a critical role in shaping our thoughts, behaviors, and interactions with ourselves and others. They're our responses to external stimuli, and they help us interpret and respond to the world around us. Without emotions, we wouldn't be able to experience or engage with the world around us fully.

However, if our behavior depends only on our emotions (Emotion Mind), we will most likely regret most of our actions. It's also worth noting that when we have a mental health problem, what we feel may not be appropriate or proportional to the situation. So what do we do? We must learn and adopt strategies to regulate intense and distressing emotions.

In DBT, **Emotion Regulation** skills aim to **decrease emotional reactivity** and **increase the ability to experience and tolerate a wide range of emotions**.

Before we proceed, I'd like to emphasize that **your emotions are valid**. Emotional invalidation damaged my healing when I suffered from mental health issues. When I was lonely and depressed, for example, and someone said, "get over it" or "stop overreacting," I felt even more alone in this world.
So please know that Emotion Regulation skills are NOT about discrediting or getting rid of your emotions. It's about learning ways to manage your emotions better so that you're not a slave to them.

I've also learned that even though my emotions are valid, they are not who I am. One of the ways I used to express my depression was through anger. I would lash out and say and do mean things whenever I felt scared, lonely, or anxious. After acting that way, I would feel remorse because I'm NOT an "angry person." I had a lot of love, kindness, empathy, and compassion to share.

So, the Emotion Regulation skills I learned in DBT helped me understand that I shouldn't let my distressing emotions run my life. I don't have to do what my emotions tell me to do. I am the one with the power to control my feelings.

Emotion Regulation skills differ from Distress Tolerance skills in that the latter focuses on surviving the moment, whereas the former focuses on **taking action to reduce the intensity of an emotional experience**.

Worksheet: The Happiness Habit

As I learned more about myself, I realized that being in a negative state of mind was easy. Due to my anxiety disorder, I had a constant feeling of dread, so my mindset was always tuned to waiting for something terrible to happen. Luckily, I found a book called *The Happiness Advantage*[27] by *Shawn Achor*.

In the book, an activity helped me make it a habit to think and remember good things and how to build happy memories. By doing so, I could slowly but surely reframe my mind to focus on the good stuff. I hope this activity also helps you.

Write down five (5) things that you are grateful for today.
1.) _____
2.) _____
3.) _____
4.) _____
5.) _____

–OR–

Write down one (1) positive event that has happened to you in the last 24 hours.

NEXT...

Think of an activity that makes you happy and commit to doing this for 30 consecutive days.

Joyful Activity: _____

Example: learning yoga

Commitment Statement:

I will _____ for 30 days.

Example: I will start my day with a short yoga routine for 30 days.

ALSO...

Be Mindful of Positive Experiences

Remember Mindfulness (page 55)? Whenever you do your Joyful Activity, give it your FULL ATTENTION. No multitasking! Experience the positive event one-mindfully.

After doing your chosen Joyful Activity, list down everything you noticed. Describe your feelings, thoughts, and even physical reactions in as much detail as possible.

Example: After my morning yoga routine, I feel at peace. I feel like I can breathe better. Physically, I'm still stiff, but I'm looking forward to being more flexible as I continue my yoga practice.

_____
_____
_____
_____
_____
_____

Learned Optimism

When suffering from a mental health disorder, it's hard to see life or the world as "half full"; it's nearly always "half empty." I know because I was an eternal pessimist.

As a kid, my OCD + GAD + depression dominated my life. I was constantly worried about doing something wrong and upsetting my dad. My parents' constant fighting made me nervous, stressed, and anxious. As an adult, I would complain A LOT. I was negative about everything and never took responsibility for anything (just like my mom).

While undergoing therapy, I realized that I had always thought that life was just something that happened to me. I had to learn that life doesn't "just happen." I'm not a bystander. In fact, I had the most significant say in what happened to me!

But first, I had to figure out how to see the world as "half full." I had to change my way of thinking from being a pessimist to an optimist. At first, it seemed impossible, but then again, we're not born pessimists. So, most likely, I learned to be a pessimist, and if I learned that, I could unlearn it.

Learned optimism is a theory developed by psychologist Martin Seligman[28]. It suggests that people can learn to be optimistic and happy by challenging negative self-talk and replacing them with positive ones.

The Three P's of Learned Optimism

1. **Personalization**: Optimistic people tend to view negative events as caused by external factors rather than blaming themselves. They see setbacks as temporary and specific to a particular situation rather than reflecting their overall worth.

    Takeaway: The next time something unpleasant happens, do your best to remove yourself from the equation so you don't self-blame. Imagine the event as a "sad movie"; experience it but don't make yourself part of the cast.

2. **Permanence**: Optimistic people view negative events as temporary and believe things will improve in the future. They don't see setbacks as permanent conditions.

   Takeaway: When something untoward happens, think, *"This too shall pass."*

3. **Pervasiveness**: Optimistic people tend to see adverse events as specific to a single situation rather than as a sign that everything in their life is going wrong. They know that even if they have challenges in one area, other areas of their lives may be doing well.

   Takeaway: For example, something unpleasant happened this morning. Say to yourself, *"That's okay. The rest of my day will still be great!"*

By practicing these three elements of learned optimism, we can become more resilient and better able to cope with unpleasant and volatile emotions.

You might think, *"That's great!"* But HOW does one change to be more optimistic? Following are some tips that will help.

Top 12 Tips to Be More Positive

1. **Develop an attitude of gratitude.** There's always something to be grateful for in life (e.g., waking up from a restful sleep, breathing fresh air, the refreshing effect of s shower, etc.) So, no matter how small, think about what you're grateful for every day. This can help you focus on the good things going on in your life.

   Write five (5) things you're grateful for in your life right now.
   1) _____
   2) _____
   3) _____
   4) _____
   5) _____

2. **Reframe pessimistic thoughts.** Whenever you have a negative thought, try to think of it better. For example, instead of thinking, "I'm a failure" when you make a mistake, think "I can learn from this and do better next time.":
3. **Spend time with people who have a positive outlook on life**, make you feel good, and inspire you.
4. **Celebrate small wins**: Instead of focusing on the big picture, take time to celebrate small accomplishments along the way.
5. **Exercise regularly**: Exercise releases endorphins, boosting your mood and increasing your overall sense of well-being.
6. **Practice mindfulness:** Focus on the 'NOW' and don't worry about the future or think too much about the past. This will help you feel more hopeful and less worried.
7. **Engage in activities that bring you joy:** Do things that make you happy and bring a sense of fulfillment to your life.
8. **Engage in optimistic self-talk.** Promote positivity by modeling positive self-talk. Simple reflections about what you enjoyed about your day, what you're grateful for, and what you intend to do to maximize your next day can be a powerful start to cultivating positive thoughts.

And don't be shy and give yourself credit whenever you deserve it! For example, did you help a friend? Called someone and made their day? Helped someone cross the street or get something at the grocery store they can't reach? Did you smile at someone?

Also, think of the strengths or skills you possess. You know there's GOOD in you, and you just need to tune into them more.

9. **Practice self-empathy.** BE KIND TO YOURSELF. Acknowledge your feelings and realize that you deserve kindness, understanding, and compassion just like everyone else. By becoming empathic with ourselves, we can understand better what we are going through.

10. **Put more emphasis on intention and effort rather than results.** Build optimism by having the right attitude to begin with. Positive thinkers always prioritize the *process* over the results. Encouraging yourself to partake in activities without thinking about the outcome is important. Be grateful for your efforts to become someone who believes in yourself and never gives up.

    And if something didn't turn out as planned, don't be too hard on yourself. Instead of judging your participation as a 'failure', commend yourself for trying and using that situation as a learning experience. Next time you'll know better, so you'll do better.

11. **Think of happier times.** Bad times are never-ending—if you keep thinking about them. Instead, remember past experiences that made you happy. Visualize that situation; remember what you felt then. Next, think of a past event that initially left you feeling sad but eventually overcame them. Now, let this motivate you. Think, *'if I overcame that, I could overcome this too now'*. (See related exercise, **The Happiness Habit**, on page 73).

12. **Change your perspective.** *What else could be true?* If you're a pessimist, you need to challenge your automatic negative way of thinking constantly. Over time, you won't even

need to shift your perspective. You'll find that you've broken the habit of thinking negatively and that thinking positively is now your nature.

13. **TUNE OUT negativity.** Look around you? Is anyone or anything contributing to your negativity? For example, are you at a job you're miserable in? Does the news depress you? Do you have a friend that does nothing but complain? (I mentioned before that it's said we're the average of our five (5) closest friends, so make an effort to find those who support and motivate. Don't surround yourself with people who bring you down.)

List these external sources and plan how to change *your* situation (not them).

As I've previously shared, I realized at one point that my family was the source of my negativity. So as hard as it was to do, living away from them (I moved to another continent!), at least for a while, was one of the best things I've ever done for myself.

Worksheet: ABCDE

This **ABCDE** exercise was developed by Martin Seligman to gauge your current mindset and to help you become more optimistic.

A	**Adversity**	**What difficult situation have you experienced recently?** *Example: Someone at work "joked" that my phone was "super-glued" to my hand.*
B	**Belief**	**What are the thoughts running through your mind about this adversity?** *Example: I'm a joke at work, and everyone's looking at me and making fun of me behind my back.*
C	**Consequence**	**What consequences and behaviors resulted from these beliefs?** *Example: I wanted to go home immediately, and I felt like every second I spent there was burning my skin, so I left. I filed for some sick leave and didn't return until the following week.*

D	Disputation	**Argue or dispute your beliefs.** *Example: I should learn to receive a joke as nothing but a joke. Also, I FELT my co-workers were looking at me and making fun of me behind my back. I don't know this for a FACT.* _____ _____ _____ _____ _____
E	Energization	**How do you feel now that you've challenged your initial beliefs?** *Example: I feel a little bit foolish and annoyed with myself. But then, I shouldn't feel that either. Next time, I should do <u>Distress Tolerance</u> (page 64) exercises before doing anything.* _____ _____ _____ _____ _____

Keep in mind that becoming more optimistic in life takes practice. I encourage you to do this exercise whenever you experience a challenging situation. Repetition is essential to move from one acquired mindset to another!

Interpersonal Effectiveness

"Relationships are like a garden. They take time, patience, and nurturing."—Unknown

We need people and relationships in our lives. If emotions are what make us human, relationships are what make life meaningful. In fact, according to the Harvard Study of Adult Development, *"close relationships, more than money or fame, are what keep people happy throughout their lives."*[29]

However, it's hard to find and form happy, healthy, and stable relationships when suffering from a mental health disorder. But it doesn't mean it can't be done.

Interpersonal Effectiveness refers to skills that foster healthy relationships. A great relationship has balance; there must be given and take. It can't be all about "me," and it can't be all about "you." Why? Because a relationship must be able to fulfill each participant's needs.

It can be very hard to effectively communicate what we want from a relationship when suffering from a mental illness. Some people ask for what they want in a way that is too pushy (aggressive), while others are too shy (timid).

We also tend to forget one crucial factor—we can only ask for our needs to be met; we shouldn't demand. And yet, when we state what we want in a relationship, we become so focused on trying to get what we want that we barely consider the other person's needs. We may also be unable to take the necessary steps to understand why someone says "no." (We feel the distressing pain of "no," but we don't comprehend why people say "no.")

So, Interpersonal Effectiveness skills cover many aspects of building healthy relationships. In DBT, the focus is on the following:

1. **How to be skillful in getting what you want and need from others.** This is to ensure that your needs in the relationship are met. You'll learn how to ask so that the other person *wants* to agree with you. But again, it's not always about trying to get what you want. You should also know when to ask and when to let things go.

2. **How to act in such a way that you maintain positive relationships.** This ensures that people have a "positive experience" with you when they interact with you.

"I've learned that people will forget what you said,
people will forget what you did,
but people will never forget how you made them feel."
—Maya Angelou

---

3. **How to maintain your self-respect in relationships.** This skill is about behaving, so you don't lose your respect for yourself. Sometimes, in our desire to keep a relationship, we might say or do things we don't really want. For example, we might bully or manipulate someone to make them cave and do what we want. This may help us attain a short-term goal, but in the long run, we may dislike ourselves and lose our self-respect.

Worksheet: DEARMAN

DEARMAN helps us ask for what we want without damaging our relationships. It allows us to be more assertive while considering the other person's feelings. DEARMAN is actually made up of two components:

- **DEAR**: <u>WHAT do you do</u> to get what you want?
- **MAN**: <u>HOW do you ask</u> effectively?

Describe the situation you want changed.

What do you want? Describe the situation clearly, and do your best not to relay any opinions or judgments. Stick to the facts.

Example: I asked if you could come home early last night, and you said "yes," but I waited until midnight.

_____
_____
_____
_____
_____

Express your thoughts and feeling about the situation.

Don't assume the other person knows your thoughts or feelings about the situation. Avoid misunderstandings by stating them clearly. Remember to use **'I'** statements. **'You'** statements might be interpreted as accusatory by the other person, increasing the likelihood of conflict.

Example: I was so worried and stressed while waiting for you to come home.

_____
_____
_____
_____
_____

Assert yourself.

Say what you want to happen, but don't be mean or aggressive about it. This will make it clear to the other person precisely what you want to happen.

Example: I want you to come home early when you say you will.

_____
_____
_____
_____
_____

Reinforce your request.

Make sure the other person knows how important your request is. Tell them you will be grateful if they give you what you want or need. You may also mention potential negative consequences if your request is not granted (but DO NOT make threats.)

Example: I'd really appreciate it if you came home early when you said you would. It would make me happy to spend more time with you. Also, it would prevent me from being so anxious and stressed.

_____
_____
_____
_____
_____

Mindfulness

Be in the moment and keep your words and feelings in check. No matter what the other person says, <u>stay on topic</u>.

Example: I understand you had to help a friend, but I would still prefer you prioritize coming home early. At the very least, I would like to have received your call.

Appear confident.

Adopt a confident demeanor through your words and body language. Also, do not apologize. Remember, you have a right to say what you want from the relationship.

Example: Sit or stand straight, roll your shoulders back, and keep eye contact. Then say, "I hope I'm making myself clear. I won't change my mind about this."

Negotiate

If the person doesn't want to do what you want, it's time to negotiate. This will allow you both to devise a solution that works for you both. You can provide them with a solution or ask what they think should happen next.

Example: How about you text when you think you're running late? This way, I at least know you're okay, and my thoughts don't go wild with worry.

Chapter Highlights:

- **Dialectical Behavior Therapy (DBT)** is the application of two seemingly diametrically opposed concepts: **Acceptance and Change**.
- **Mindfulness, Distress Tolerance, Emotion Regulation, and Interpersonal Effectiveness** are the four (4) core DBT skills.
- **Mindfulness** is a state of awareness or being fully present in the present moment.
- **Distress Tolerance** is the ability to endure unpleasant, painful events.
- **Emotion Regulation** is the awareness of painful emotions and how to control them so that you do not act destructively (a.k.a. acting on your emotions).
- **Interpersonal Effectiveness** is the ability to understand your own needs in a relationship and learn how to ask for them to be addressed while also acknowledging the needs of the other person in the connection.

Chapter 4: Dialectical Behavior Therapy for Borderline Personality Disorder (DBT for BPD)

> *"Mental health...is not a destination, but a process.*
> *It's about how you drive, not where you're going."*
> — Noam Shpancer, PhD

Studies show that DBT is a highly effective treatment for BPD.[30,31,32] In one study, it was discovered that after the first year of DBT treatment, 77% of individuals no longer fit the diagnostic criteria for BPD.[33]

DBT is effective for BPD because it directly addresses one of the main struggles of people with this disorder: emotion dysregulation.

Emotional dysregulation is the inability to manage or control one's emotional responses to stimuli (triggers). People who have trouble managing their emotions often react disproportionately to the situation. (This is why people often think that people with BPD are always overreacting.)

Further, individuals with emotion dysregulation find it challenging to return to a baseline emotional state after they've been triggered. This affects people with mental health problems two-fold. One, we suffer longer from our distress; two, we can't help but give in to our volatile emotional urges.

> Content Warning: the following story contains distressing material.

This is what Denise**, a reader, had to say: *"Sometimes, it feels as if I'm just watching myself from the outside. Before I learned how to better cope with my BPD, I would get easily triggered by my boyfriend, and things would escalate so quickly.*

One time, I offered him coffee, and he was so busy on his laptop that I guess he didn't hear me. Part of my brain registers this, "he is deep in thought with work." But I can't help how I feel.

I dumped the whole pot of coffee on the sink and stomped away. But he still didn't hear me! So I started having thoughts like, "He has forgotten me." And then I panicked and thought, "Maybe he met someone else." And then I got furious and thought, "HOW DARE HE." And then I felt so lonely and empty that I started crying and throwing stuff around in our bedroom.

My boyfriend heard me and came running upstairs. He had no clue what triggered me this time, but he still tried to touch me, and even though I KNOW it wasn't right, I started saying the worst things I could think of against him. And then, just like watching a movie or a stranger doing it, I saw my hand grab the heavy flashlight he keeps on his side of the bed and threw it right at him as hard as I could.

I can totally relate to Denise's story. Before DBT, when my OCD or GAD got bad, I often resorted to anger or self-isolation. Now I know that I only prolonged my suffering by being unable to control my emotions. And that by not being able to keep myself from acting based on my emotions, I only made the situation worse.

However, DBT is more than learning to control emotions. It helps significantly to *prevent* emotional reactions to triggers from happening in the first place. In my opinion, DBT is a highly effective way to deal with what happens *before*, *during*, and *after* a mental health episode.

** Name changed for privacy.

Worksheet: Radical Acceptance of Triggers

Individuals with BPD often struggle with intense emotional reactions because they find it difficult to accept the situation(s) that trigger their emotions. It's hard to accept things AS IS, and thoughts immediately go to doubt, fear of abandonment or rejection, feelings of low self-worth, and so on.

Now, you already did a [Radical Acceptance exercise](#) on page 48. For this particular activity, take a moment to think and write down some acceptance statements you can use specifically when triggered.

Remember:
- Be kind to yourself.
- You are NOT your illness. (You're not BPD. You have BPD.)

Examples:
1) *Okay, I'm having BPD symptoms now.*
2) *This is not me; this is my BPD talking.*
3) *I've just been triggered. I can't press "Rewind" and undo what happened so that I won't replay it in my mind.*

Your turn:

_____
_____
_____
_____
_____
_____

Worksheet: Turning the Mind to Cope

Radical Acceptance of triggers takes practice. In fact, you might find yourself often *rejecting* rather than *accepting* that you've been triggered. Turning the Mind (page 52) is a practice that involves repeatedly trying to move toward acceptance. The following activity is how to turn your mind to cope after being triggered.

Write down coping statements you can tell yourself after you've been triggered.

Examples:
1) *This is temporary. This is temporary. This is temporary.*
2) *I will be okay. I will be okay. I will be okay.*
3) *What happened, happened. The thing I can influence now is how I respond to it.*
4) *I don't need to do anything.*
5) *I don't need to react.*

Your turn:

_____
_____
_____
_____
_____
_____
_____

Worksheet: Desire to Change

You have to be open to change to live better and be happier. So, recommit to change by writing down some Change Statements below. Whenever you feel disheartened or discouraged, go back to what you wrote here to remind yourself why making changes in your life benefits you.

Examples:
1) *NOW isn't working for me. NEW will help me live better.*
2) *I want to change because I don't want life to pass me by.*
3) *CHANGE will help me LIVE, not just survive.*
4) *I want to change because I'm tired of constantly feeling angry, scared, and doubtful.*
5) *CHANGE will take me out of the shadows.*

Your turn:

_____
_____
_____
_____
_____
_____
_____
_____
_____
_____

Mindfulness

When struggling with a mental health illness, it's hard to stay "still." Our thoughts race like an avalanche, tumbling without any real reason or purpose. When this happens, we usually react to events without thinking. And often, our reactions DO NOT help the situation.

This is why I think of mindfulness as a "mental pause." It's a mental breather we give ourselves to take stock of the situation *before* we act.

In DBT, the goal of mindfulness is three-fold:

(1)   Reduce suffering and increase happiness.
(2)   Increase control of your mind.
(3)   Experience reality AS IS.

The above benefits may not seem evident at first. But to me, that's part of the beauty of this. When I began with DBT, I committed to having an open mind. I thought, *"I'll do what DBT teaches, and I won't judge it until I've tried it."* So, I learned mindfulness skills; I practiced them, and I lived them. And lo and behold—the above benefits did materialize.

One of the important things I also learned is that mindfulness is not something you utilize only when you need it. It's a quality you must cultivate in yourself to be constantly mindful. Also, note that mindfulness is the basis of all other DBT skills, so embracing this skill first is crucial.

Worksheet: One-Mindfully

Pick a task and give it your FULL ATTENTION. Do this one thing and one thing only. If you get distracted, that's okay; just say to yourself, *"Oops, I got distracted,"* and then pull yourself back to what you're doing. If you get distracted again, that's fine again. Keep pulling yourself back to the task on hand until it's finished.

Remember, this is not a contest. You're trying to learn a new skill. When you finish your activity, please answer the following questions.

What activity did you choose? _____
Example: washing my car

How long did you do this activity? _____
Example: 30-ish minutes

Did you get distracted? If so, what happened?
Example: Yes, my neighbor's kids were noisy. I couldn't concentrate.
Example: Yes, I kept having intrusive thoughts about my girlfriend, who was out.
Your turn:
_____
_____
_____
_____
_____

What did you do to pull yourself back from the distractions?
Example: I said to myself, "STOP," and then continued washing my car.
Example: I grabbed the sponge and squeezed and released it a few times to bring myself back to what I was doing.
Example: I took two deep breaths and continued washing my car.

Your turn:
_____
_____
_____
_____
_____

NEXT:

Pick an activity you can do one-mindfully for the next 30 days. The activity can be anything like brushing your teeth, washing dishes, eating breakfast, walking, etc.

The goal is to train yourself to focus on the task at hand and not get easily distracted.

Worksheet: Mindfulness Using Your Five Senses

Hold something, anything (e.g., a coffee mug, a pet, a sweater, etc.). Describe the object using your five senses—sight, smell, sound, touch, and taste. This exercise helps you take the time to engage in an experience fully and to do so *without judgment*. Stick to the facts when describing what you're holding. No opinions.

What object did you choose? _____

Example: a piece of dark chocolate

Describe what you SEE:

Example: it's dark; it's glossy; it's small

_____
_____
_____

Describe what you SMELL:

Example: it smells sweet

_____
_____
_____

Describe what you HEAR:

Example: my own breathing as I try to smell the chocolate

_____
_____
_____

Describe what you're TOUCHING:

Example: it's soft; it's sticky

_____
_____
_____

Describe what you TASTE:

Example: it's sweet and bitter at the same time

_____
_____
_____

Worksheet: Mindful Body Scan (Self-Observation)

Do this exercise to get better at paying attention to yourself. Try to do it every morning to center yourself *before* the day begins.

1. Sit or lie down, whatever is most comfortable for you.
2. Close your eyes.
3. Do the Box Breathing exercise (page 58) for at least two cycles.
4. Starting with the top of your head, become aware of your scalp.
5. Notice any areas of tension. Breathe in deeply and as you breathe out, soften and relax that part.
6. Next, become aware of your forehead.
7. Notice any areas of tension. Breathe in and as you breathe out, soften and relax that part.
8. Continue down until you've covered your whole body.

Worksheet: 4-7-8 Breathing

This breathing exercise is an advanced awareness technique. Concentrating on your breath calms your mind and brings your attention to the present. This is also an excellent exercise to do when stressed, anxious, or feeling any distressing emotions. By slowing down your breathing, you're calming your nervous system and inducing feelings of calm and relaxation.

1) Find a comfortable position. Take a few relaxing breaths to prepare your mind and body.

2) INHALE for 4 counts through your nose.

3) HOLD YOU BREATH for 7 counts...

4) EXHALE for 8 counts through your mouth.

5) Do steps 2-4 for at least four cycles.

Distress Tolerance Skills for BPD

Distress is excessive or continuous stress. It's a state of emotional and mental suffering caused by unpleasant circumstances. Before DBT, many mental health treatments were *change-focused*. That is, the purpose was to change upsetting events or situations so that the individual with the mental illness does not have to confront them or to reduce the likelihood of them experiencing them.

However, life likes to throw curveballs. Whether we like it or not, distressing events WILL happen in our lives. And so what we need to know is how to survive those moments.

In DBT, **Distress Tolerance skills are all about crisis survival**. In reality, when we're in distress, we cannot just "walk away." Somehow, we need to deal with it, but we shouldn't deal with it in ways that will worsen the situation. So, we must learn how to accept the situation—not ignore, deny, escape, or fight it— and learn how to bear our distress skillfully.

In the end, distress tolerance is the ability to see and be in our environment without trying to change it, to feel our distressing emotions without trying to change them, and to watch our own thoughts and actions without trying to stop or control them, but also... without having to act on them.

Worksheet: Grounding Activities

Following is a list of quick, easy-to-do grounding exercises. Whenever you're in distress, use any of these exercises to bring your attention back to the present moment and create distance from your distress.

- ☐ **Pick up or touch any object** near you and then do <u>Mindfulness Using Your Five Senses</u> (page 96).
- ☐ **Take a short walk.** Let nature distract and soothe you.
- ☐ **Bring yourself to a happy place or time.** Think of a happy memory or look at a picture that makes you happy. Mentally list down as many things as you can remember about this event. Really push yourself to recall as many details as you can. Challenge yourself to list at least 20 things about it.
- ☐ **Do, think, or say the mundane.** Think of something you do regularly, such as cooking breakfast, making coffee, showering, folding the laundry, etc.
  - If you're alone, do the task, but this time do it slower and really pay attention to all the steps.
  - If you're alone, say each step of the process aloud as if explaining how to do the task to someone.
  - If you're not alone, mentally go through each step of the process.
- ☐ **Make a "self-reward" list.** Grab a pen and paper (or do this mentally) and list how you will reward yourself after surviving your moment of distress. For example:
  - Go to the gym. (No excuses!)
  - Buy new, cozy pajamas.
  - Eat my favorite ice cream flavor.
    (Important: Ensure you don't always reward yourself with food.)
  - See a movie.
  - Buy a plant.
  - Get a haircut.

Worksheet: TIPP

The following exercise is about changing your body's chemistry to eliminate distressing or highly unpleasant feelings or urges. **TIPP** skills are easy to do and work fast to bring you down from overwhelming thoughts and emotions.

	TIPP *Change Your Body Chemistry*	
T	**Temperature**	Distressful situations make our body temperature rise. Cool down to counteract this physical response to stress. *Examples: Splash your face with cold water, hold an ice cube, take a walk in the cold, place your head inside the refrigerator for a few seconds*
I	**Intense Exercise**	Release pent-up frustrations and distress in a positive way by intensely exercising. Use up your body's stored physical energy by jumping jacks, walking quickly, jogging, running, etc. Exercising is a great mood enhancer[34], so engaging your body relieves you of emotional or mental burdens. If you don't have much time, try investing in some low-cost fitness equipment that you can use at home. For example, a set of resistance bands can help you squeeze in a quick 5-10 minute strength training routine at home. Can't get away from your desk? Purchase an inexpensive under-desk bike (desk cycle) to get some exercise in *while* working. You can also turn to apps like [5 Minute Home Workouts](#) by Olson Applications, [7 Minute Workout](#) by Workout Apps, [FitOn Workouts](#) by FitOn, and others to get in some fast exercise throughout the day.

	TIPP *Change Your Body Chemistry*	
P	**Paced Breathing**	Slow down your swirling thoughts and emotions by pacing (slowing down) your breathing. For example, do [Box Breathing](#) (page 58), [Belly Breathing](#) (page 59), or [4-7-8 Breathing](#) (page 99). **Tip**: If you need guidance, use apps such as *[Prana Breath](#)* or *[Breathe](#)* to stay on track.
P	**Paired Muscle Relaxation**	You can combine Paced Breathing above with Paired Muscle Relaxation. You should slowly tighten your muscles as you take a deep breath in, but not so much that they cramp. When you exhale, release all of your stress while reminding yourself to relax. **Tip**: Flex and relax your muscles as though you were performing a body scan. Flex and relax your face muscles first, then go on to your neck and shoulders. After that, flex and release your arms and hands before moving on to your core muscles. Repeat until you've reached your legs and feet.

Worksheet: ACCEPTS

ACCEPTS is an exercise in *distraction*. When we're in distress, we tend to focus or zero in on what's causing our distress, which is actually the opposite of what we should do. This is because the more we focus on our pain, the more agitated we become. Distracting ourselves limits our physical, emotional, and mental contact with whatever caused our distress. Distraction also helps us avoid giving in to dangerous emotional urges or behaviors.

ACCEPTS
Turn Your Attention to Something Else to Reduce Distress

A	**Activities**	What activities give you joy? Make a list of things that interest you and require you to pay attention while doing them. *Examples: painting, drawing, writing, meditating, etc.* Your turn: _____ _____ _____ _____ _____
C	**Contributing**	When you help someone, you stop thinking about yourself and start thinking about what you can do for others. Helping can help you forget your own problems, even for a while, and many people find that helping others gives their lives more meaning. And this isn't just a feeling—studies show that helping others activates the "reward" part of our brains.[35] So, by contributing, we make ourselves feel good. *Examples: run a food drive, assemble a care package for someone, make some soup and bring it to a sick friend, etc.* Your turn:

ACCEPTS
Turn Your Attention to Something Else to Reduce Distress

		_____ _____ _____ _____ _____
C	**Comparisons**	Compare your situation to a previously distressing one, and then try to see your circumstance more positively. *Example: A year ago, I was clueless about how to handle a BPD episode. I almost always end up harming myself or doing something to "punish" myself. Now, I can calm myself down most of the time.* Your turn: _____ _____ _____ _____ _____
E	**Emotions**	Distressing events or emotions are triggered. So, do something that will trigger *other* emotions. As much as we want to, we cannot summon other emotions on demand (by willpower only). To feel something else, we need to do an activity that will trigger that other emotion. *Example: Read an old love letter to bring up feelings of love and nostalgia; watch cute cat or baby videos on YouTube to feel happy; read a joke book to make yourself laugh, etc.*

ACCEPTS
Turn Your Attention to Something Else to Reduce Distress

		Your turn: _____ _____ _____ _____
P	**Push Away**	Instead of giving in to distressing emotions and unpleasant urges (behaviors), push them away. Select an activity from the list below. Please feel free to add more options as well. ☐ Physically leave the space where you are now. As you leave the room, imagine leaving your distressing thoughts and emotions in that room (i.e., do not bring them with you). ☐ Write down exactly what you're feeling on a piece of paper. Crumple that paper or tear it into shreds, and then throw it in a trash can. ☐ Go out for a walk. Grab a stone. Think of the stone as a representation of your distress, and then throw it away as hard as possible. ☐ Others: _____ _____ _____ _____
T	**Thoughts**	Think of something else other than your current situation. Following are a few ideas. Feel free to add more options if you want to.

ACCEPTS
Turn Your Attention to Something Else to Reduce Distress

		☐ Sing your favorite song in your mind. ☐ Look around and count how many people are passing by, or count how many people are wearing red, or count colors on wall painting; count anything. ☐ Pick a puzzle book and solve a puzzle. ☐ Play a game on your mobile phone or tablet. ☐ Others: _____ _____ _____ _____ _____
S	Sensations	Subject yourself to different physical sensations. Here are a few examples. Feel free to add more as you see fit. ☐ Take a hot or cold shower. ☐ Chew very sour candy. Hold an ice cube, ice pack, or bag of frozen vegetables. ☐ Squeeze a stress ball as hard as you can. ☐ Taste tabasco sauce or anything spicy. ☐ Listen to very loud music. ☐ Others: _____ _____ _____ _____

Worksheet: IMPROVE

IMPROVE is a selection of strategies designed to help you improve your moment of crisis by replacing immediate negative situations and feelings with more positive ones.

		IMPROVE *Make the Moment Better*
I	Imagery	Imagine or visualize a "happy place" you can mentally go to. Be as detailed as you can. *Example: I imagine going to that cozy coffee place in my neighborhood. It's quiet, and the smell of dark, delicious coffee fills my nose. I order my favorite drink, go to a quiet corner, and prepare to read for an hour in blissful solitude.* Your turn: _____ _____ _____ _____
M	Meaning	When life gives you lemons, make lemonade. That is, try to find or even create meaning from your painful or distressing situation. Ask yourself questions like, *"what good can come out of this?"* or *"what can I learn from this?"* or *"how can I use this situation to make things better?"* *Example: I've been through hard times, and they've strengthened me. I'll get through this, too, and be even stronger for it.* *Example: This is a wake-up call for me to seek more help.*

IMPROVE
Make the Moment Better

		Your turn: _____ _____ _____ _____
P	Prayer	For strength and comfort, turn to a higher power. Prayer has religious connotations, but its basic definition is to "make an earnest hope or wish." So, truly, you don't need to be religious or be a "believer" to pray. *Example: I wish for strength to get me through this.* Your turn: _____ _____ _____ _____ _____
R	Relaxation	Relaxing activities help you relax and calm your mind. Make a list of ten (10) calming activities. *Examples: drinking a hot or cold beverage, writing in my journal, doing a mindfulness exercise, attending a yoga class, etc.* What activities do you find relaxing? 1 _____ 2 _____ 3 _____ 4 _____

IMPROVE
Make the Moment Better

5 _____
6 _____
7 _____
8 _____
9 _____
10 _____

O	One thing at a time.	Do something one-mindfully. Don't think of the past, and don't think of the future. Just be present in this one thing that you're doing.

What did you do one-mindfully?

Example: I cooked chicken soup.

_____
_____
_____
_____
_____

Describe the moment.

Example: I ensured I was alone and played relaxing music in the background. I printed a recipe so that my whole focus went into each step of making the soup.

_____
_____
_____
_____

V	**Vacation**	Disengage and take a short break from adulthood. *Example: go to the beach and take the morning (or afternoon) off, put your phone on silent and take a walk for exactly one hour, etc.* Your turn: _____ _____ _____ _____ _____
E	**Encouragement**	Be your own cheerleader and talk to yourself as you would a friend. *Example: I am stronger than my fears.* *Example: I can do this!* *Example: This feeling won't last forever. I WILL survive.* Write down five (5) positive affirmations for yourself. 1 _____ 2 _____ 3 _____ 4 _____ 5 _____

Worksheet: PROs and CONs

When we're in distress, we're not just feeling emotions such as sadness, loneliness, anger, emptiness, and others. We also have this almost irresistible urge to do something about it! As mentioned before, unhealthy emotional urges or crisis behaviors usually worsen things instead of improving them.

This PROs and CONs exercise aims to show you the positives and negatives of acting on your impulses and the positives and negatives of not acting on your impulses. Hopefully, you'll see that radically accepting the situation and tolerating your distress is better than acting on your emotional urges.

PROs and CONs
Advantages and Disadvantages of Acting Out and Not Acting Out Urges

What situation is causing you distress?

Example: I'm at a party. I go get some drinks in the kitchen, and suddenly I hear everyone erupt in loud laughter in the living room. My mind goes, "They're laughing at me!" and I feel this intense sense of embarrassment. I feel ganged up upon by everyone. I can feel the temperature rising inside me to my face as my intense feeling turns into rage.

_____
_____
_____
_____
_____

Emotional Urge:

Example: I want to grab a beer bottle, return to the living room and throw it at them.

_____
_____
_____
_____
_____

PROs and CONs
Advantages and Disadvantages of Acting Out and Not Acting Out Urges

	PROS	**CONS**
Acting Out Emotional Urge	*Example:* *I'll feel some instant relief.*	*Example:* *I might seriously hurt someone if I throw that beer bottle.*
<u>**NOT**</u> **Acting Out Emotional Urge**	*Example:* *I prevent possibly hurting someone.* *I prevent "making a scene."*	*Example:* *My friends won't know it hurts me when people laugh when I'm out of the room.*

Emotion Regulation Skills for BPD

As mentioned before, DBT is about the coming together of two seemingly opposing ideas: Acceptance and Change. **Emotion Regulation** is part of that change process inside you.

You're not just fully aware now (Mindfulness, page 55) or trying to survive a crisis (Distress Tolerance, page 64). You will now learn the skills to effectively take action to CHANGE the intensity of unpleasant emotional experiences.

You may wonder, *"Why do I have such overwhelming emotions?"* It's crucial to remember that feeling an emotion is not what causes problems. How you understand or interpret the emotion tends to make the feeling worse and make you feel like you can't handle it.

For example, say a colleague walks right by you in the hallway without saying a word. You have an almost tsunami-like rush of feelings like confusion, disappointment, anger, rejection, or maybe even fear. These feelings quickly turn into a series of thoughts such as, *"Why didn't they say "hi"?", "Did I do something wrong?", "Is this about the report I filed last week?", "Is there a rumor about me at the office I don't know about? "Am I going to get fired?!"*.

These raging emotions (feelings) and thoughts (assumptions) may lead you to behave (act) in ways you regret. For example, you might think of resigning because you can't bear the thought of getting fired.

Emotion regulation skills are all about breaking this cycle of negative emotions, thoughts, and behavior.

Worksheet: Check the Facts

When we're in distress, it's challenging to take a step back and consider whether our feelings are proportionate to what just happened. **Check the Facts** is a technique for pausing, reflecting, and fact-checking our emotions. This allows us to make rational sense of a situation and avoid overreacting.

Let's start with a reflective exercise. Go back and think of a couple of incidents where you overreacted. It could also be an occurrence that seemed significant at the time but turned out to be insignificant after all.

Question: What emotion do you want to fact-check?
Example: my extreme loneliness
Your answer:

Question: What happened? What triggered this emotion?
Example: A friend of mine told me that I'm always overreacting.
Your answer:

Question: What assumptions did you make about the event?
Example: I can't share ANYTHING with anyone... ever.
Your answer:

Question: What did you do?

Example: I bottled up everything inside me, making me feel so alone in the world.

Your answer:

CHECK THE FACTS!

You listed your assumptions above, but <u>WHAT ELSE</u> could the situation mean? Try to think of the situation as a whole, not just your reaction. Consider what happened before, during, and after the event, if possible.

Example: I told my friend I wanted to resign that day because I felt I was not connecting to anyone at work. That's why she said I was overreacting. Looking back, my friend was not in the best of moods that day because her son got into a fight at school, so she probably didn't mean what she said.

Your answer:

Question: Why do you think you reacted that way?

Example: I didn't have the tools yet to think things through. My emotions go through me like a raging river I can't keep up with.

Your answer:

Question: Looking back, on a scale of 0-5, did your emotion fit the facts? (0 = not at all, 5 = yes):

Example: 1, a tiny bit, I guess

Your answer:

Question: If your emotion DID NOT fit the facts, what would you do differently?

Example: I would do some grounding exercises first to ease my pain. Then I would think about why she said what she said. (Before, I couldn't think so much about other people's WHY. I just felt what I felt.)

Your answer:

Question: If your emotion DID fit the facts, would you do anything differently?

Example: Yes. Bottling up my emotions DID NOT do me any good. I know now that I just prolonged my suffering, and I should have found other ways to deal with my pain.

Your answer:

Note: **Check the Facts** can help you whenever you feel an unpleasant emotion. This exercise is not just about previous experiences. But I do suggest you do the above exercise at least twice more. This way, you train yourself to get into the habit of fact-checking your feelings.

Worksheet: Opposite Action

When what we feel doesn't fit the facts of the situation, acting opposite to these emotions can make us feel better. There are also many times when what we feel matches the facts of the situation, but acting on those feelings still won't help us.

For example, say that you and your friend have been planning a weekend getaway for months. Days before the planned vacation, your friend calls and cancels but cannot tell you exactly why yet. They promise to explain everything in a day or two. You're disappointed, upset, angry, and feeling very alone. You feel abandoned, so you ghost your friend for weeks. They call, text, email—but you refuse to reply. They eventually got tired of trying. To you, this *proves* that they truly abandoned you. Months pass, and you and your friend accidentally meet. You get talking and know now that your friend's reasons for canceling were valid. You regret ghosting your friend because you really missed them and know that you wouldn't have felt so lonely for months if you hadn't.

In this case, you can see that even if we think we're "justified" to act the way we want to, it doesn't make things better for us. So, what do we do?

First, [radically accept](#) (page 48) the situation.
Second, do any of the [distress tolerance](#) exercises in this book (page 100) to survive the crisis.
Third, do the **Opposite Action** exercise below.

Opposite Action not only prevents you from acting out your emotional impulses. By doing the *opposite* of what you want to do, you're influencing how you feel about the situation. For example, say you're angry, but instead of punching someone (which is what you want to do), you watch cute and funny baby videos on YouTube instead. After a few minutes, you'll most likely realize that you're not as angry as you were before.
Column A covers unpleasant emotions. **Column B** shows what you would ordinarily want to do when you feel these emotions. **Column C** lists a counter-action to your initial natural

inclination. When an unpleasant situation arises, and you feel an emotional urge, turn to this table and what you wrote in Column C.

OPPOSITE ACTION
Do the Opposite of What You Feel to Start Feeling Better

A Emotion *What you are feeling.*	B Emotional Impulse *What you would usually do when you feel this way.* *(If you want to do something other than what's on this list, please write it down on a separate sheet.)*	C Opposite Action *Write down a counter-action to what you're feeling.*
Emptiness	Ghost everyone	*Promptly reply to messages I receive*
Guilt	Self-blame or blame others (deflect)	
Anger	Break something, shout, punch, or throw something	
Fear	Stay indoors	
Sadness	Self-isolate, eat all day, turn to alcohol	
Loneliness	Self-harm	
Frustration	Throw-out things	
Helplessness	Cry all day	
Resentment	Spread rumors about someone; plan some form of revenge	

OPPOSITE ACTION

Do the Opposite of What You Feel to Start Feeling Better

A	B	C
Emotion	**Emotional Impulse**	**Opposite Action**
What you are feeling.	*What you would usually do when you feel this way. (If you want to do something other than what's on this list, please write it down on a separate sheet.)*	*Write down a counter-action to what you're feeling.*
Feel free to add more emotions and scenarios in the extra rows below.		

Worksheet: PLEASE

Your physical health has a direct effect on how you feel.[36] So, if you want to feel better emotionally, you must also take care of yourself physically.

	PLEASE *Take Care of Your Mind by Taking Care of Your Body*	
PL	**Physical Illness**	If you're feeling physically ill, don't put off seeing a doctor or taking any prescribed medications. It is also advisable to contact someone (e.g., a friend, a family member, a loved one, a neighbor, etc.) so that you are not alone at this difficult time. If you don't want to see a doctor or are physically unable to do so, then go for a holistic approach to well-being, such as reiki, acupuncture, aromatherapy, acupressure, yoga, etc. The goal is to get the help you need as soon as possible so your sickness doesn't worsen. **Tip**: Please see your doctor for a yearly checkup to avoid getting any physical illnesses.
E	**Balanced Eating**	Adopt a healthy and balanced diet. According to the American Dietetic Association, when people are stressed or unhappy, they tend to eat too much or too little. Yet, these behaviors are not beneficial at all. If we eat too much, we experience sluggishness and weight gain. If we eat too little, we end up with no energy. The best way is to eat a healthy and balanced diet, but what does that look like? According to the Healthy Eating Plate:

PLEASE
Take Care of Your Mind by Taking Care of Your Body

S		½ your plate should be made up of fruits and vegetables, ¼ of your plate should be whole grains, and the final ¼ of your plate should be devoted to protein.[37] Also, try to consume foods that make you feel good. For example, if eating a piece of chocolate makes you happy, then do that. However, do not overconsume or develop a routine around it. For instance, don't eat a piece of chocolate at the end of each day so you don't feel bad. Eat a small piece of chocolate on really stressful days to feel good! Remember, when it comes to food: everything is in moderation.
A	Avoid Unhealthy Substances	Consuming unhealthy substances such as caffeine, alcohol, and prohibited drugs can exacerbate your anger, so avoid taking them. Instead, consume water or lemon water, green tea, healthy smoothies, etc.
S	Sleep	According to the American Academy of Sleep Medicine and Sleep Research Society, adults need seven (7) or more hours of quality sleep each night.[38] Quality and quantity of sleep are important because chronic sleep debt contributes to emotional stability.[39,40] Establishing a healthy sleep routine is one of the best ways to ensure you have a good night's rest. Here are a few helpful tips: 1. **Establish "sleep time."** Create and stick to a predictable sleep pattern, especially on weekends. Sleep

PLEASE
Take Care of Your Mind by Taking Care of Your Body

and wake up at the exact times every day, and take no more than a 10-minute nap during the day.

2. **Establish a relaxing "before bedtime" ritual.** Make a relaxing routine for going to bed, such as taking a warm bath, reading a book, or listening to soothing music. This signals your body that it's time to relax and go to sleep.

3. **Bed = sleeping only.** Don't use your bed for any other activity other than sleeping. Don't watch TV, read, mindlessly scroll social media sites, etc., in bed.

4. **Avoid stimulants before bedtime.** Don't consume caffeine or alcohol or any big meals just before bedtime.

5. **Do things that induce sleep.** Turn off the lights and keep the room silent. Make sure your blankets are thick during cold months, or use an electric blanket. During the warm months, consider using a fan. Use earplugs or turn on a white noise machine if it's noisy outside. Do what you need to do to fall asleep.

6. **Don't "mentally stray" too long.** Give yourself 30 minutes to an hour to fall asleep. If you're still awake, think about what's preventing you from sleeping. For example, if you're thinking about work, tell yourself, "Stop," and then visualize yourself in a calm and relaxing space.

7. **Consider natural sleep aids.** Natural sleep aids like valerian root, melatonin, or chamomile tea may help you feel more relaxed and sleep better.[41,42] (Please note that you should always consult your doctor before taking supplements.)

PLEASE
Take Care of Your Mind by Taking Care of Your Body

		8. **Do not overanalyze or catastrophize.** Tell yourself that you need to rest your mind and body to have a great day tomorrow and that you're still resting if you can't sleep. That is, don't think being unable to sleep is a catastrophe.
E	Exercise	Research shows that engaging in physical activities can increase happy feelings while decreasing negative ones.[43,44] The general recommendation is to exercise for at least 30 minutes a day. If you haven't worked out in a while, start with shorter, less intense workouts such as walking or power walking for just 10 minutes and build your routine from there. The beauty of picking up this healthy habit is that there's no need for any "preparation." You don't need to join a gym or sign up for a class. You can just go out for a walk or run, follow a yoga, Pilates, or Zumba class online, and so on.

When doing **PLEASE**, don't forget that these are not one-time things to do. The goal is to establish a consistent routine to reap the benefits mentioned in this exercise truly.

Since individuals with BPD experience intense and unstable emotions, staying on track with our intentions can be difficult. For example, say you want to schedule a 30-minute jog thrice a week. However, when you wake up, you first grab your mobile phone to check for messages. When someone you expect to message doesn't, it throws off all your plans to jog. So, how do you increase the probability of sticking to a new routine? Here are some helpful tips.

Top 10 Tips to Start and Stick to a Routine

1. **Focus on one change first.** Don't overhaul every aspect of your life in one go. If you try to take on too many changes, you won't be able to stick to any of these new routines.

2. **Think "small steps."** Start by establishing simple, attainable goals that you can easily achieve. For example, if you're a night owl who usually sleeps at 2:00 AM, then drastically changing your bedtime to 10:30 PM might be too big a change. So, gradually adjust your bedtime by sleeping 15 minutes *earlier* each night until you reach your target bedtime.

3. **Create a strategy.** Write down your routine and stick to it. Make changes to your daily schedule and prioritize accordingly. For example, if you usually have dinner at 8:00 PM, then a 10:30 PM bedtime is neither advisable nor feasible. So, this means having to adjust what time you eat dinner too. In this scenario, aim to eat at 6:30 PM at the latest.

4. **Think of positive consequences.** For example, suppose you want to sleep seven (7) hours each night consistently. In that case, a positive consequence might be that you'll have more energy during the day and thus be more productive at work.

5. **Be consistent.** Establishing a new routine requires consistency. Make it a habit to do the same things at the same time every day. For example, say you want to establish a morning yoga routine. You've determined that you need to sleep by 11 PM to wake up at 6 AM in order to fit in an hour of yoga. You've set this schedule because you must hit the shower by 7 AM, have breakfast by 8 AM at the latest, commute to work and be on your desk by 9 AM. The first few days may be difficult, but if you stick to this schedule, yoga WILL become a part of your morning routine.

6. **Find accountability.** Find someone to hold you accountable, whether it's a friend, family member, coach, Facebook group or other online support group. This will help you stay motivated and on track.

7. **Reward yourself!** Acknowledge your accomplishments and reward yourself for keeping to your regimen. This can assist in pushing you to continue and make the habit more fun. For example, say you're successful in establishing a morning yoga routine. Good for you! Reward yourself by purchasing a yoga mat, yoga clothes, or other yoga gear.

8. **Stay positive.** Even when things are unpleasant, focus on the positives of your new regimen. Be patient with yourself, and remember that transformation takes time and effort.
9. **Be flexible.** Be willing to make changes to your routine as needed. Life happens, and you may need to alter your routine to accommodate your shifting schedule or circumstances. For instance, say that after weeks of successfully shifting to a healthier diet, you're asked by your boss to join a 3-day seminar where you know you won't be able to stick to your new eating plan and will most likely be confronted with less-than-healthy food options. Instead of panicking or stressing out, be flexible and adjust. Prepare healthy snacks to bring, check out restaurant menus in the area, so you have healthier food options to order, and so on.
10. **Manifest success.** Picture yourself completing your routine and reaching your goals. Visualizing success might assist you in being motivated and devoted to your new routine. For example, imagine yourself entering your bedroom extremely relaxed. You pull your silk bedsheet and spray some lavender mist. (You discovered this helps you sleep, so you bought some.) Picture yourself lying down, feeling calm, and slowly drifting off to sleep. Visualize this happening night after night. Next, imagine yourself waking up from your restful sleep feeling energized and ready for the day's opportunities.

Worksheet: COPE AHEAD

COPE AHEAD is an exercise that helps you identify situations that are likely to trigger a BPD episode. (**Tip**: If you don't know your triggers, please see the Trigger Journal on page 150.)

Knowledge is power. So, if you know your triggers, you can devise a plan so that you know what to do whenever you're triggered. This way, you're less of an enslaved person to your emotions and will feel less pain and suffering from the situation.

However, coping ahead is not just about planning but trying to really live and execute that plan in your mind. Why? Research shows that visualizing activity in detail activates many of the same parts of the brain as doing that activity. (i.e., thinking is doing).[45]

COPE AHEAD
Plan for Difficult Situations

Triggering Event or Situation:
Example: My birthday

Your turn:

_____

_____

_____

Why is this event a trigger?
Example: Days before my birthday, I panic and stress out. I'm afraid people will forget to greet me, and then I spiral into feelings of distress, pain, loneliness, anger, shopping sprees, alcohol, and just about anything I can think of. I want people to remember me and show love on my birthday, but when they do, I don't think I deserve any of it.

Your turn:

_____

_____

_____

What DBT skills do you want to use to handle this situation?

Example: I need A LOT of Mindfulness (page 55) and Distress Tolerance (page 64) days before my birthday. My plan is to start EACH day with some Mindfulness exercises. And then have my go-to grounding exercises ready.

Your turn:

_____

_____

_____

Imagine the situation happening RIGHT NOW.

(Be as detailed as you can.)

Example: It's my birthday; my parents greet me and remind me of the birthday dinner they booked at my favorite restaurant. I start to panic, so I do the following:

    (1) Box Breathing (page 58)

    (2) Wise Mind (page 60)

    (3) Self-Soothe Using My Five Senses (page 67)

    (4) IMPROVE (page 108)

And then I repeat to myself over and over and over, "I'm good. I deserve this."

Your turn:

_____

_____

_____

Role-play; imagine in your mind how the situation is going to unfold.

Example: Waiters burst out with a birthday cake during my birthday dinner and sang 'Happy Birthday.' I feel like I'm drowning. I look at my mom, who's always been my rock, and stare at her supportive face. I then smile and say Thank You to the servers. I look at my watch and time myself for two minutes. Next, I stand up and go to the washroom to splash cold water on my face. I return, look at my dad, and say, "Where's my slice of cake?"

Your turn:

_____
_____
_____

> **Take a break.** Mental role-playing can be tiring. Also, since you're thinking about a stressful situation, the role-playing itself may distress you. As such, taking a break after this step is critical.
>
> *Example: walk outdoors, attend a yoga class, take a relaxing shower, etc.*

Your turn:

_____
_____
_____

Interpersonal Effectiveness Skills for BPD

You have a relationship with everything and everyone around you. Say you have a plant at home. If you want to keep that plant, you need to water it, put it out to get some sun, fertilize it, and so on. If you do these things, you're keeping the plant alive for its benefit and for yours. If the plant grows and thrives, it will help improve indoor air quality, reduce your stress[46], help with your mental well-being[47], and so on. It will wither and die if you don't care for the plant. Pretty much the same can be said about human interactions and relationships.

Relationships are about individuals trying to form a bond to fulfill their needs. You don't get into a relationship for the sole benefit of others. You do it also for your benefit. **Interpersonal Effectiveness** is about finding that "balance" to find and keep healthy relationships.

As someone with co-existing mental health problems, it was hard to see other people. Most of the time, I was focused on getting rid of the dark cloud of my OCD, anxiety, and depression that I either self-isolated (not wanting to deal with people at all) or wanted everything my way whenever I did deal with people. As you can imagine, it's not a way to build lasting relationships.

Thankfully, with DBT's interpersonal effectiveness skills, I could adjust and finally find and feel relationships that last.

Before doing the following exercises, I suggest you do the DEARMAN exercise again on page 84.

Worksheet: GIVE

GIVE is an exercise in maintaining positive relationships. The goal is to ensure that the person you're communicating with leaves your interaction feeling good about it. You see, people often say no to what we ask for, not because they don't agree with us, but because of *how* we ask. No one likes to feel like they're being manipulated into agreeing with something or made to feel bad if they don't agree with us. **GIVE** teaches us how to say what we want in a way that makes others want to give us what we want.

GIVE
How to Create Positive Interactions

G Gentle

Be gentle. Be nice and respectful, and don't offend others with which you interact. If someone disagrees with you, don't be judgmental or make personal attacks or threats.

What can you SAY to convey gentleness?

Example: I see that we don't agree, but I respect your opinion.

Your turn:

_____

_____

_____

What can you DO to convey gentleness?
List three ways.

Example: DON'T fold your arms across your chest, DO look at the other person directly when they speak

1.
2.
3.

GIVE
How to Create Positive Interactions

I	**Interested**	**Act interested.** Actively listen when other people speak and truly try to understand their point of view.
		
		What can you SAY to convey your interest?
		Example: Hmmm, I didn't know that. Thanks for telling me.
		Your turn:
		
		_____
		
		_____
		
		_____
		
		What can you DO to convey your interest?
		List three ways.
		Examples: make eye contact, physically face the other person with your whole body, don't keep checking your phone, etc.
		   1.
		   2.
		   3.

V	**Validate**	Demonstrate that you understand the other person's words with WORDS and ACTIONS. **What can you SAY to convey that you're validating the other person?** *Example: If I understand you correctly, getting the report in by Friday is impossible because Greg from another department gave you another task.* Your turn: _____ _____ _____

GIVE
How to Create Positive Interactions

What can you DO to show *validation* to others? List three ways.

Examples: touch the other person (if appropriate), nod your understanding, move to a more private place if you see the other person acting uncomfortably, etc.

1.
2.
3.

E | Easy Manner

Take on a **friendly, easygoing attitude**. When you have a friendly and non-threatening attitude, people will feel more at ease and be more open to what you want. This also means that you shouldn't argue, shout or make demands.

What can you SAY to convey in an easy manner?

Example: I understand entirely, but are you sure you can't squeeze this short report in? Please?

Your turn:

_____

_____

_____

What can you DO to convey an easy manner to others? List three ways.

Examples: smile, adopt a relaxed demeanor (e.g., don't fidget, tap your nails on a table, or look as if you're about to end the conversation abruptly), etc.

1.
2.
3.

Tip for a Great Read: Consider getting *How to Win Friends and Influence* people by Dale Carnegie.[48] It's an excellent resource for improving your communication skills and building relationships.

Worksheet: FAST

FAST is an exercise where we learn to try to get what we want from interactions while keeping or improving our self-respect. When we want someone to like us, agree with us, or do what we want, we might use "drastic measures" like begging, coercing, or even threatening. However, when we do this, we lose our self-respect sooner or later.

> Content Warning: the following story contains distressing material.

This is what Cori[††], a reader, had to say: *"I was 30 and living with my girlfriend for nearly two years. TWO YEARS. That's actually something I'm proud of, as most of my previous relationships lasted only a few months.*

I love Gina with all my heart, but my BPD meant going through a lot of "idealization" and "devaluation" cycles. One day I would shower her with love, praise, and gifts, and then a few days later, I would think of her as worthless and criticize everything about her.

One time, she got so fed up that she said, "I love you. Remember that." I can't describe what I felt. It was as if someone stabbed me in the chest and kept on twisting and twisting and twisting that knife. As she gathered some stuff to leave, I hugged her hard and begged her not to go. I kept crying, apologizing, and begging over and over. When she seemed unmoved, I said, "I'll kill myself if you go." As soon as the words left my mouth, enormous shame engulfed me like a tidal wave.

Gina stayed for the next 5 days and 12 hours. She told me she didn't want to leave me in that state. She also told me that what I said was when she knew I wasn't the right man for her. I completely understood, of course.

It took me MONTHS to get my life back on track. It felt like all the progress I'd made so far with this disease had been wiped out. One day, during a session with my therapist,

---

[††] *Name changed for privacy.*

we uncovered that the reason it was taking me so long to get better wasn't just because of my failed relationship but also because I had lost my self-respect. When I realized this, things started to improve because I knew what I should focus on first.

		FAST *How to Ask and Still Maintain Self-Respect*
F	**(Be) Fair**	Be reasonable and fair to yourself and the other person. Remember that your thoughts, opinions, and feelings have EQUAL value. Don't get dramatic, act out, or say angry things. Stick to the facts. *Example: I prefer if you don't just drop by for a visit. I truly appreciate your gesture, but it disrupts my routine, and it's something I need for my BPD.* Your turn: _____ _____ _____ _____
A	**(No) Apologies**	There's no need to apologize for communicating what you want or when you want to say "No" to someone. Your thoughts, opinions, and feelings are valid, so you don't need to apologize for them. And if you did something wrong, apologize only once; do not over-apologize. *Example: So, thanks in advance for understanding my need for routine. NOT: I'm so sorry you can't visit whenever you want to. I feel terrible about it.* Your turn: _____ _____ _____ _____

FAST
How to Ask and Still Maintain Self-Respect

S	**Stick to Your Values**	Don't give in just because the other person dislikes or wants to do what you want. Stick to what you believe in. *Example: A person you asked not to visit unannounced dropped by again without letting you know in advance. Open the door a little, but not too much, to show that you're not letting them in. And then say something like, "Hi. I mentioned before that unannounced visits disrupt my routine terribly. Thanks for thinking of me, but please call next time." Usually, this prompts the other person to apologize quickly and leave. Wait for that before gently closing the door. If they still try to persuade you to let them in, by all means, close the door on them now.* Your turn: _____ _____ _____ _____ _____
T	**Truthfulness**	Don't lie, act helpless, make excuses, or exaggerate to get what you want. *Example: Don't say, "Oh, thanks for visiting, but I'm just about to leave RIGHT NOW for a very important appointment," if that's not true.* Your turn: _____ _____ _____ _____ _____

Self-Harm

> Content Warning: the content contains distressing material.

When a person with BPD feels emotionally overwhelmed, there is a strong need to do something to alleviate the intensity. Self-harm is frequently used as a temporary cure to alleviate the overwhelming nature of their terrible feelings.[49] The Diagnostic and Statistical Manual of Mental Disorders, Fifth Edition (DSM-5) says that up to 80% of people with BPD hurt themselves at some point in their lives.

Self-mutilation, a form of self-harm, is when a person destroys or changes their body tissue on purpose but not intending to take their own life. This pattern of behavior is believed to be common in BPD (50-80% of cases) and highly repetitive (more than 41% of patients who self-mutilate do it more than 50 times).[50]

I have had "brushes" with self-harm. On several occasions, I would step out to my then 17th-floor balcony and wonder what would happen if I jumped. Would I make it? Was I going to be paralyzed? What would my last thoughts be before collapsing? Would anyone even care? Luckily, I was always able to bring myself back from the edge.

So, my sincere wish for you is this: whenever you feel like harming yourself, I hope you pull yourself back too. You may not see it now, but I assure you, life IS worth living.

The Vicious Cycle of Self-harm

One of the things that helped me overcome my self-harming thoughts was understanding the cycle of self-harm.

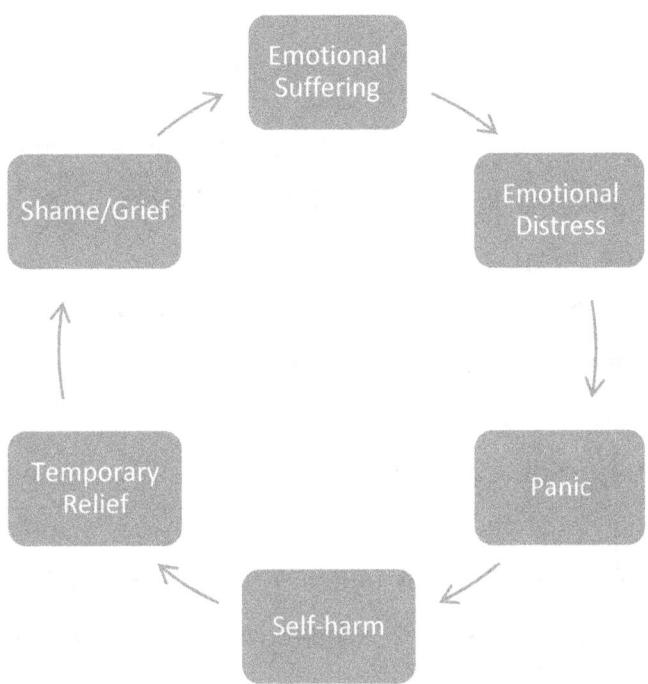

Self-harm usually starts with emotional suffering, and then the feelings get so intense that we panic because it feels like there's no way out. In our intense desire to feel some relief, we self-harm. We then get the "relief" we are after, but it's so short-lived because it's followed by intense shame and grief. The shame and grief become so big that emotional suffering kicks in, jumpstarting the cycle all over again.

If we don't break this cycle, self-harm becomes a standard way of dealing with problems. And then one day, pinching becomes burning, burning becomes cutting, and even that does not provide the relief we seek. To stop this cycle, we must learn new behaviors and apply healthier ways to deal with emotional suffering.

Top 6 Tips to Stop Yourself from Engaging in Self-Harm

1. **Identify triggers**: Try to identify the triggers that lead to self-harm, such as stress, anxiety, certain situations, specific emotions, and others. Once you recognize these triggers, you can take steps to avoid or manage them.
2. **Develop healthy coping strategies**: Find alternative ways to cope with difficult emotions. For example, do any or all of the Mindfulness and Distress Tolerance exercises in this book.
3. **Reach out for support**: Connect with friends, family members, or mental health professionals for support and guidance. You don't need to suffer alone or in silence. You can choose to reach out and talk to someone about your feelings.
4. **Create a self-care plan**: Develop a self-care plan that includes healthy activities such as exercise, healthy eating, getting enough sleep, and engaging in hobbies and interests that bring you joy. (**Tip**: See the Happiness Habit and PLEASE.)
5. **Remove self-harm tools**: If you have specific tools or objects you use to self-harm (e.g., razor blades, pocket knives, cigarette lighters, pieces of broken glass, etc.), completely remove them from your environment.
6. **Create a safety plan**: Develop a safety plan that includes the steps to take when you feel the urge to self-harm. Be as detailed as you can when making your plan. (Note that you don't need to do every step on your plan.) For example:
    a) Play my favorite, feel-good dance music.
    b) Consult Wise Mind (page 60).
    c) Look at a picture of my happiest vacation.
    d) Do TIPP (page 102).
    e) Call my best friend.
    f) Call mom.
    g) Call my therapist.
    h) Call the local suicide hotline.

Chapter Highlights:

- Research has shown that DBT is highly effective in treating people with BPD.
- Mindfulness, Distress Tolerance, Emotion Regulation and Interpersonal Effectiveness worksheets with BPD-specific situation examples are provided.
- A high percentage of people with BPD engage in self-harming behaviors. Tips are provided to break the cycle of self-harm.

Conclusion

Your body has the capacity of self-healing. What you have to do is allow it, to authorize it to heal.
—Thich Nhat Hanh

BPD is one of the most challenging mental health disorders there is. I know that life can be very bleak at times, but I would like to share—from one person dealing with mental health issues to another—**there is hope, and you can feel better**.

Dr. Marsha Linehan said that she developed DBT because there must be a way to "live a life worth living." That truly resonated with me because before I decided to take steps to heal, I really felt that life was not worth living. Now I know that that's not true. Yes, it takes a lot of work, but I can honestly tell you that I've never been happy with life as I am today. I hope that someday you'll feel this way too.

Here's a quick recap of what we covered in this book:

- Borderline Personality Disorder (BPD): what it is, causes and symptoms, and currently known treatments.
- Living with BPD: Understand how this disorder affects the brain and the importance of knowing your triggers.
- Dialectic Behavior Therapy (DBT) and its core concepts fundamentals (Acceptance and Change) and its primary skills (Mindfulness, Distress Tolerance, Emotion Regulation, and Interpersonal Effectiveness).
- DBT for BPD: An in-depth presentation of DBT exercises you can use when experiencing BPD symptoms and episodes.
- Additional tips: BPD self-assessment, BPD trigger journal, tips on preventing self-harm, and others.

Appendix A – BPD Self-Assessment

McLean Screening Instrument for BPD

The following self-evaluation quiz is for anyone who thinks they might have BPD. It's a 10-item questionnaire adapted from the McLean Screening Instrument for Borderline Personality Disorder (MSI-BPD)[51]. Please note that this is NOT a diagnostic tool; only a licensed mental health professional can diagnose BPD. Please answer the questions below to the best of your ability.

Question	Yes	No
1. Are your closest relationships characterized by a lot of arguments? Do constant breakups plague your romantic relationships? Are you constantly fighting with your family, friends, and co-workers?	1	0
2. Have you ever engaged in self-harming activities such as cutting, hitting, or burning yourself? Do you have frequent thoughts about or have you ever tried taking your own life?	1	0
3. Are you quite impulsive? On at least two (2) occasions, have you ever given in to eating binges, drinking sprees, uncontrolled retail therapy (shopping), and other similar activities?	1	0
4. Are you a very moody person? Do you often feel happy one moment and then sad or depressed the next?	1	0
5. Do you have anger issues? Do you often give in to angry urges such as shouting, breaking things, slamming doors, using sarcastic or abusive language, pushing or hitting someone, etc.?	1	0
6. Are you often suspicious of others (trust issues)?	1	0

Question	Yes	No
7. **Do you ever experience dissociation? Do you ever feel that you're in a dream or that the world around you isn't real?**	1	0
8. **Do you often succumb to feelings of loneliness or boredom?**	1	0
9. **Do you have an unstable image or sense of yourself? Do you often feel you don't know who you are or what you truly believe in?**	1	0
10. **Do you engage in many frantic and desperate things to prevent rejection or abandonment by people close to you? For instance, have you ever physically embraced someone to prevent them from leaving, made repeated phone calls to someone to reassure yourself that they still care, or begged someone not to leave you?**	1	0

Scoring:

Yes = **1** | **No** = 0

Using the above scale, please tally up your score.

My Score: _____

Interpretation:

A score of 7 or higher indicates you are above the cutoff for BPD. If your score is 5 or 6, additional evaluation is advised.[52] A score of 4 or less indicates you likely don't have BPD.

Important:

This BPD self-assessment questionnaire is NOT meant to be used as a substitute for a visit with a doctor or health care professional. However, the truth of it is people don't get help because they think their problems aren't real or "bad enough" to warrant it. So, if you suspect you're suffering from BPD after this self-evaluation (even if you score 4 or less), please don't hesitate to contact a licensed mental health professional for an official diagnosis.

How to Convey Your BPD to Others

If you're experiencing symptoms or have been diagnosed with BPD, discussing your situation with others to help them understand you better is a good idea. Hopefully, they'll understand your condition more, which will help your relationship with them.

Here are some tips that might help you when communicating your condition:

1. **Educate yourself first**. Educating yourself about BPD is essential to effectively communicate what it is and what it feels like to others. This will also help dispel the myths often associated with BPD. Also, the people you talk with will likely have questions, so be prepared—and willing— to answer them. This does not mean you need to be an "expert" in BPD. It's simply best to know more about it so you can talk about it better.

2. **Find a way of communication that works for you.** Face-to-face conversations are great. However, if you're not ready for this, it might be easier to talk on the phone or write a letter before engaging in a face-to-face meeting.

3. **Pick the right time and place.** Not everyone is ready to talk about mental health at any time. So choose a time and place where the other person will be most receptive to your information.

4. **Practice what you want to say**. It might be easier to discuss your BPD by practicing what you want to say or making some notes. Here are some examples that might provide a starting point:

   - *I have an illness called Borderline Personality Disorder. I want to discuss it with you because I'd really appreciate it if you could understand me better.*

- *I'm struggling to cope with what's happening in my life, and I think I know why...*
- *I'm struggling with...*

5. **Be honest**. Be truthful when communicating your illness. This includes being honest about your experiences, including your difficulties and how BPD affects your daily life. And if you receive a question to which you don't know the answer, be honest about that too.

6. **Use clear language**: Use language that is easy to understand. For example, "*I find it really difficult to control my emotions*" is better than "*My amygdala, the part of the brain that processes emotions, is hyperactive.*" Try to use non-judgmental statements too. For instance, "*I know it's a bit hard to take this all in*" is better than "*You probably don't understand what I'm saying.*"

7. **Emphasize that BPD is treatable**. Explain that BPD is a treatable mental health condition and that with the proper support and treatment, people with BPD can lead fulfilling lives.

8. **Encourage support**. Emphasize the importance of support and understanding from others in managing BPD. Let others know how they can help and what kind of support is most helpful for you. For example, you might say that when you have a BPD episode, you need the other person to:

   - **Just listen.** Most people especially loved ones, tend to show support by wanting to "fix" the problem. Mention that listening—real, active listening—is already healing and that you don't need them to find solutions for you. You want to share, not be fixed.
   - **Stay calm.** The other person might be tempted to reply when you're expressing your fear of abandonment, but perhaps you just need the other person to stay calm and not react. If this is the case, let them know.

- **Be patient.** Emphasize that your BPD episode will pass and that the type of support you need is patience.

9. **Don't expect too much from just one conversation.** It takes time to understand mental health conditions. Some people may be confused, shocked, or even react badly. Give them time to think about what you just shared.

Are you afraid to discuss your mental illness because you're concerned about how others will see you? This is understandable because many stigmas are associated with mental health issues. However, stigma causes significant harm.

A Mental Health Million Project report found that 22% of respondents, or about one in five, did not get help for their mental illness because they were afraid of being judged or did not want other people to know about their mental health problems.[53]

How to Deal with Stigma

> *"I fight stigma by choosing to live an empowered life. To me, that means owning my life and my story and refusing to allow others to dictate how I view myself or how I feel about myself."*
> – Val Fletcher

In my opinion, seeking treatment for BPD, or any mental disorder is one of the best things you can do for yourself. So, if mental health stigma is preventing you from seeking treatment (or revealing a diagnosis), the following suggestions can help you manage the situation:

1. **Practice self-care.** Self-care activities, such as exercise, meditation, or simply doing anything you enjoy, can help you feel better and increase your resilience in the face of stigma.

2. **Explain that you are NOT your illness or diagnosis.** Enlighten people that BPD is a disorder you have. It's not who you are. For instance, say, "*I have a bipolar personality disorder*," not "*I'm borderline*."

3. **Take care of the language you use.** If you want others to be mindful of the words they use about your illness, let them take the cue from you. Avoid using harmful words and descriptions such as "nuts," "wacko," "crazy," "weak," or "weird" when talking about yourself.

4. **Find a supportive community**. It's normal to want to share what's happening in our lives with those closest to us. However, suppose you feel that these are the very same people who will judge you negatively. In that case, getting support from others first might be a good idea, such as an online BPD support group or forum, a therapist, and others.

5. **Advocate for yourself**. Focus on what you need to get better. Often, this means deciding to seek treatment *despite* any fear you may have about others "finding out" about your illness. Also, remember that therapy helps you develop the coping strategies you need for dealing with stigma.

Appendix B – Trigger Journal

One DBT exercise to help identify triggers is to create a "Trigger Journal." Here are some tips to help you increase awareness of your triggers and develop coping strategies.

1. Start by keeping a journal to **record your daily experiences**, including any emotional reactions to specific situations or events.

2. When you notice that you have had an intense emotional reaction, please take a moment to reflect on what might have triggered it. Write down the event, situation, or person that triggered your response and the thoughts, feelings, and physical sensations you experienced. Here's an example:

Event: _____
Who/What triggered your emotions: _____
_____
_____
_____

What were your thoughts? Be as detailed as you can.
_____
_____
_____

What exactly did you feel?
_____
_____
_____

What physical sensations did you experience while feeling these emotions?
_____
_____
_____

3. **Look for patterns** in your triggers, such as specific people or situations that tend to elicit strong emotional reactions. Try to identify the specific thoughts or beliefs associated with these triggers. Here's an example:

   I've noticed that I'm triggered every time Brad, my office mate, passes me with his back turned to me. It makes me feel as if he doesn't want to see me. He does this all day.

4. Once you've seen a pattern, **develop coping strategies** to manage your emotional reactions in these situations. (See Distress Tolerance, page 64.)

   These are the Distress Tolerance coping strategies that work best for me:

   _____
   _____
   _____

As you apply your coping strategies, you'll discover that your emotional reactions to your triggers become less intense and easier to manage.

If you want to take this a step further, you can also add a **What Next** step. For example:

What Next: *I'll talk to Brad about how he passes me at work makes me feel. Hopefully, he'll understand and stop doing it (or at least do it less).*

Review Request

If you enjoyed this book or found it useful...

I'd like to ask you for a quick favor:

Please share your thoughts and leave a quick REVIEW. Your feedback matters and helps me make improvements to provide the best books possible.

Reviews are so helpful to both readers and authors, so any help would be greatly appreciated! You can leave a review here:

https://tinyurl.com/complete-dbt-review

Or by scanning the QR code below:

Also, please join my ARC team to get early access to my releases.

https://barretthuang.com/arc-team/

THANK YOU!

Further Reading

Be sure to check out my other bestselling DBT books in the Mental Health Therapy series. Here are some of the titles you can find:

- DBT Workbook for Adults
- DBT Workbook for Kids
- DBT Workbook for Teens
- The DBT Anger Management Workbook
- DBT Workbook for PTSD
- DBT Workbook for BPD
- DBT Workbook for Depression

You can get them here:

https://tinyurl.com/mental-health-therapy

DBT Workbook For PTSD

Proven Psychological Techniques for Managing Trauma & Emotional Healing with Dialectical Behavior Therapy

DBT Skills to Treat Post-Traumatic Stress Disorder for Men & Women

By Barrett Huang

https://barretthuang.com/

FREE Guide: Mastering DBT Essentials

FREE DOWNLOAD ALERT!

Master Dialectical Behavior Therapy Skills in 5 Simple Steps with my Free DBT Quick Guide. Access the 'Mastering DBT Essentials' quick guide at:

https://barretthuang.com/dbt-quick-guide/

Or scan the code below:

Contents

FREE Guide: Mastering DBT Essentials 155
Introduction 158
    Who Should Read This Book 162
    Goals of This Book 162
    How to Use This Book 163
    Content Warning 163
    Safety 163
    About Me 165
    You Can Feel Better 165

Chapter 1: What is PTSD? 166
    What Causes PTSD? 168
    What are the Symptoms of PTSD? 173
    What are the Different Types of PTSD? 176
    PTSD Treatments 177
        Cognitive Behavioral Therapy (CBT) 177
        Prolonged Exposure Therapy (PET) 178
        Eye Movement Desensitization and Reprocessing Therapy (EMDR) 178
        Dialectical Behavior Therapy (DBT) 179

Chapter 2: Living with PTSD 181
    How PTSD Affects Your Brain 182
        Amygdala – Your Alarm System 182
        Hippocampus – Your Memory Center 183
        Prefrontal Cortex – Your Learning Center 183
    How PTSD Affects Your Life 184

Chapter 3: What is Dialectical Behavior Therapy? 188
    DBT History 188
    DBT Concepts: Radical Acceptance and Desire to Change 190
    DBT Worksheets in this Book 193
    DBT Core Skills 198

    Mindfulness 198

    Distress Tolerance 207

    Emotion Regulation 211

    Interpersonal Effectiveness... 228

Chapter 4: DBT for PTSD 234

  Why DBT for PTSD? 234

    Avoidance and Radical Acceptance.. 235

    Desire to Change... 239

    Mindfulness Skills for PTSD 240

    Distress Tolerance Skills for PTSD 248

    Emotion Regulation Skills for PTSD 262

    Interpersonal Effectiveness Skills for PTSD 272

Chapter 5: Continuing the Road to Coping and Healing 285

Chapter 6: Conclusion 290

Appendix A – Trauma Resiliency 291

Appendix B – PTSD Self-Evaluation 293

Appendix C – Establishing a Sleep Routine 297

  Top 3 Tips to Set a Sleep Routine 298

Review Request 303

Further Reading 304

Introduction

"There is no timestamp on trauma. There isn't a formula that you can insert yourself into to get from horror to healed. Be patient. Take up space. Let your journey be the balm."
– Dawn Serra

I was a very troubled and lonely teen. My parents moved from China to Canada to provide a better life for our family. But I looked different, talked differently, and even the food I ate was different. So, growing up, I never felt like I belonged—anywhere. Even today, as an adult, it's very hard for me to describe the pain that comes from loneliness. But that's not all.

My father was a hoarder who had Obsessive Compulsive Disorder (OCD). My mother suffered from severe anxiety and showed PTSD symptoms due to a childhood accident (more on that later). Because of all the chaos and instability at home and the loneliness and isolation I felt as a teenager, and it's no surprise that I was diagnosed with OCD and General Anxiety Disorder (GAD) as an adult. And although I was not clinically diagnosed with it, I knew I also suffered from depression.

I knew I had to do something when I left home for college. Although I didn't fully understand what was going on with me, I knew this to be true: something had to change because I couldn't go on with life that way.

I started seeing a mental health professional and was prescribed anti-anxiety medication. It somewhat improved my ability to handle daily life. However, this was only the start of my journey.

I tried different types of therapy. But the one that worked for me, allowing me to cope and overcome my various mental health issues, is the one I am sharing in this book—Dialectical Behavior Therapy (DBT).

During one of the DBT group therapy sessions, I met Paul[**] and learned about his post-traumatic stress disorder (PTSD).

> Content Warning: the following story contains potentially distressing material.

"I was about 16 years old, I think. I was working part-time at a popular coffee shop in the city center. One payday, I and a bunch of other teens working there decided we'd treat ourselves to a burger and movie that night. We were going to watch The Matrix!

It was a great and fun night... until it wasn't.

After the movie, I gallantly escorted one of the girls home. She was just a few blocks from the cinema anyway. From there, I had to walk back and take the subway back home.

I didn't notice anything at all after I dropped her off. I turned a corner, and suddenly a group of guys was on me. To this day, I don't remember how many.

Even though I wasn't beaten to a pulp, I was shoved around roughly enough to know that this was serious. All of a sudden, someone took out a gun.

I don't remember what was said or what happened in what order. What I remember, always so clearly, was how the cold, hard barrel of the gun felt against my temple.

[**] *Name changed for privacy.*

They wanted my wallet, but I remember hands patting me up and down, over and over, everywhere. Many years later, I would process this part as sexual assault.

After taking my wallet, they laughed as they left.

I don't remember how I got home. I remember locking my bedroom door shut. I would do this every night from that moment on.

The following morning, I went down for breakfast, and I remember my mom asking how last night had gone. I remember taking a moment before I looked up and said, "It was great!"

I didn't decide beforehand to keep what happened a secret. I guess, when confronted, I just wanted to forget about it. I was young enough to foolishly think, "If no one knows, it didn't happen."

But it did happen, and I've been living with it since. I don't want to, but I do."

Paul had a tough time after that traumatic incident. One of the things he mentioned during therapy that struck me so much was when he said, *"After what happened, it's like "Paul" disappeared, and I don't know why."*

Just like me, Paul went through years of loneliness, anger, shame, frustration, fear, depression, severe anxiety, and others. His life was an endless story of failed relationships and attempts to keep a job. Paul was eventually diagnosed with PTSD and tried various therapies before trying DBT.

Since that first DBT group therapy session, Paul and I have become friends. We've seen each other through some tough times in our lives, and I'm happy to say that today, Paul and I no longer see ourselves as "just surviving" but as "survivors."

So, why did I write this book? Well, as cliché as it sounds, I want to help.

One component of mental health disorders that Paul, myself, and a significant number of people discuss is that, for years, we don't understand what's going on with ourselves.

If you're hungry, you ask for food. If you're thirsty, you ask for something to drink. If you have a mental health problem, you might not even know you should be asking for something, let alone know what to ask for.

We don't have the vocabulary to describe what we're going through. We're not equipped to look at ourselves and how we should start healing. And even if there's some awareness, we don't know what to do about it.

We don't start to understand things until much later. And this only happens if we are lucky enough to: 1) realize that life can be better, 2) know we need help, 3) ask for, seek, or be open to help, and 4) use the help we get.

Today, as an adult, I often look back at my teenage self and feel a lot of empathy. If only that kid understood that his parents were suffering from mental health problems and that his chaotic, traumatic, and unbalanced home life was not normal. If only that teen understood how "not belonging" left him empty. If only he knew what to do to start making friends in a strange country, then perhaps he wouldn't have spent years being lonely and depressed.

As an adult, Paul knows that he couldn't have known what would happen that night and that he's lucky to be still alive. However, as a teenager, *"How do you even begin to describe the feeling of having a gun to your head? Even now, I have trouble putting it in words."* He also knows that he is a victim and shouldn't feel shame. But as a teen, *"Just the thought of telling someone that grown men touched me all over made me want to throw up."*

So I wrote this book to help you.

- I want to help you know **you're not the only one going through this**.
- I want to help you **see your incredible strength** for coming this far. That you have this book in your hands speaks volumes of your courage because confronting trauma is nothing but an act of bravery.
- I want to help you realize that **you're not broken but are hurt** and need support, compassion, and kindness.
- I want to help you **live the life you want to live**.

I will not sugar-coat it. You deserve honesty. The journey to healing from PTSD, or any mental health disorder, is never a linear process. There will be ups, and there will be downs. But this I promise you: keep at it, and you'll always be going forward.

But where do you start? What do you do? How do you proceed? Hopefully, this DBT for PTSD book provides the answers you seek.

Who Should Read This Book

This book is for anyone who has suffered trauma. You might be showing PTSD symptoms or have already been diagnosed with PTSD. You may be undergoing therapy and want to use this book and its exercises as part of your healing, or you may want to go through this material yourself. Either way, you want to address at least one aspect of the trauma you experienced or witnessed to lessen its impact on your life.

This book is also for anyone with a partner, friend, or family member exhibiting PTSD symptoms or diagnosed with it. Understanding is one of the first steps we can take to help and support anyone living with PTSD.

Goals of This Book

This book aims to teach you Dialectical Behavior Therapy (DBT) skills and how to use them to deal with the stress symptoms associated with trauma. Within these pages are mindfulness, stress coping, emotion regulation, and interpersonal exercises and techniques to help you feel better.

How to Use This Book

The first part of this book introduces PTSD, what it is, its causes, what happens inside and outside of your body, etc. Trauma is a very sensitive topic that is often misunderstood. So to move forward, I believe it's essential to know what you want to move forward from.

The second part of this book discusses DBT (e.g., its history, what it's all about, what to expect, why it can help with PTSD, and so on). Here, you'll understand what makes DBT different from other forms of therapy and why it's an excellent means to address PTSD.

The third part of this book discusses using DBT skills to help you deal with PTSD. You see, learning is not just reading and gaining information. Real learning happens when you put what you've just learned to use and do something with it. So this part of the book is full of step-by-step DBT exercises designed to help with PTSD.

Content Warning

Please note that this book contains content that might be troubling to some readers. Some stories, topics, and examples might be considered distressing material that can trigger adverse reactions. Content may include but is not limited to childhood trauma, adult trauma, abandonment, self-harm, anxiety, emotional abuse, mental illness, eating disorders, night terrors, and others. Please be mindful of these and other possible triggers. Above all, never hesitate to seek assistance or professional help when you need it.

Safety

What does it mean to be safe? What does "safety" look or feel like to you? This book talks about trauma and how to deal with its repercussions. In going over its content, it's essential to *be safe* and *feel safe*. Here are some tips:

- Think about moments in your life when you felt safe, and write about them in as much detail as possible. Whenever you feel any unpleasant emotions or reactions, turn to your journal and let the memory and feeling of safety come over you.

- Know your safety vulnerabilities. For example, if the traumatic event occurred at night, go over this book and its exercises during the day. If the traumatic event resulted in you fearing for your physical safety, then perhaps you should not be alone when you go over this book and its exercises. Visit the library or sit down at a local café.
- Plan B. Write down what you should do when you start feeling unsafe. Here are a few ideas:

    - Stop and take a walk in nature.
    - Call _____.
    - Stop and hug your pet.
    - Look at a picture of _____.
    - Stop and listen to _____.
    - Others:

    _____
    _____
    _____

About Me

> *"I'm not saying I will heal you.*
> *But I am sharing what healed me." – Barrett Huang*

My journey into mental healing has inspired me to learn more about the mind and behavior. So I majored in psychology and have completed the DBT Skills certificate program of Dr. Marsha Linehan, the founder of DBT. I have also taken to heart Dr. Linehan's philosophy of "living a life worth living." So I've spent years broadening my philosophy, happiness, and self-improvement knowledge. Still, I'd like to emphasize that the contents of this book draw primarily from my personal struggles with mental health disorders and the struggles of people I know that are gracious enough to allow me to share their stories. DBT has helped us cope, survive, and thrive. I sincerely hope that it helps you as you take your own journey to mental healing.

You Can Feel Better

You and I know that life is not easy. Add traumatic experiences into the mix, and life becomes even more difficult. But there is hope. You can feel better.

When I was suffering from my mental health problems, I was lost and constantly struggling. I felt like I was living in a tiny, very tight maze that I didn't want to be in but couldn't get out of. The following pages taught me how to get out of that maze.

I can honestly say I have never felt better about myself and my life as I do today. And I wholeheartedly believe the same can happen to you. All you need to do now is turn the page, start your journey, and keep going until you're free from your maze.

Chapter 1: What is PTSD?

"PTSD: It's not the person refusing to let go of the past, but the past refusing to let go of the person." – Anonymous

Post	Traumatic	Stress	Disorder
After	Trauma	Stress	Irregular Function of Mind or Body

Post-traumatic stress disorder (PTSD) is a specific set of reactions that can develop in anyone who has ever experienced or witnessed a terrible, distressing event that threatened their life, safety, or the lives of people around them.

PTSD was once thought only to affect war veterans. This was because soldiers who returned home from war showed high levels of stress, depression, anxiety, fear, and other physical and psychological problems. Terms such as "shell shock," "combat fatigue," and "war neurosis" were coined.

In the 1980s, however, the American Psychiatric Association officially recognized "post-traumatic stress disorder" in the third edition of its Diagnostic and Statistical Manual of Mental Disorders (DSM-III). This is a turning point in the history of PTSD because it highlights that a traumatic event triggers the mental condition. In short, a person does not cause PTSD; a traumatic event does. Trauma is at the core of PTSD.

Trauma can happen anytime. How many times have you started your day feeling happy and awesome, and then something happens that changes the course of your life forever?

Content Warning: the following story contains potentially distressing material.

My friend Myrah[§§] has this to say: "Greg and I have been married for 11 wonderful years. We have a 7-year-old daughter. We've been trying for a second child for years, but it seemed like it wouldn't happen anymore, so Greg and I eventually said to each other, "We have a great daughter. Our little family of three is more than enough."

Nearly a year later, my belly started to hurt unexpectedly, and I began to bleed a bit. I thought I had a bad PMS case (premenstrual syndrome). The following day, I went to work and had the most horrendous pain in my belly in the middle of a meeting. I also started bleeding a lot. I was rushed to the hospital, and after a thorough examination, I discovered I had just had a miscarriage.

I was stunned. I couldn't speak. Tears just kept falling and falling. I was pregnant, and I didn't know it! I lost a baby I didn't think I had. What did I do wrong?!

I can't describe what happened after because everything was just a blur. I was just in a haze of sadness and agony. Since I couldn't explain how I felt, no one understood the depth of my grieving, not even my husband. Eventually, Greg and I divorced."

Trauma can happen to anyone. It can happen to a child with no defenses or an adult who feels at the peak of their life.

Trauma doesn't have to happen in the "first person." You don't need to experience trauma to develop PTSD personally. Witnessing a traumatic event can also bring about this condition.

For example, the September 11 terrorist attacks[54] on the World Trade Center and the Pentagon in the US were highly traumatic to people on ground zero and those exposed to

---

[§§] *Name changed for privacy.*

the event through the enormous and almost non-stop media coverage. People worldwide, not just in the US, suddenly felt scared, unsafe, and uncertain about the future because this was not an accident but *intentional violence*.

Reaction to trauma comes in various shapes and sizes. Why does trauma affect us differently? How can the same event be traumatic for one person but not for another? This is because of our individual personalities, histories, life experiences, and situations.

My friend Myrah (page 167) suffered from clinical depression in her teens. This vulnerability, coupled with the trauma of losing a child who was so desperately wanted, triggered her PTSD.

When the 9/11 attacks occurred, a friend who had *aerophobia* (fear of flying) developed PTSD even though he was nowhere near ground zero. This is called *secondary trauma*.[55]

"Secondary" means that the original (primary) trauma happened to someone else, but the situation is having a traumatic effect on your life nonetheless. Secondary trauma is NOT any less severe or more straightforward to deal with than any other kind of PTSD.

So, even though a traumatic event is an *external phenomenon*, our experience is filtered through our cognitive and emotional processes.

However, despite all of the above variations, one thing is sure: **trauma is anything that endangers your feeling of safety**.

What Causes PTSD?

PTSD can develop after experiencing or witnessing a single distressing, traumatic event (e.g., the unexpected loss of a loved one) or after being consistently exposed to it (e.g., abuse, bullying, etc.).

The following are the types of traumatic events that can lead to PTSD:

- Serious accidents (e.g., being involved in a car crash)
- Criminal activities (e.g., robbery, kidnapping, cybercrime, etc.)
- Sexual assault or abuse (e.g., rape, human trafficking, etc.)
- Physical assault or abuse (e.g., child abuse, spousal abuse, bullying, racism, being kidnapped, being held hostage, etc.)
- The sudden death of someone you love or someone very close to you
- Serious health problems (e.g., being diagnosed with a life-threatening illness)
- Childbirth experiences (e.g., miscarriage, problems during childbirth)
- Witnessing traumatic events over and over due to your job (e.g., cops constantly exposed to gun violence, first responders exposed to life and death situations daily, etc.)
- Natural disasters (e.g., earthquakes, fires, floods, hurricanes, pandemics such as COVID-19, etc.)
- Acts of terrorism (e.g., school shootings, bombings, hijackings, etc.)
- War and conflict
- Torture

Question: **I experienced/witnessed one of the items above. Does it mean I have PTSD?**

No. It's important to remember that **not everyone who goes through a traumatic event develops PTSD**.

Even though there are situations when exposure to trauma is so great that the chance of developing PTSD is very high (e.g., surviving a car accident in which your whole family perishes, participating in combat, etc.), there are some things that greatly influence it. Here are a few examples.

Before the Trauma

Your personal situation before a traumatic event influences your resilience to trauma. These factors may include the following:

- **Previous exposure to trauma or experiencing emotional problems at a very young age.** For example, say you were bullied every day at school, and despite this, you grew up to be a healthy, happy, and well-adjusted adult. However, you experienced being the victim of a crime and were held at knifepoint. This recent trauma might be the "straw that breaks the camel's back" and cause PTSD.
- A personal or family **history of mental illness**.
- Having **unhealthy and ineffective coping strategies** like blaming yourself when something unpleasant happens.
- A **history of substance abuse**.
- **Problems with school** such as low academic performance, frequent fights with teachers and students, always skipping school, etc.
- **Experience early losses** such as previously losing your home or losing money in an investment gone wrong.
- **Lack of a healthy support system.**

During the Trauma

Factors present during a traumatic event are also relevant. These factors may include the following:

- **Proximity to the trauma.** For example, after 9/11, a study showed that people who were in the New York City metropolitan area during the attack were more likely to develop PTSD than those who were physically further from that area.[56]
- **Suffering an injury.** For example, let's say you and your friends were at the movies when a fire broke out. As you and your friends try to exit the movie house, you trip, get trampled and suffer a broken leg.
- **Personal meaning of the traumatic event**. For example, a person who has grown up with an abusive parent might develop PTSD if they find themselves in an abusive relationship. Note that the type of abuse doesn't have to be the same.

Content Warning: the following story contains potentially distressing material.

My friend Angie*** had this to say: *"My father was an alcoholic and was emotionally abusive to my mother. He was never physically or emotionally abusive to us, just my mom. Later, I had a boyfriend who had anger management issues, and one day, in a fit of jealousy, he just lost it. He grabbed me by the shirt, dragged me to the kitchen, and hit me on the head with a frying pan. It happened once, as I ended the relationship immediately after that.*

However, soon after, I started to have panic attacks whenever I heard loud things in the kitchen. I was also constantly in fear. I was afraid of running into my ex every time I left home. It got so bad that I quit my job and started working online. I ordered food and groceries so I wouldn't have to go out. I avoided my friends.

One day, my mom came to visit, and when I opened the door, she looked at me from head to toe and cried. She was the one who convinced me to seek help.

After undergoing therapy, I learned that unresolved issues from my childhood triggered my PTSD. My father's abuse of my mother always had my siblings and me on pins and needles. For years, we feared he would finally turn on us, and my ex-boyfriend brought that fear into reality."

- **Duration of the trauma.** For example, being held hostage in a bank robbery that lasted for hours.
- **Risk of trauma occurrence.** For example, living in a neighborhood where crime rates are high.
- **Accidental vs. intentional violence**. Domestic abuse, racism, bullying, terrorist attacks, and others leave us more prone to develop PTSD because this type of violence provokes higher emotional responses.[57]
- The **atrocity of the traumatic event**. For example, witnessing a heinous crime.

After the Trauma

*** *Name changed for privacy.*

Your environment after a traumatic incident also influences the likelihood of developing PTSD. These factors may include the following:

- **Absence of a good support system** (e.g., family, friends, colleagues).

> Content Warning: the following story contains potentially distressing material.

One of our readers, Kian[†††], said: *"During the pandemic, I lost my mother in the worst circumstances. Like so many others, I wasn't with her and didn't get to say goodbye. I'm an only child, and my father died when I was a baby, so I lost my one and only anchor in this world when she passed away. I was in shock. I was traumatized. I was alone.*

I reached out to a few friends, but they were also dealing with their stuff, so I locked myself in my apartment for a whole year. I didn't talk to anyone, and no one talked to me.

I don't know what I would've done if I had not encountered an online group on DBT. I'm still not where I want to be, but at least now I have some hope I'll get there. "

- **Rumination and feelings of helplessness.** For example, re-living the traumatic event over and over in your head, thinking of the "what ifs," and ending up feeling helpless again.
- **Self-pity or victimizing yourself.** For example, having thoughts of *"Why me?"*, *"What did I do wrong?"*, *"What did I do to deserve this?"*.
- **Self-neglect** or not taking care of yourself. For example, it's understandable that you might lose appetite[58] or have sleep problems[59,60] after a traumatic event. However, if you keep this up, you'll hurt your physical and mental health[61], making you more vulnerable to PTSD.

[†††] *Name changed for privacy.*

 *Many factors affect how you react to a traumatic experience. For instance, if you're an optimistic person, if you've previously handled setbacks and bounced back, and so on.*

If you want to quickly check your ability to effectively handle trauma, you can check the Trauma Resiliency exercise on Appendix A (page 143).

But, surely, STRESS is a normal reaction to trauma? Yes, absolutely. If you notice that you're agitated or overly cautious after a traumatic event, that's normal. Physical reactions such as sweating or an increased pulse rate are also expected. Emotional responses such as anger or fear are also natural reactions to trauma. It is when everyday stress becomes *distressed*, when your stress lasts way after the traumatic incident is over, or when it becomes severe to the point that it interferes with your health, your relationships, and your daily life—this is when stress evolves into post-traumatic stress disorder (PTSD).

What are the Symptoms of PTSD?

There is no specific timeframe when PTSD symptoms show up after a traumatic event. Some people experience symptoms immediately after the event. For others, it can take months or even years before any symptoms appear (as a result of being triggered).

Since PTSD symptoms can take many different forms, four broad categories or "clusters" have been established by experts: *intrusive symptoms, avoidance symptoms, negative changes in mood and thoughts*, and *hyper-reactivity (being on edge)*.

1) Intrusive Symptoms (Re-Experiencing)

Intrusive symptoms, also known as *re-experiencing*, are when we re-live the trauma we experienced or witnessed whether we want to or not. These may include:

- Unwelcome and frequent recollection of the terrible event.
- Re-living the traumatic experience as though it were happening again (flashbacks).
- Having disturbing nightmares involving the trauma.

- Emotional distress or involuntary physical reactions to something that reminds you of the traumatic event. For example, a woman who has had a miscarriage might suddenly be overcome with extreme sadness and cry uncontrollably when she sees a pregnant woman.

2) Avoidance Symptoms

Avoidance is when we avoid or disengage from anything and everything that might remind us of the trauma we experienced. It is considered a maladaptive (unhealthy) coping mechanism[62]. Still, we do it because it gives our minds an escape from difficult thoughts, feelings, and experiences. These may include:

- Avoiding thinking about or discussing the painful event.
- Avoiding people, places, or things that remind you of the trauma.
- Engaging in distracting activities such as throwing yourself into work or a new hobby.

3) Negative Changes in Mood and Thoughts

This is when we start thinking and feeling unhealthy because of the trauma. These may include:

- Negative thoughts and feelings that lead to incorrect beliefs about oneself (e.g., *"I'm not a good person," "Maybe I deserve what happened,"* etc.)
- Negative thoughts and feelings that lead to incorrect beliefs about others (e.g., *"I can't trust anyone," "Everybody lies,"* etc.)
- Feeling disconnected from other people (alienation).
- Feelings of panic, horror, anger, guilt, or shame that never goes away.
- Unable to feel happiness, contentment, safety, or any other positive emotions.
- Loss of interest in hobbies and activities that you used to find joyful.
- Loss of interest in life in general.

4) Hyper-Reactivity (Being on Edge)

This is when we are over-reactive or display strong reactions to stimuli. These may include:

- Uncontrollable outbursts of anger.
- Being highly aggressive or irritable.
- Engaging in self-destructive or risky behavior (e.g., self-harm, impulsive and reckless sexual behavior, gambling, using alcohol and drugs, etc.)
- Hypervigilance or being overly suspicious of what's happening around you.
- Being easily startled or frightened.
- Unable to focus or sleep because your mind is always in "alert mode."
- Seeing danger everywhere.

Question: **I'm experiencing some of the above symptoms. Does it mean I have PTSD?**

To be officially diagnosed with PTSD, there must be:

- At least one symptom of re-experiencing or re-living the traumatic event;
- At least one symptom of avoidance;
- At least two symptoms of negative changes in mood and thoughts; and
- At least two symptoms of hyper-reactivity.

The symptoms must last for more than a month and be so severe and distressing that they interfere with your daily life.

Important: Not having an official PTSD diagnosis doesn't mean you don't need help or shouldn't deal with whatever symptom(s) you're experiencing. Self-help or asking for help is always essential and doesn't need to meet any criteria.

What are the Different Types of PTSD?

There are different types of PTSD: *uncomplicated PTSD*, *dissociative PTSD*, *complex PTSD*, and *comorbid PTSD*. Following is a quick breakdown of their differences.

1. Uncomplicated PTSD

Uncomplicated PTSD usually comes from a single traumatic event, as opposed to experiencing multiple or repeating trauma.

For example, someone in a severe car accident might become afraid to drive, get startled when a car honks, get uncontrollably angry while driving, take longer routes to avoid the area where the traumatic car accident happened, and so on.

2. Dissociative PTSD

Dissociation means disconnection. As such, a person with dissociative PTSD is someone diagnosed with PTSD who shows depersonalization (feeling detached from one's own body) or derealisation (viewing things as unreal or dreamlike) symptoms.

For example, a child subjected to abuse and diagnosed with PTSD as an adult might also show symptoms of "blanking out," numbness, inability to connect with others, and so on.

3. Complex PTSD

Complex PTSD, or c-PTSD, is considered the most severe type of this mental health disorder. It's usually caused by experiencing recurring or long-term traumatic events, and symptoms are generally more behavioral.

For example, someone who's suffered domestic abuse for years might develop low self-esteem, anger or rage issues, severe mood instability, and others. They may also develop other mental health problems, such as depression.

4. Comorbid PTSD

Comorbid means "to exist simultaneously." As such, comorbid PTSD is when a person has PTSD in addition to other trauma-related disorders that aren't part of their PTSD diagnosis.

For example, someone with PTSD may also concurrently be diagnosed with generalized anxiety disorder (GAD), major depressive disorder (MDD), borderline personality disorder (BPD), substance abuse problems, and others.

PTSD Treatments

I believe there's no single, one-size-fits-all solution to addressing mental health problems. When I was suffering from OCD, GAD, and depression, I underwent Cognitive Behavioral Therapy (CBT). I was prescribed anti-anxiety medication, which helped jumpstart my healing.

After some time, I adjusted enough that taking prescribed meds was no longer necessary. However, I was still suffering from many mental health challenges. At that point, I knew CBT wasn't what I needed anymore. That's how I discovered and consequently stayed with Dialectical Behavior Therapy (DBT).

So, I guess I'm trying to say that seeking and undergoing treatment is a journey. Helping yourself to get better takes time, so my advice is to, first and foremost, **have an open mind; be curious; be kind to yourself, and give yourself time to heal**.

Following are some of the more known treatments for PTSD today.

Cognitive Behavioral Therapy (CBT)

Cognitive means "mind." As such, Cognitive Behavioral Therapy or CBT focuses on how you process your thoughts and feelings related to the traumatic event and for you to understand your resulting behavior from the trauma.

During therapy, which is usually administered over 12-16 sessions in either individual or group format[63], you might be asked to talk about your traumatic experience and how your thoughts about it affect your daily life.

For example, say you're prone to uncontrollable outbursts of anger due to trauma. CBT can help you understand what goes on inside your mind and body and teach you how to cope with your anger. Another example: suppose you've become afraid and overly pessimistic about people or the world because of the trauma you experienced or witnessed. In that case, CBT will help you re-evaluate these negative thinking patterns.

Prolonged Exposure Therapy (PET)

Prolonged Exposure Therapy (is a specific type of CBT wherein you're taught to slowly face the memories, emotions, and situations related to the trauma. If you remember, Avoidance (page 174) is one of the major symptoms of PTSD. The problem with this symptom is that *avoidance coping* never addresses underlying issues. It's a short-term, Band-Aid solution.

PET gives you the tools to slowly confront things related to the trauma, identify the things that you're avoiding, and finally, how to slowly and effectively face your fears one item at a time. Hopefully, with continuous effort, you'll learn that there's no need for avoidance because the trauma-related memories and triggers do not pose any real danger to you in the present.

Eye Movement Desensitization and Reprocessing Therapy (EMDR)

Eye Movement Desensitization and Reprocessing Therapy (EMDR) is made up of a set of structured protocols and procedures that are based on the adaptive information processing (AIP) model (how your brain stores memories).[64]

During therapy, you will be asked to think or talk about the trauma you experienced or witnessed while moving your eyes in response to stimuli in the room. The general idea is that EMDR helps your brain *reprocess* how the event has affected you emotionally.

If you remember, involuntary [Re-Experiencing](#) (page 173) is one of the major symptoms of PTSD. When things are normal, your brain captures memories smoothly and links them together to remind you of other things.

For example, say you had a great family vacation to Disneyland when you were a kid, and that first night you had "the best burger ever!". Today, you recall that happy memory whenever you eat the same burger. But even though you remember that memory, you know it happened years ago. You smile and move on.

During a traumatic event, that brain networking doesn't function as it should. The brain can go "offline," and there is a gap between what you feel, hear, and see and what your language-based memory stores. There's a sort of involuntary time loop.

For example, say you and your friend were victims of a robbery. When this occurred, you were in a dark alley, and your friend got stabbed and killed. Months or years later, you're out with some friends and find yourself walking down a dark path. All of a sudden, you break into a sweat. You can hardly breathe and feel very afraid. You're involuntarily re-experiencing the trauma. Your brain is not telling you that the danger is over, and it has been for some time now.

The goal of EMDR is to help your brain reprocess what you remember from the traumatic incident (through rhythmic eye movements). And in doing so, repair the mental injury you suffered from the trauma so that involuntary re-experiencing happens less (or not at all).

Dialectical Behavior Therapy (DBT)

And, of course, there's Dialectical Behavior Therapy or DBT, which we will cover in great detail in [Chapter 3](#).

A note about medication: There are medications prescribed for PTSD, usually antidepressants. When used to treat PTSD, they work to lessen PTSD symptoms. I believe that if you're not suffering from any other underlying mental health condition, such as depression, trauma-focused psychological treatment should be the first option. Please consult a doctor regarding the option that's best for you.

 *Are you showing a normal stress response to a traumatic experience or is it PTSD? For clarity, you can go over the PTSD Self-Evaluation exercise on <u>Appendix B</u> (page 150).*

Chapter Highlights:

- TRAUMA is at the core of PTSD.
- Stress is a normal response to trauma. PTSD is when normal stress turns into *distress* or *chronic stress* that gets in the way of your daily life.
- People with PTSD are not just war veterans but anyone who has experienced or witnessed a traumatic event.
- PTSD Symptoms: intrusive symptoms, avoidance symptoms, negative changes in mood and thoughts, and hyper-reactivity (being on edge).
- PTSD Types: uncomplicated PTSD, dissociative PTSD, complex PTSD and comorbid PTSD.
- PTSD treatments: Cognitive Behavioral Therapy (CBT), Prolonged Exposure Therapy (PET), Eye Movement Desensitization and Reprocessing Therapy (EMDR), and Dialectic Behavior Therapy (DBT).

Chapter 2: Living with PTSD

"It isn't in my past. It's in my every day." – Helen Wilson

According to the National Center for PTSD of the US Department of Veterans Affairs, *"about 6 of every 10 men (or 60%) and 5 of every 10 women (or 50%) experience at least one trauma in their lives"*. Women are more likely to be sexually assaulted or sexually abused as a child, while men are more likely to be involved in accidents, physical assaults, battles, natural disasters, or witness deaths or injuries.[65] Globally, 3.9% of the population has PTSD.[66]

Despite the above already concerning statistics, **PTSD is considered one of the most undiagnosed disorders**.[67,68,69] That's not surprising since Avoidance (page 174) is one of its symptoms. In my personal experience, *cultural norms* play a role too.

Content Warning: the following story contains potentially distressing material.

Here's my mom's story: My mom had a very difficult childhood growing up. However, talking about such things is not in Chinese culture. But when I was a kid, my mom would often experience nightmares. The silence of the night would be pierced by her screams, which were so loud that I would wake up in my room down the hall. This didn't happen every night, but it went on for years.

When I was older, I finally mustered up the courage to ask her why she thought she had these nightmares. She said she didn't know. When I asked her if something terrible happened when she was a kid, she said, *"Well, when I was six or seven, a pot of boiling water accidentally tipped over and poured all over me."*

I stared at my mom in disbelief and asked her what had happened afterward. *How badly was she burned? Did anyone bring her to the doctor? How long did it take her to heal?* She said she didn't remember that part. I wanted to know more, but my mom didn't like to discuss it further, and that was that.

She has never gone through any therapy, and I doubt she ever will because mental health was, and still is, very much a taboo in Chinese culture.

How PTSD Affects Your Brain

PTSD affects brain function.[70] Specifically, it affects our brain's *context processing* abilities, which is our ability to recognize that a particular stimulus may call for various reactions depending on its context.

For example, suppose the trauma you experienced involved a gunshot. In that case, sounds such as a door banging or fireworks might trigger intense fear even though you are in no danger. Your brain does not take into context that you are in a safe environment now.

This diagram[71] shows a cross-section of the parts of the brain discussed below.

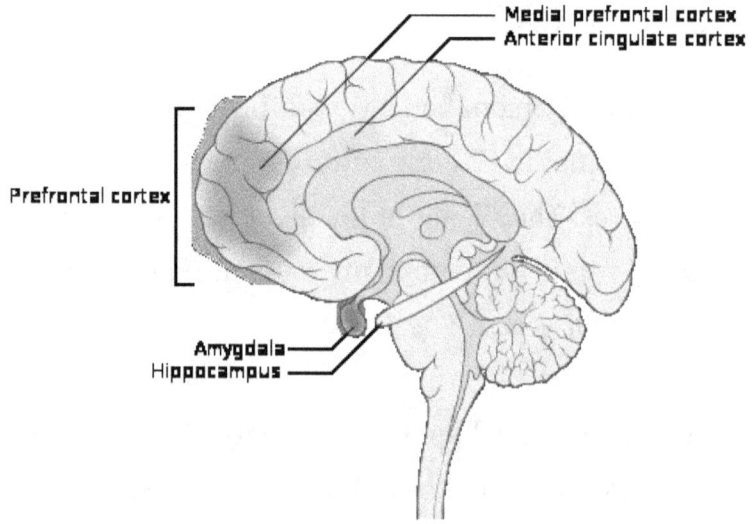

Amygdala – Your Alarm System

The **amygdala** is an almond-shaped structure in the middle of the brain that helps control our emotions (how we feel) and behavior (how we act). Under normal circumstances, the amygdala processes frightening or threatening stimuli and instructs our brains and bodies on how to respond. For this reason, the amygdala is considered our natural alarm system.

The amygdala in people with PTSD is overstimulated, and it has trouble distinguishing between a threat *then* and a threat *now*.[72] So, when frightening or threatening stimuli are encountered, we overreact so that even common or normal triggers, such as door banging, can send us into a complete panic.

Hippocampus – Your Memory Center

The **hippocampus** is the brain's memory center. As previously mentioned in this book (AIP, page 178), our brains capture memories smoothly when all's well. The hippocampus should be able to recall a traumatic incident and make sense of it afterward.

However, the trauma is so overpowering during a traumatic event that the hippocampus does not store and properly categorize all the information. In fact, research shows that the hippocampus is smaller and less active in people who've experienced trauma.[73]

This implies that because your hippocampus is working so hard to make sense of things, you might have problems recalling crucial parts of the incident (memory loss), or you might find yourself thinking a lot about what happened. (Hence, the involuntary re-living or re-experiencing of the event.)

Prefrontal Cortex – Your Learning Center

The **prefrontal cortex** aids in decision-making and mental observation. When presented with frightening or threatening stimuli, the prefrontal cortex helps us evaluate what's going on and, if necessary, stops us from our emotional urges or impulses.

Research shows that the prefrontal cortex in people with PTSD underperforms.[74] For example, when we hear loud fireworks, and the amygdala (*alarm system*) triggers feelings of fear, the prefrontal cortex cannot always evaluate that there is no danger.

This indicates that people with PTSD are in a never-ending cycle of stress. And as long as the cycle continues, your pain and suffering will too.

How PTSD Affects Your Life

> *"Even if you've accumulated a house full of nice things and the picture of your life fits inside a beautiful frame, if you have experienced trauma but haven't excavated it, the wounded parts of you will affect everything you've managed to build."*
> – Oprah Winfrey

PTSD needs to be addressed because it affects all parts of your life. Here are some ways PTSD can hurt you in the long run if you don't take steps to heal or get help.

Tired, just tired. When your brain uses so much energy to protect you from perceived danger and threats, you might feel totally depleted of energy. Initially, you might lack the energy to do daily tasks, but this can progress to self-neglect and self-harming thoughts.

Low self-esteem. Many people who show PTSD symptoms find it hard to seek help. So one of the most damaging things that can happen is to reach out to someone you know only to be invalidated.

Content Warning: the following story contains potentially distressing material.

This is what Nicko[***], a reader, had to say: *"I won't go into details about what I saw, heard, and did during the war, but I was a 26-year-old war vet when I first tried to reach out to someone. This person told me, "What did you expect? You're a soldier. You knew what you signed up for." Since I trusted this person, their*

[***] *Names changed for privacy.*

reaction made me question if I was overreacting or maybe I was just not "man enough."

This made me want to keep what I was going through a secret. The years went by, and things just got worse for me. My sleeping problems worsened, and I turned to alcohol. At one point, I was in a relationship and tried to tell her about it, but then she said, "That was YEARS ago. Don't hide being an alcoholic to this PTSD."

I can't tell you how much it took from me just to try and talk to someone. The fact that I wasn't taken seriously bothers me to this day."

(**Note**: Nicko met Anna** in 2014 in an AA meeting. She was the one who finally listened and encouraged Nicko to join her and try DBT.)

Please note that *invalidating* and *gaslighting* are not the same, but they are both very damaging.[75,76] Invalidating is when someone tells you that you shouldn't feel what you're feeling. Gaslighting is when someone is trying to convince you that you don't actually feel that way. People who invalidate or gaslight you make you question yourself, which harms your self-esteem. In addition, it delays you from seeking treatment for your PTSD.

Broken relationships. Trauma can make you distrustful of others and overprotective of yourself. Since trust is an issue, closeness also becomes a problem. You might have difficulties communicating or connecting with others and may even begin to self-isolate. Unfortunately, the painful opposite is also true. That is, if others don't understand, can't connect, or can't sympathize with you, they might avoid or leave you.

Psychological problems. Humans are not meant to be alone. We thrive when we can share this journey called life. However, PTSD promotes loneliness, which is linked to various mental health problems, such as depression and anxiety.[77,78,79] With increased isolation, other issues such as substance abuse, alcoholism, self-harm, intermittent explosive disorder (impulsive and violent anger), suicidal thoughts[80,81], and others may develop.

Physiological problems. You've heard this before: stress can kill you. Actually, "everyday stress" or "normal stress" does not kill you, but chronic stress does. Studies show that PTSD can cause many physical health problems, such as obesity, diabetes, heart disease, autoimmune disease, etc.[82]

Financial problems. When PTSD interferes with your capacity to do daily tasks, this can negatively affect your employment (potential job loss). Another symptom of PTSD is engaging in self-destructive or risky behavior. This might cause you to make bad financial decisions such as gambling, entering bad investments, etc.

There are many other ways that PTSD can negatively affect your life. You can develop sleep disorders, eating disorders, lack of peace of mind, lack of life enjoyment, etc. In my journey, I've come to think of these negative consequences as "costs."

For example, my OCD and GAD led to my depression (*mental costs*). My loneliness led to my low self-esteem, which made it very hard for me to have and keep relationships (*social costs*). My way of coping was to engage in unhealthy eating, which led me to gain weight and develop a weakened immune system (*physical costs*).

One day, after another night of restless sleep, I opened my eyes and stared at the ceiling. I had absolutely ZERO energy and enthusiasm for the day ahead. And then, a thought popped into my head—*"Life can be better, right?"*

One thought. One sentence. One wish. That's what started my mental healing journey. And in the next chapter, I'll share with you what worked for me. It's my sincere hope that it works for you too.

Chapter Highlights:

- About 6 of every 10 men (or 60%) and 5 of every 10 women (or 50%) experience at least one trauma in their lives.
- PTSD is one of the most misunderstood or undiagnosed mental health disorders.
- PTSD changes how certain parts of our brains function, sending us into a never-ending cycle of stress.
- PTSD affects every aspect of our lives (mentally, socially, physically, financially, emotionally, etc.)

Chapter 3: What is Dialectical Behavior Therapy?

"Life is very interesting, because in the end, some of your greatest pains become your greatest strengths."
- Drew Barrymore

DBT History

Dialectical Behavior Therapy, or **DBT**, was created by Dr. Marsha Linehan[83], Ph.D., in the 1980s. It was initially meant to treat people with borderline personality disorder (BPD). This mental health condition makes it hard for people to control their emotions.

DBT is a variation of Cognitive Behavioral Therapy (CBT). However, while CBT focuses on discovering a client's unhealthy thinking patterns and changing them into positive ones (*change-focused*), Dr. Linehan believes it's more effective to apply two opposing (*dialectical*) concepts instead: **Acceptance** AND **Change**.

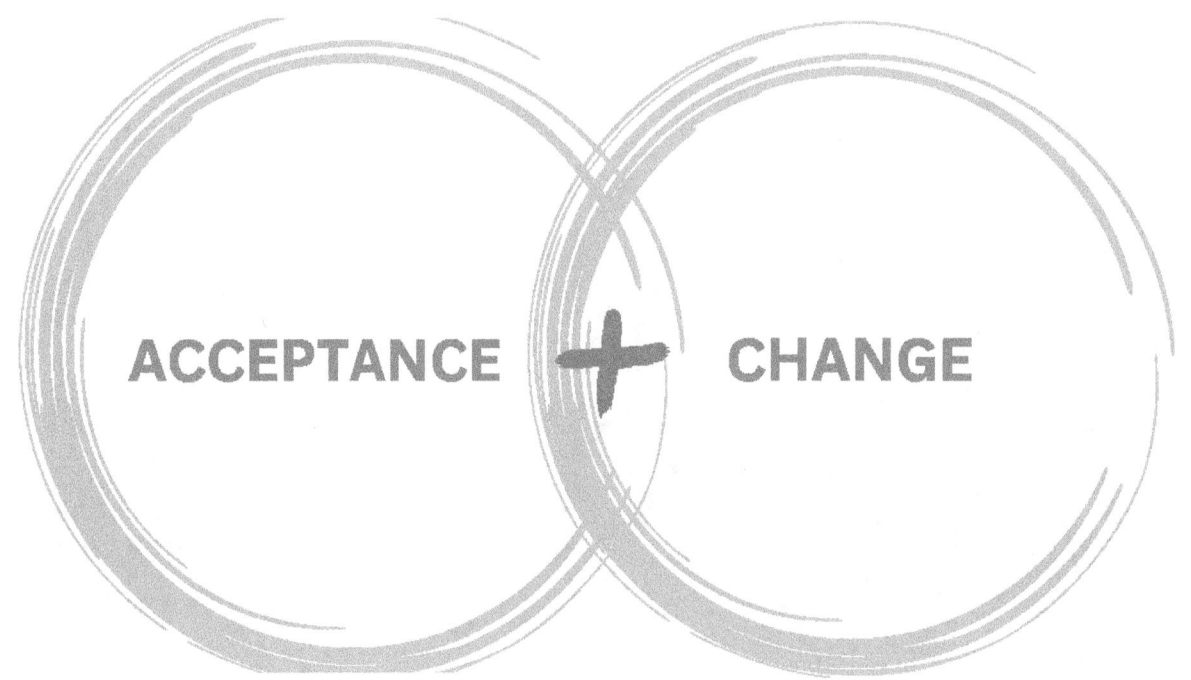

DBT proposes that before a person can start to heal, they should first accept the reality of their situation. Dr. Linehan's personal story[84] underlines this belief.

In the 1960s, Dr. Linehan, then only 17 years old, was admitted into the *Institute of Living*, a psychiatric facility for her "extreme social withdrawal." While at the clinic, she engaged in self-harming activities and displayed suicidal behavior, so she was kept in isolation for her own safety.

Dr. Linehan believed that she had *bipolar disorder* (BPD) then, but since the illness was not yet known in the 1960s, she was misdiagnosed with *schizophrenia*. She was subjected to electroconvulsive therapy for this illness and given Thorazine and Librium as treatment. However, since she did NOT have schizophrenia, these methods did not work to alleviate her mental health problems.

After more than two years, Dr. Linehan was released from the clinic, but she was far from well. It would be another four years before she would have an epiphany about her mental health.

Dr. Linehan says that she was praying at church when she started to think that her suicide attempts were because the gap between *who she was* and *who she wanted to be* was so big that it made her feel hopeless and desperate. She wanted a better life but didn't know how to get it. This was when she realized that she needed to do more than focus on CHANGE.

Yes, CHANGE is necessary for growth and happiness, but ACCEPTANCE is the first step down that road.

Dr. Linehan realized that she had to accept her reality "as is" before moving on. Even though her emotions, behavior, and actions were destructive, they made sense because she was so unhappy and suffering from her present reality. Dr. Linehan would eventually call this concept

Radical Acceptance.

Radical Acceptance is when you acknowledge the facts of your reality, whatever they may be. You don't need to dissect, evaluate, judge, fight, or even react.

So, Radical Acceptance is accepting your reality; now what? This brings us to the second concept of DBT—**Change**.

You have this book in your hands because you want to feel better. You want your situation to be better so that you can go on and live a better life. Change is what makes that happen.

For example, say you're in a room with the door closed. Outside the room is a small gathering of your family and friends. You can hear them having a great time over there. They sound happy, and you believe joining them will make you happy too. But they will not go into your room and bring the party to you. So, what do you do?

Radical Acceptance = I'm unhappy in this room. The door is locked.
Change = Get up, open the door, walk out, and join the party.

DBT Concepts: Radical Acceptance and Desire to Change

Dialectic means looking at things from more than one point of view. In DBT, it means the fusion of two seemingly opposing concepts: **Acceptance** and **Change**.

At first glance, it might seem unclear. How can you *accept* and *change* at the same time? But you see, you're not accepting and changing the same thing.

What you are accepting is the reality of your current situation. You're also accepting your emotions regarding the situation. What you're changing is your normal reaction to that situation.

Why do I need to practice Radical Acceptance? It's essential to accept the reality of your situation because if you don't, you're ignoring or denying it. And doing this *prolongs your suffering*. You cannot change something you cannot accept.

Imagine being in a maze. If you ignore or deny that you're in it, you stay inside that maze. However, if you accept reality (*I'm in a maze*), you can proceed to the next step—getting out of it.

When you're radically accepting, remember that you should do it without judgment. Do your best to free the mind of your own opinions. You're in a maze. That's it for now.

RADICAL ACCEPTANCE = IT IS WHAT IT IS

Why do I need to change? Because whatever you're doing, they're not working for you. Let's go back to our maze example.

> *David is in a maze, and he doesn't like it! He's angry, and when David's furious, he lashes out, so he starts clenching his fists, breathes rapidly, shouts, and walks in any direction. After 10 minutes, David is STILL in the maze and even angrier.*

> *George is in a maze, and he's filled with dread. He can't stand confined spaces, and he's stressing out. He's sweating bullets, clenching his teeth, and breathing rapidly. George is panicking and is frozen in place. He can't seem to take a single step or move a muscle. After a few minutes, George is STILL in the maze, and his anxiety levels are higher.*

The above examples illustrate that reacting to one's emotional impulses (i.e., doing what you would typically do) does not improve the situation.

For David, learning how to control his anger instead of reacting to it gives him a better chance of getting out of the maze sooner. For George, learning to manage his distress instead of acting according to it gives him a better chance of getting out of the maze sooner.

And there's another layer here: by learning new behaviors, you avoid suffering from the weight of your unpleasant emotions. For me, this is one of the most essential lessons in DBT.

CHANGE = LEARNING NEW BEHAVIORS TO FEEL BETTER

Here's how I applied **Acceptance** and **Change** in my life: As mentioned, my teen years were filled with loneliness. I didn't want to accept the reality of my situation (having zero friends) because, in my mind, that meant admitting I wasn't loveable or likable in any way or that I really didn't belong in our new environment. My response to this was to self-isolate. It was my way of protecting my ego and my feelings. But that way of dealing with things meant I never went out and met anyone, which worsened my loneliness, low self-esteem, and depression. I was caught in a dark, vicious cycle of my own undoing.

I discovered DBT as an adult, so I cannot go back and rewrite my teen years. (Believe me, I wish I could.) However, I can make my adult years better.

So, as painful and challenging as it was, I accepted the reality of my situation:
I still had no real friends, was very lonely, and felt empty. I felt invisible, too, as if I was walking around and no one saw or heard me. It hurts to live like this.

Now, the "old me" would react by self-isolating as usual. But that wouldn't work. It never did, so why would it work now, right? So, I changed. I learned new behaviors to get a different outcome.

> *"Your life does not get better by chance;*
> *it gets better by change." – Jim Rohn*

I wish I could tell you that things got better overnight. It didn't. Change takes time—but it's time well spent.

But <u>HOW</u> does one change? Ah, that's the real question. How do you get from A to Z? Well, that's one of the many things I like about dialectical behavior therapy. It's not just theory. DBT gave me the "HOW" I needed to change.

DBT Worksheets in this Book

We learn when we apply what we know in what we do (knowledge + action). So, this book not only talks about the DBT principles but also gives you worksheets to help you put these principles into action in your own life. Many of these exercises are adapted from Dr. Linehan's *DBT Skills Training Manual*[85], while the rest are ones I've found helpful when practicing DBT skills.

When doing these exercises for the first time, I recommend you do them in a place you feel safe, comfortable, and unlikely to be disturbed.

Lastly, I encourage you to keep doing the exercises until the DBT way of feeling, thinking, and behaving becomes natural. Also, if there are any exercises or worksheets you're not ready to do, that's okay. You can always go back to then when you're ready.

Worksheet: Radical Acceptance

Radical Acceptance is reality acceptance. So, for your first exercise, please write down inside the circle below what your reality is right now. Write down whatever comes to your mind. Try not to judge your situation. Imagine your current situation as if you're watching a movie and just taking notes.

Examples: (1) I'm in pain. (2) I'm tired. (3) People confuse me. (4) Loud noises scare me. (5) I am not okay.

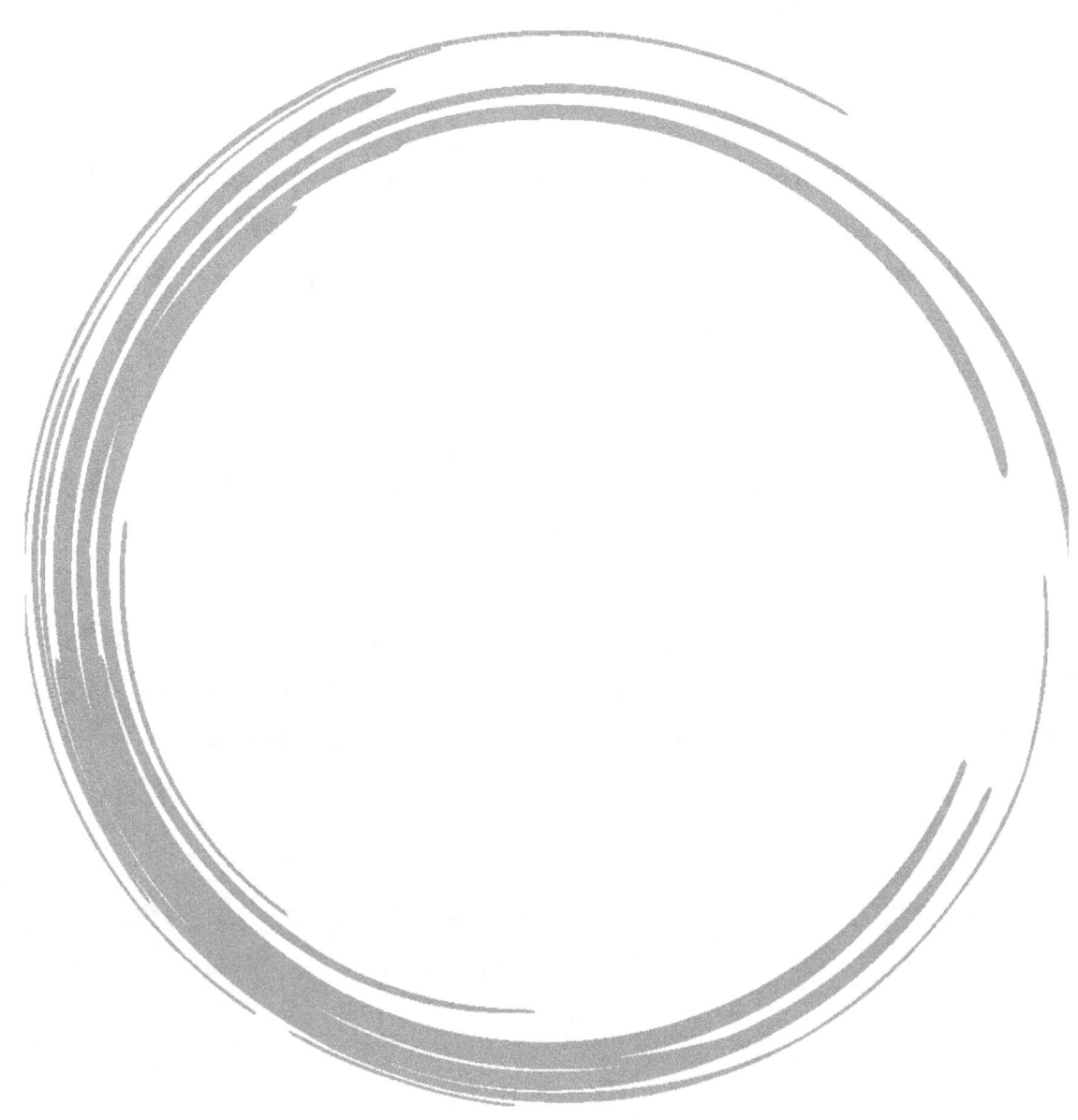

Worksheet: Desire to Change

Set yourself up to welcome change in your life. You don't need to make any plans here. Just be kind to yourself and imagine why change can benefit you. Write down whatever comes to your mind inside the circle below.

Examples: (1) I'm open to change. (2) I'm ready for "new." (3) I'm ready for "better." (4) I know I can be happier. (5) It's time for "more."

Worksheet: Acceptance + Change

Now, let's complete the picture. Under Radical Acceptance and Desire to Change, copy what you wrote in the previous exercises. In the middle, write down a Statement for yourself. Acknowledge today and what you want for tomorrow.

Here's an example:

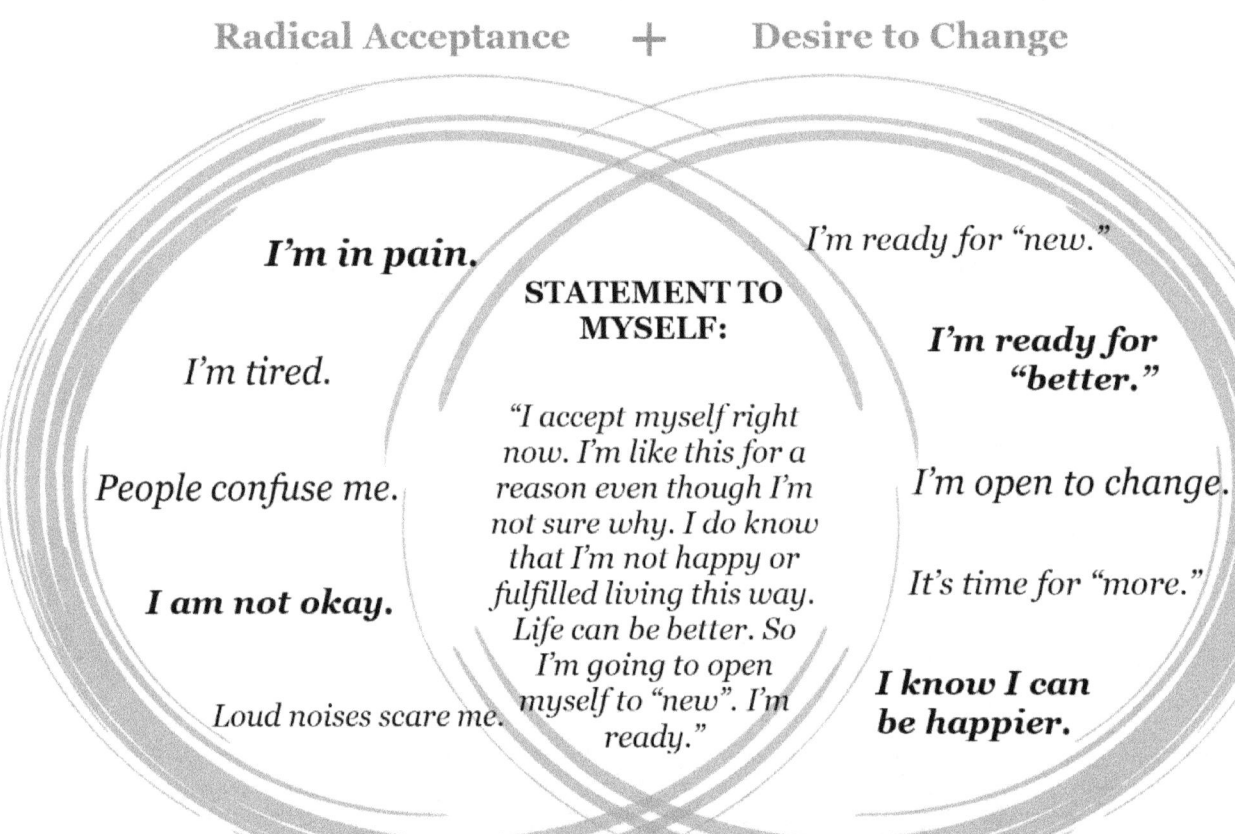

It's your turn on the next page:

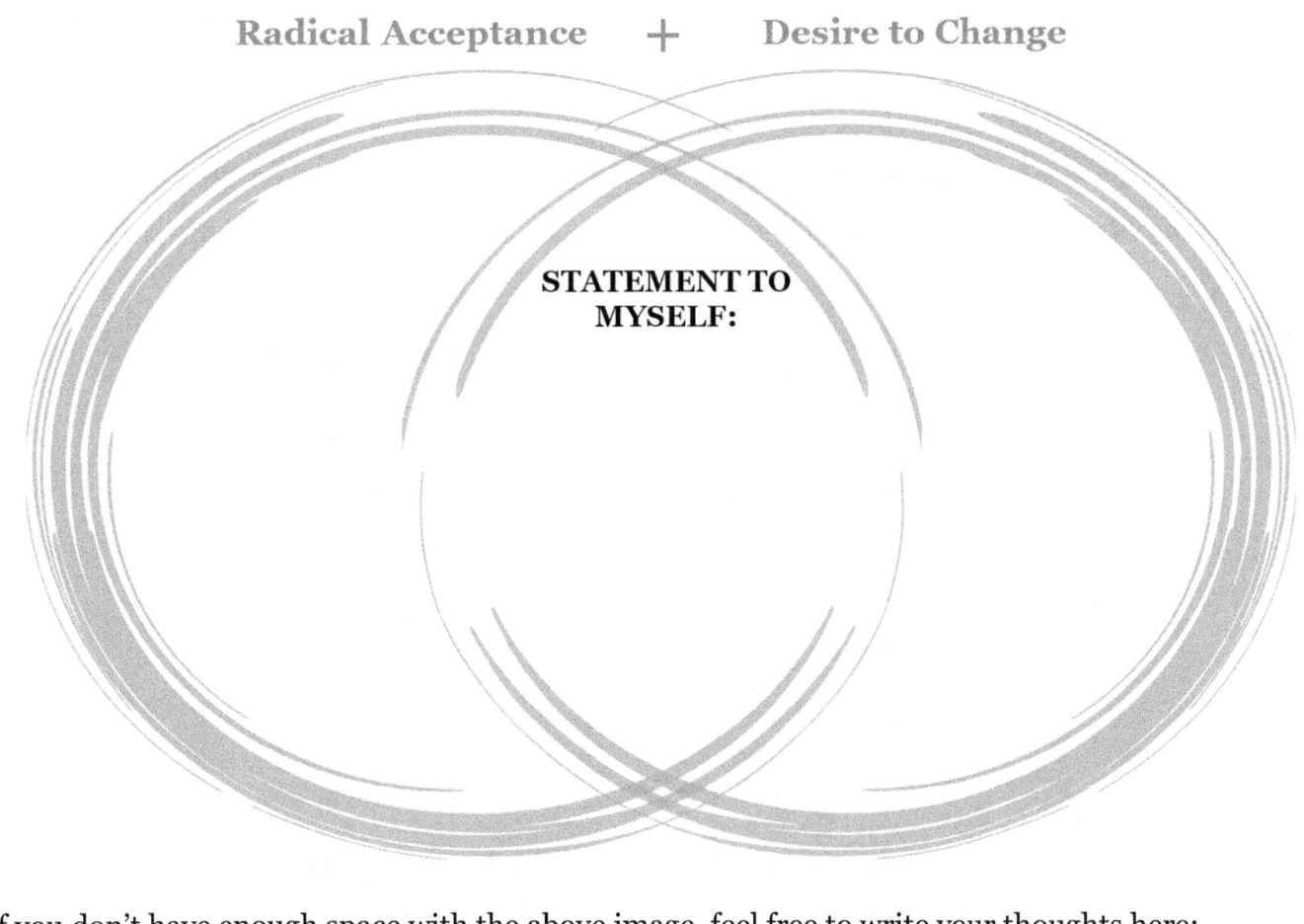

If you don't have enough space with the above image, feel free to write your thoughts here:

___
___
___
___
___
___
___
___
___
___
___
___

DBT Core Skills

Adopting **Acceptance** and **Change** in your life requires practicing four primary skills: *Mindfulness, Distress Tolerance, Emotion Regulation,* and *Interpersonal Effectiveness.*

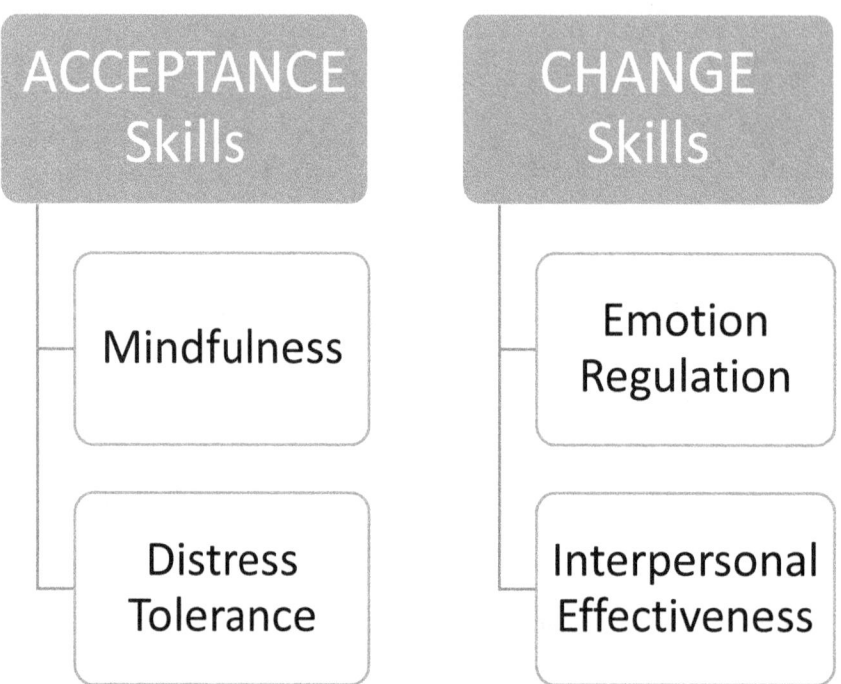

As the image above shows, Acceptance is possible by learning *Mindfulness* and *Distress Tolerance* skills. At the same time, Change takes place by learning *Emotion Regulation* and *Interpersonal Effectiveness* skills.

Mindfulness

What comes to your mind when you hear the word "mindfulness"? You're probably picturing someone meditating on a mat with their eyes closed, hands gently clasped, and legs crossed. However, there's a BIG difference between the two: mindfulness is a way of being (*who you are*), while meditation is a practice (*what you do*).

Mindfulness is a state of awareness or being fully present in NOW. Meditation is a technique to help you achieve mindfulness.

But how does one become mindful? In DBT, this is achieved by learning WHAT and HOW skills.

WHAT Skills

These skills are about WHAT we have to do to be mindful.

- **Observe.** Pay attention to what's happening inside and around you. Open your eyes and your senses entirely to whatever you're experiencing.

    For example, when was the last time you really paid attention to eating a meal? Eating is so basic, normal, and routine that most of us don't really give food or how we eat much attention. So, for your next meal, take the time to observe yourself and your food a bit more closely.

    Here are a few things to which you may want to pay attention:
    After a spoonful, what's the first thing you taste (sweetness, sourness, saltiness, bitterness, or savoriness)?
    What are the different textures you feel in your mouth as you chew?
    How often do you take a sip of something to drink while eating?

- **Describe.** Define or discuss what you observe. Often, we're in such a hurry living our lives that we gloss over what's happening around us. One way to "slow down" is to take the time to describe what we observe.

    For example, say you're eating dinner. Describe the scenario. Are you sitting down? If so, describe the chair. Is it new or old? Is there a glass of water next to you? Who put it there? Do you always drink water during a meal? What are you eating? Did you make it? Is it a favorite of yours? Why or why not?

- **Participate**. You get the most out of an experience when participating fully. You're probably not even aware of it anymore, but you do A LOT of things at once.

    For example, what else do you do while eating? Are you on your phone? Are you watching TV? Are you reading something? When was the last time you JUST ate a meal?! You miss so much when you multi-task and don't participate fully in the moment.

HOW Skills

These skills focus on HOW to be more mindful in our everyday lives.

- **Non-Judgmentally.** When mindful of something, we don't need to express our opinion. Just observe and describe but don't label anything as "good" or "bad."

    For example, you're mindful that it's raining hard outside. That's it—no need to state how it might ruin your plans for the day.

- **One-Mindfully.** When practicing mindfulness, focus on one thing and one thing only because mental multi-tasking divides awareness.

    For example, you're mindful that it's raining hard outside. Stay with the rain. Watch it fall on the ground and splash brilliantly. Watch it hit the window pane and glide against the glass. Close your eyes and listen. What music is the rain playing for you?

- **Effectively.** Whatever you are mindful of, you are a part of it, so you must participate effectively. Doing so will enable you to get the results you want out of the situation.

    For example, you're working from home and must turn in a report at the end of the day. However, your partner is going in and out of your home office, trying to discuss weekend plans with the kids. You're mindful (aware) of your growing stress and annoyance. However, losing your cool and shouting will lead to an argument (less time to do your report), which can ruin your weekend (more stress you don't need). In this situation, it's far more effective to say something like, *"I hear you, honey, but give me an hour to finish this first. You'll have my full attention then."*

Mindfulness is not just a switch we turn "On," especially today when many things entice and demand our attention. Also, when we're tired, sad, exhausted, hungry, running late, etc., it's hard to be mindful—but it's not impossible.

Like most things we want to master, mindfulness needs practice, practice, practice!

Worksheet: Box Breathing

This deep breathing exercise is a great way to practice mindfulness. It will help limit your focus and allow you to be in the here and now. Another benefit to Box Breathing, also known as *four-square breathing*, is that you can do it anywhere.

1. Sit up straight on a chair, lie on a mat or on your bed, or stand, whatever is most comfortable for you.
2. Breathe in deeply for a count of four (4).
   Mentally count 4-3-2-1.
3. Hold your breath for a count of four (4).
   Mentally count 4-3-2-1.
4. Exhale for a count of four (4).
   Mentally count 4-3-2-1.
5. Hold your breath for a count of four (4).
   Mentally count 4-3-2-1.
6. Do this for at least five rounds or cycles.

Worksheet: A Mindfulness Habit

This exercise will help you practice Mindfulness **WHAT** and **HOW** skills.

Tip: This exercise is best done when you're alone and not likely to be interrupted.

- Get some "ME" time and choose any of these activities.
    - Coffee/tea break.
    - Take a leisurely walk.
    - Walk your pet.
    - Sit in nature.
    - Take a bath.
    - Listen to music.
    - Others:

    _____
    _____
    _____

- Next, fill out this Mindfulness table. If one aspect does not apply to what you're doing, just write some notes about it, but DO NOT leave it blank. I've done one for you as an example.

ME Time Activity: *Coffee break.* Time you started: *4:15 PM*	
Observe. *Use your senses (eyes, nose, ears, hands, and tongue). Don't describe anything. Just focus and pay attention to what your senses are picking up.* • *I'm looking at the coffee.* • *Smelling the coffee.* • *I'm putting my hands around the mug.* • *I just took a sip of the coffee.*	**Non-Judgmentally.** *Free your mind of any opinions. Nothing is good or bad. Nothing is right or wrong. Just state facts.* *When I first smelled the coffee, I immediately thought, "this smells strong; I won't like it." I had to smell it again and focus on the scent itself.*

ME Time Activity: *Coffee break.*
Time you started: *4:15 PM*

Describe. Put into words what you've observed.	**One-Mindfully.** Pull yourself back to NOW and your selected activity whenever your mind wanders.
• Sight: it's a very dark color; coffee is swirling; I still see smoke • Smell: deep aroma • Touch: the mug's really warm to touch • Taste: dark, almost bitter	*Wow, how the mind wanders! To re-focus, I would trace the mug's rim with my fingers to bring me back to just drinking coffee.*
Participate. How are you engaging with this activity?	**Effectively.** What is your goal with this activity? Ask yourself if you're achieving it. (If not, you're not engaging in it effectively.)
I'm sitting alone in the dining room. I didn't turn on any music or anything to distract me. I left my mobile phone (on Silent!) in another room.	**Goal:** *Practice mindfulness; stop my mind from thinking about a dozen different things for a while.* **Am I achieving it?** *Yeah, I think I am. It's been eight minutes, and I'm still here. Just me and my coffee.*

Your Turn:

ME Time Activity:
Time you started:

Observe. Use your senses (eyes, nose, ears, hands, and tongue). Don't describe anything. Just focus and pay attention to what your senses are picking up.	**Non-Judgmentally.** Free your mind of any opinions. Nothing is good or bad. Nothing is right or wrong. Just state facts.

ME Time Activity:	
Time you started:	
Describe. *Put into words what you've observed.*	**One-Mindfully.** *Pull yourself back to NOW and your selected activity whenever your mind wanders.*
Participate. *How are you engaging with this activity?*	**Effectively.** *What is your goal with this activity? Ask yourself if you're achieving it. (If not, you're not engaging in it effectively.)* ***Goal:*** ***Am I achieving it?***

Self-Analysis:

1. After doing your "ME" time activity, rate your Mindfulness level from 1-10, with 1 being completely unable to focus on your activity and 10 being easy for you to 100% concentrate on what you're doing. Mark or encircle your answer.

1	2	3	4	5	6	7	8	9	10

In all likelihood, you'll find it challenging to practice Mindfulness at first; that's okay. That's normal. I promise that you WILL get better at it with constant practice. So I suggest you do this exercise at least once a week, choosing whatever activity you want and noting your progress.

2. Which Mindfulness skill were you having the most difficulty with? Mark or encircle your answer.

Observe	Non-Judgmentally
Describe	One Mindfully
Participate	Effectively

Spend a few extra minutes on the skill you need to work on the next time you do this exercise.

For example, if you consistently offer an opinion (judgment) about something, re-focus and keep trying to state only FACTS.

Distress Tolerance

Stress is a natural response to anything that we deem unpleasant, and it's not always a bad thing. For example, if you're starting a new job, stress can help you focus, drive you to do well at work, and improve your performance.

Eustress is stress that is positive or constructive. It's the type of stress that pushes you just enough outside your comfort zone to be beneficial in the end. For example, if you're stressed about traveling to a new country, doing it anyway will most likely result in a positive experience. (New places, new people, and new experiences help you grow as a person.[86,87])

Distress is stress that is negative or harmful. It's the type of stress that's crippling and makes you feel unable to cope with a situation. Chronic distress can damage your self-esteem and harm your physical and mental health.[88]

Eustress and distress: what's the difference? One way to differentiate between the two is to evaluate events in terms of "challenges" or "threats."[89] If you view something as a "challenge," there's this belief in you that no matter how difficult it is, you can overcome it and that the experience, good or bad, will benefit you. If you perceive an event as a "threat," you feel unsafe, and the situation is harmful to you. You might feel overwhelmed and anxious so that you cannot respond (feel, think, or act) appropriately to the event.

With PTSD, you may perceive everything as a threat. In that case, increasing your Distress Tolerance levels is your first line of deference.

Distress Tolerance is one's ability to withstand psychological discomfort effectively. And people with mental health problems have a *low* distress tolerance level.

When we cannot handle stressful, upsetting, and demanding situations well, we tend to ignore, deny, fight or run away from whatever's causing our distress. The problem with this coping mechanism is that the next time you deal with the same thing—you will be in distress all over again.

This is why **Distress Tolerance** skills are part of **Acceptance** in DBT. This way, you are not ignoring, fighting, denying, or escaping anything. You accept that a situation is distressing. Now, you can start tolerating (surviving) your emotional response (your distress) about it.

Also, when we don't deal with our distress (as it's happening), we might lash out or behave in ways that might make the situation worse. We do this because we want to get the pressure off and feel better immediately.

For example, say you're in a very heated argument with your boss again. People are watching. Your heart is racing, your head is pounding, and you feel overwhelmed. You're starting to see red. If you can't tolerate your distress, you might shout back, throw something, or even shove your boss. But then what? You might lose your job.

Distress Tolerance skills help you accept reality (the situation as it is *in the moment*, not forever) even though you don't like it and endure them without making them worse.

The following exercises are some of the first DBT distress tolerance skills I learned. I still use them today whenever something distresses me. I hope they come to your aid too.

Worksheet: 5-4-3-2-1 Grounding Technique

Grounding techniques help pull you away from distress by bringing your attention to the present. This grounding exercise calls upon your five senses.

Name five (5) things you can see.
Examples: pen, coffee mug, post-it note, sanitizer, speaker
1.
2.
3.
4.
5.

Name four (4) things you can touch.
Examples: keyboard, apple, water bottle, my clothes
1.
2.
3.
4.

Name three (3) things you can hear.
Examples: car, kids, radio
1.
2.
3.

Name two (2) things you can smell.
Examples: coffee, cologne
1.
2.

Name one (1) thing you can taste.
Example: candy
1.

If you're still in distress, try this exercise again or list down AS MANY things as you can per sense.

Worksheet: The Grounding Wheel

When in distress, choose an activity from the Grounding Wheel below. Depending on where you are, you may not be able to do some of the activities below, so feel free to make your own **Grounding Wheel** with activities easily accessible to you. *Examples: hold my dog and feel its fur, listen to my Spotify "feel good" playlist, grab my journal and list positive things, etc.*

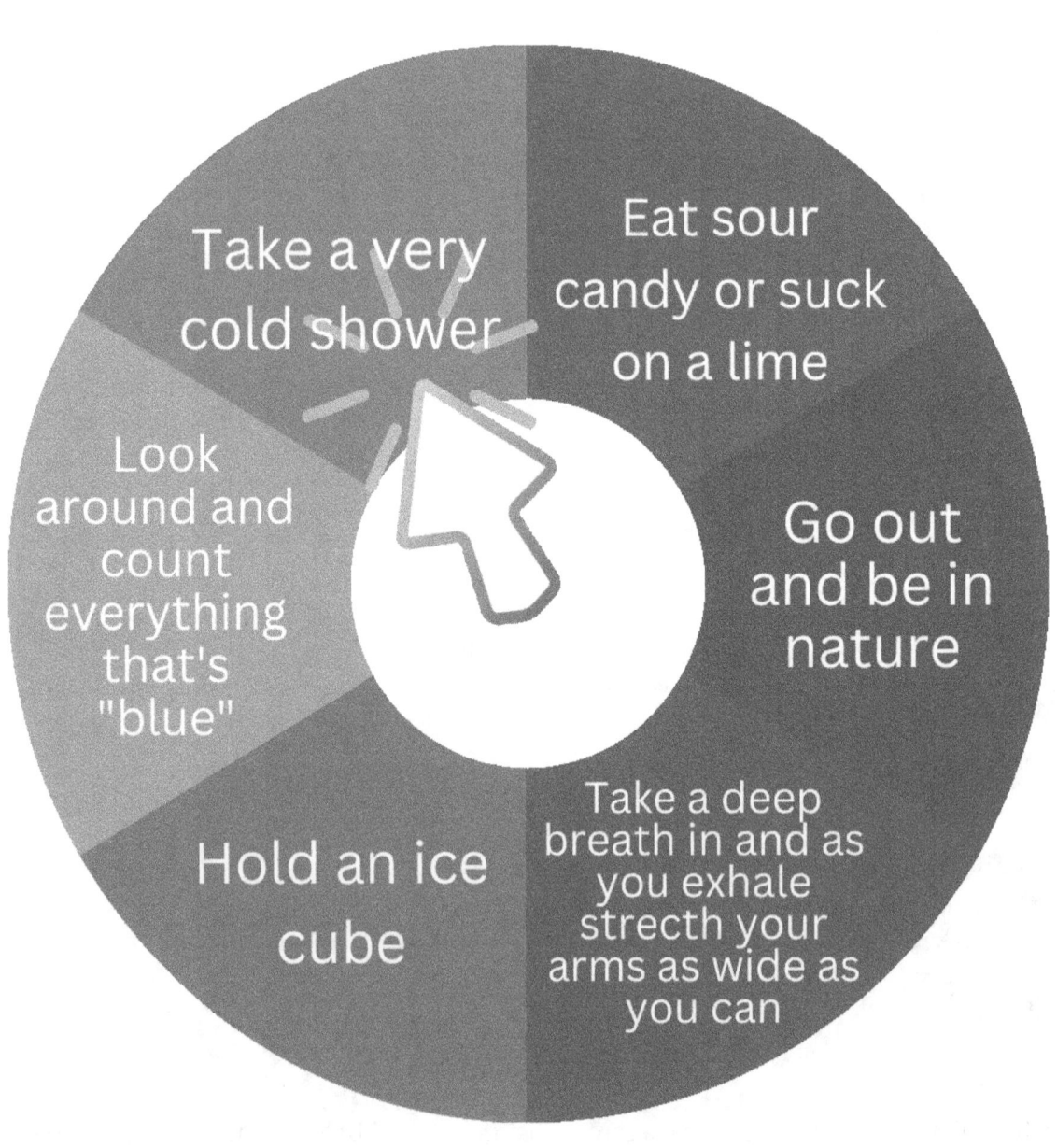

Emotion Regulation

Emotions are reactions to stimuli. According to the *American Psychological Association* (APA), emotions are "a complex reaction pattern involving *experiential, behavioral,* and *physiological* elements."[90]

Experiential Elements

All emotions are prompted. Someone or something is causing the emotional effect. However, the actual emotion produced is based on our personal experiences.

For example, hearing someone sing *Happy Birthday* may prompt happiness *if* they have happy memories of their childhood or birthdays. In contrast, if a loved one suddenly passes away during their birthday, hearing the song might trigger feelings of sadness or even anger.

Behavioral Elements

The actual expression of emotion is the behavioral component of an emotional response. Several factors influence this element, such as our upbringing, individual personalities, cultural norms, and others.

For example, it always amazes me how easy it is for some people to say *"I love you"* or give hugs when they're happy. This is not the norm in *my* family. I didn't grow up with such free expressions of love and happiness, so this is not a behavior I would regularly show.

Physiological Elements

How our body reacts to the emotion we feel is the physiological element of an emotional response. Our autonomic nervous system (ANS) responds when an emotion is triggered. The ANS controls involuntary body responses, such as heart rate, blood flow, respiration, and digestion. A branch of the ANS is the sympathetic nervous system (SNS), which controls our fight-or-flight response.

However, the ANS and the SNS are not the only things that control our bodies' reactions to emotions. Studies show that the amygdala also plays a vital role in our emotional responses.

(If you remember, we discussed that the amygdala in people with PTSD is overstimulated (page 182), making it one of the reasons why people appear to be constantly "on edge" and overact to stimuli.)

So this is the process of emotions: there's a prompting event, and based on our personal experiences (*subjective experience*), an emotional response is produced. Our bodies react to the emotion we're feeling (*physiological response*), and we show this emotion externally through our behavior (*behavioral response*).

Now, what does this have to do with our mental health? **When we struggle to manage or regulate painful emotions such as sadness, anger, fear, and disgust, we are more likely to engage in dysfunctional behavior.** And when we act this way, we harm ourselves the most.

> Content Warning: the following story contains potentially distressing material.

This is what Kris[§§§], a reader, had to say: *"I was raped when I was 14 by someone I knew at a home party my parents forbade me to attend. I was confused. I was ashamed. I was afraid. I was angry. I was disgusted. And a huge part of me was blaming myself. If only this… if only that… I didn't tell anyone and internalized everything because I couldn't deal with what had happened.*

It would take me a long time to list down all the bad things I did and all the bad decisions I made over the years. So, I'll just say this: when I was 27, I found myself at a rooftop party for the company I was working for. I didn't hear anything around me. All I could think of was walking towards the ledge. Although I have no recollection of moving, I physically walked towards the ledge because a colleague grabbed my wrist and dragged me inside. She stared at me and asked softly, "Do you need help?" I cried as I had never cried before in my life. I visited a psychiatrist after that and was diagnosed with PTSD.

[§§§] *Name changed for privacy.*

I'm still seeing my psychiatrist, and she was actually the one who introduced me to DBT. I've learned a lot of important things from DBT that really helped me. I discovered that Acceptance can be very healing. I realized that I was victimizing myself repeatedly because I couldn't manage my painful and disturbing emotions. And although hard to deal with, I learned that I was sort of "suffering by choice" and that I could end that suffering if I wanted and was willing to do the work."

"Pain is inevitable. Suffering is optional."
– Haruki Murakami

In many ways, **Emotion Regulation** is about understanding yourself. It's **awareness of painful emotions and how you can regulate them so that you don't act in destructive ways (**thereby causing or prolonging your suffering).

IMPORTANT: Emotion Regulations skills are NOT about denying or getting rid of emotions. We are human because of our capacity to feel, so we will not judge or invalidate our emotions. The goal is to reduce our vulnerability to unpleasant feelings and to find ways to manage or regulate them effectively.

Your emotions are not who you are. You can (and should) **feel your feelings; just don't act on them all the time**.

Worksheet: Accumulate, Build, Cope (ABC)

This exercise will help you become less sensitive and vulnerable to painful emotions. It will build your resilience so that if and when an unpleasant situation happens, you can cope with it.

Imagine your life as a bucket. If it's filled with pleasant events, then there's not a lot of room left for negative ones. That's what this exercise is all about.

A	Accumulate Positive Emotions
B	Build Mastery
C	Cope Ahead

Accumulate Positive Emotions (Short- and Long-Term)

Short Term: List down **10 positive activities** that bring you joy that you can do today.

Examples: swimming, doing yoga, gardening, etc.

1. _____
2. _____
3. _____
4. _____
5. _____
6. _____
7. _____
8. _____
9. _____
10. _____

Long Term: List down **10 positive changes** you want to make, so that positive events happen more often in the future. *Examples: stop smoking TO improve my health, start limiting my time on the phone TO be more present in my own life*

1. _____ to _____
2. _____ to _____
3. _____ to _____
4. _____ to _____
5. _____ to _____
6. _____ to _____
7. _____ to _____
8. _____ to _____
9. _____ to _____
10. _____ to _____

Build Mastery

Engage in **activities that make you feel skillful and competent**. Knowing that you're proficient in something is good for your self-esteem and fights feelings of helplessness and hopelessness. *Examples: take online or offline cooking lessons, start CrossFit, etc.*

1. _____
2. _____
3. _____
4. _____
5. _____

Cope Ahead

If you know that certain situations stress you out or trigger unpleasant emotions, create a plan to be ready whenever the event occurs. Whatever your plan is, rehearse it in your mind or roleplay it with someone. This helps you be prepared to do and say what you need to when the time comes.

Stressful Event: _____
Example: mom's birthday

What usually happens? / What are you concerned about?
Example: my oldest brother feels he has achieved the most amongst us siblings and always makes me feel "less." I get furious, which usually ends with me saying or doing something I regret. This, of course, upsets my mom, and I don't particularly appreciate doing that.

_____
_____
_____
_____

Plan to cope ahead:

1. Rehearse the situation in your mind.

2. State what you plan to DO. Be as detailed as possible.
   Example:
   - I will practice Box Breathing (page 58) and go over my Distress Tolerance (page 64) exercises before I go to the party.
   - I will sit furthest away from my brother all the time.
   - I'll leave the room each time he says something negative about me.
   - I'll go to the kitchen when I get angry and hold an ice cube.

   Your turn:

   _____
   _____
   _____
   _____

> 3. State what you plan to SAY. Be as detailed as possible.
>   *Examples:*
>   - *Hey dude, I do not appreciate you teasing me. Please stop.*
>   - *Hey, how about we give the teasing this year a rest?*
>   - *Happy for you. I've got a lot of good stuff going on right now too. (Mention activities I'm doing under* Build Mastery *(page 215).*
>
>   Your turn:
>   _____
>   _____
>   _____
>   _____

Important: When you rehearse your coping ahead strategy, it's normal to experience unpleasant emotions because you are, in effect, recreating the unpleasant situation as if it were happening. As such, it's essential to take a break and relax afterward.

Write down some of the things that make you feel calm right away.

Examples: walking in nature, hugging my dog Lizzie, sitting down and having coffee with my partner, taking a nap

1. _____
2. _____
3. _____
4. _____
5. _____
6. _____
7. _____
8. _____
9. _____
10. _____

Worksheet: PLEASE

This DBT exercise emphasizes how important it is to take care of our physical health because it directly affects our emotional health.[91] If your body is healthy, you're better equipped to regulate your emotions.

PL	Treat Physical Illness
E	Balanced Eating
A	Avoid Unhealthy Substances
S	Quality Sleep
E	Exercise

Following is an explanation of each acronym with some exercises where applicable.

PL   Treat Physical Illness

If you're unwell, don't wait to see a physician or refuse to take prescribed medication for your illness. I suggest you also talk to someone (e.g., a friend, a family member, a colleague, etc.) so that you are not alone during this time. If you don't want to see a doctor, then be open to trying a holistic approach to wellness (e.g., reiki, acupuncture, acupressure, etc.). The objective is to GET HELP, so your illness doesn't worsen.

When was the last time you were physically ill?
_____

Did you see a doctor?   Y / N
Why or why not?
_____
_____

Are you open to alternative therapies? Y / N

If so, which treatment would you like to try?

Examples: reiki, Ayurveda, meditation, yoga, acupuncture, acupressure, aromatherapy, etc.

_____

_____

_____

E Balanced Eating

We are what we eat.[92] The food we consume affects not just how we look but how we feel. As such, eat as close to its natural state as possible because highly processed food has a lot of added sugar, sodium, fat, and chemical preservatives, which harm your health.[93,94] For example, make your own sauce using fresh tomatoes instead of opening a jar or processed pasta sauce.

A 21-day Healthy Swaps log is provided below. For 21 consecutive days, write down an unhealthy food item (e.g., candy, potato chips) and/or an unhealthy food habit (e.g., skipping breakfast, binge-eating, etc.) that you're replacing with a healthy one. For example, switch to whole-wheat or plant-based pasta instead of consuming white pasta; swap a store-bought processed muffin for a homemade oatmeal cookie, etc.

Tip: Check out sites like *MyFitnessPal* or books like *Eat This, Not That*[95] for advice on achieving a balanced diet.

Why 21 days? In the 1960s, *Dr. Maxwell Maltz*, a plastic surgeon, observed in his book, *Psycho-Cybernetics*[96] that *"[Experiences take] a minimum of about 21 days for an old mental image to dissolve and a new one to jell."* Many studies would prove or disprove this "21 days to form a habit" theory in the succeeding years. Still, in the end, it boils down to what you're trying to do and your determination. For example, giving up chewing gum may be easy for you and require less than 21 days to stick, while wanting to do 30 minutes each day of physical activity will most likely take longer. My opinion is that either way, 21 days is a great way to start.

Note: Please always check with your doctor or a dietitian before making any significant changes in your diet.

21-Day Healthy Swaps

What unhealthy FOOD ITEM are you swapping for a healthy one?
Example: white rice and white bread for brown rice and whole wheat bread

What unhealthy food HABIT are you swapping for a healthy one?
Example: midnight snacking

Were you able to stick to your swap?

Day	Yes	No
Day 1	(Y)	N
Day 2		
Day 3		
Day 4		
Day 5		
Day 6		

21-Day Healthy Swaps

What unhealthy FOOD ITEM are you swapping for a healthy one?
Example: white rice and white bread for brown rice and whole wheat bread

What unhealthy food HABIT are you swapping for a healthy one?
Example: midnight snacking

Were you able to stick to your swap?

Day	Yes	No
Day 7		
Day 8		
Day 9		
Day 10		
Day 11		
Day 12		
Day 13		

21-Day Healthy Swaps

What unhealthy FOOD ITEM are you swapping for a healthy one?
Example: white rice and white bread for brown rice and whole wheat bread

What unhealthy food HABIT are you swapping for a healthy one?
Example: midnight snacking

Were you able to stick to your swap?

Day	Yes	No
Day 14		
Day 15		
Day 16		
Day 17		
Day 18		
Day 19		
Day 20		

21-Day Healthy Swaps

What unhealthy FOOD ITEM are you swapping for a healthy one?
Example: white rice and white bread for brown rice and whole wheat bread

What unhealthy food HABIT are you swapping for a healthy one?
Example: midnight snacking

Were you able to stick to your swap?

Day	Yes	No
Day 21		

A — Avoid Unhealthy Substances

Avoid unhealthy substances like caffeine, alcohol, and illegal drugs as much as possible. According to health experts, adult males need about 15.5 cups of fluids daily. In comparison, females need around 11.5 cups daily, so it's a good idea to switch to drinking water or lemon water. If water is too bland, try green tea or matcha tea. These teas are known for their antioxidant properties, promoting good health.

S — Quality Sleep

According to the American Academy of Sleep Medicine (AAS) and Sleep Research Society (SRS), adults need seven (7) or more hours of quality sleep each night regularly.[97] Lack of sleep increases our emotional reactivity and sensitivity to unpleasant stimuli and experiences.[98]

So, are you getting enough sleep? Find out with this **21-Day Sleep Log** below. Every morning write down what time you slept and when you woke up and calculate your total sleep hours.

21-Day Sleep Log			
Day	**Sleep Time**	**Wake Time**	**Total Sleep Hours**
Day 1	*Example: 12 midnight*	*Example: 6 AM*	*Example: 6 hours*
Day 2			
Day 3			
Day 4			
Day 5			
Day 6			
Day 7			
Day 8			
Day 9			
Day 10			
Day 11			

21-Day Sleep Log			
Day	Sleep Time	Wake Time	Total Sleep Hours
Day 12			
Day 13			
Day 14			
Day 15			
Day 16			
Day 17			
Day 18			
Day 19			
Day 20			
Day 21			

Suffering from sleep deprivation? See <u>Appendix C – Establishing a Sleep Routine</u> (page 297) for tips on sleeping faster, better, and longer sleep.

E Exercise

According to the World Health Organization (WHO), adults aged 18-64 years should engage in at least 150 minutes of moderate-intensity aerobic physical activity (e.g., brisk walking, bike riding, etc.) or at least 75 minutes of vigorous-intensity aerobic physical activity (e.g., jogging, running, swimming laps, etc.), or a combination of both each week.[99] For optimum health, two days of muscle-strengthening activities (e.g., lifting weights, doing push-ups, etc.) should be added per week too.

So, are you moving enough? Find out with this 21-Day Exercise Log below.

21-Day Exercise Log		
Day	**Exercise Activity**	**Time Spent**
Day 1	*Example: brisk walking*	*Example: 25 mins*
Day 2		
Day 3		
Day 4		
Day 5		
Day 6		
Day 7		
Day 8		
Day 9		

Day 10		
Day 11		
Day 12		
Day 13		
Day 14		
Day 15		
Day 16		
Day 17		
Day 18		
Day 19		
Day 20		
Day 21		

Are you exercising enough? Y / N

If not, make a list of things you can do to do more.

Examples: *wake up an hour earlier, park your car as far as possible from work, so you're forced to walk, take the stairs instead of the elevator, make fitness appointments with friends, etc.*

I was guilty of not exercising enough too in the beginning. I wanted to increase my daily steps, so I bought a pedometer. After seeing my step count improve, I joined a gym just two blocks from work. The goal is to make exercise an "easy choice" so that it easily fits right into your daily life.
1.
2.
3.

Interpersonal Effectiveness

Relationships are what make life worth living. We are social creatures who want to belong to a unit, want to share what we know, and want to learn from others. Healthy relationships are also critical to our mental and emotional well-being[100,101]. This is because it's not only the good times we want to share. We want to know that when tough times come, we are not alone and have people who will support us.

A great relationship has balance. When there's "give and take," the needs of the people in the relationship are satisfied. So for a relationship to prosper, it's crucial that you:

- Identify your needs and express them;
- Understand the needs of the person in the relationship;
- Know how to communicate your needs; and
- Learn when to compromise to meet the other person's needs.

If one person's needs are met more than the other, then there's an imbalance that can damage the relationship.

Sometimes, though, this imbalance is not intentional. For example, you (or the other person) might not know exactly what you want or need from a relationship. It can also be that you (or the other person) want to stay in the relationship so badly that you compromise your needs. (You never say "No.") In the end, the imbalance always brings dissatisfaction and pain.

Now, it's one thing to KNOW your needs, but it's another to COMMUNICATE them.

For example, when I was in my teens and suffering from extreme loneliness, I knew what I wanted: friends. But whenever I met someone, I didn't know how to start a friendship. I would get all tongue-tied and awkward. (This, of course, would make me self-isolate again, feeding my anxiety and depression.)

So it's these two, identifying needs and effectively communicating them, that's at the heart of **DBT Interpersonal Effectiveness**. When we learn to prioritize ourselves and respect our own wishes while at the same time considering the needs and desires of others, that's when we achieve that relationship balance.

The following exercise is one of the first DBT interpersonal exercises I learned and fully embraced. You see, when I finally got around to identifying my needs and building the courage to speak them out, I would quickly back down the minute I sensed the other person was not inclined to give in to my request.

I didn't want to hear "No," and I didn't like to push because I didn't want the other person to not like me anymore. (All due to my low self-esteem.) I always gave in, which left me empty, angry, and unhappy. The exercise below helped me finally get what I deserve in my relationships.

Worksheet: DEARMAN

This exercise lets you say what you want to say and get what you want to get without harming your relationship. It helps you be more assertive in communicating what you want without being aggressive or inconsiderate.

D	**D**escribe the situation.
E	**E**xpress what you want clearly.
A	Be **A**ssertive.
R	**R**einforce.
M	Stay **M**indful.
A	**A**ppear Confident.
N	**N**egotiate.

Following is an explanation of each acronym with some exercises for you.

D	**D**escribe the situation.

Before asking, describe the situation first. This way, you and the other person are on the same page regarding the topic. When describing the situation, don't offer opinions or accuse anyone of anything. Be objective and stick to the facts.

Example: You told me you would return home by Friday night, but you didn't.

Your turn:

_____
_____
_____

| **E** | **E**xpress what you want clearly. |

When you talk, use "**I**" statements. "**You**" statements can be taken as accusations by the other person, which might turn the conversation into an argument. This is the time when you do convey your emotions and feelings.

Example: I feel taken for granted when you don't bother to tell me where you are. I start to worry about you too.

Your turn:

_____
_____
_____

| **A** | Be **A**ssertive. |

Clearly state what you want (or don't want). Don't assume that the other person knows or "gets it." And even if they do, it's still important to say it yourself.

Example: I would like you to call me if you're not coming home.

Your turn:

_____
_____
_____

| **R** | **R**einforce. |

Make sure the other person knows how important your request is. So tell them how grateful you will be if they give you what you want or need.

Example: I would feel much better and not get so worried and stressed if you did that.

Your turn:

_____
_____
_____

| **M** | Stay Mindful. |

Keep your words and feelings in check. Remember that you're in a conversation, so if the other person is not inclined to give in to what you want, they might want to change the subject or start to argue with you. If this happens, control your emotions (feel your feelings, but don't act on them), stay on topic, and maintain your position.

Example: I would still like you to call. I deserve no less.

Your turn:

_____
_____
_____

| **A** | Appear Confident. |

Show your self-assurance through your words and body language. Do not beg or apologize. Also, maintain a consistent demeanor. For instance, do not express what you want confidently and then lower your voice or fidget.

Example: Sit or stand up straight, keep your voice level, maintain eye contact, and then say: I hope you understand where I'm coming from because my stand on this won't change.

Your turn:

_____
_____
_____

| **N** | **N**egotiate. |

If the other person is not budging, it's time to negotiate. The goal now is to devise a workable solution to the situation. You can suggest what to do moving forward or ask the other person what they believe should happen next.

Example: How about you send a quick SMS? Surely you can do that.

Your turn:

_____

_____

_____

Chapter Highlights:

- **Dialectical Behavior Therapy** (DBT) is the practice of two seemingly opposite concepts: **Acceptance** and **Change**.
- There are four (4) primary DBT skills: Mindfulness, Distress Tolerance, Emotion Regulation, and Interpersonal Effectiveness.
- **Mindfulness** is the state of awareness or being fully present in NOW.
- **Distress Tolerance** is about surviving unpleasant, painful situations.
- **Emotion Regulation** is awareness of painful emotions and how to control them so that you don't act in destructive ways (a.k.a. acting on your emotions).
- **Interpersonal Effectiveness** is identifying your needs in a relationship and learning how to ask for them (to be met), while at the same time acknowledging the needs of the other person in the relationship.

Chapter 4: DBT for PTSD

"Healing doesn't mean the damage never existed. It means the damage no longer controls your life."—Akshay Dubey

In Chapters 1 and 2 (pages 166 and 181, respectively), you learned about PTSD and how it affects your brain chemistry and your life. In Chapter 3 (page 188), you discovered DBT, its concepts (Acceptance + Change), and core skills (Mindfulness, Distress Tolerance, Emotion Regulation, and Interpersonal Effectiveness). This chapter is where we bring everything together. Here, you'll learn how to use DBT skills for PTSD.

IMPORTANT: This chapter is full of DBT skills exercises that will help you with your mental healing recovery. But since PTSD is about trauma, please have your safety plans ready at all times. (An example of Safety protocols can be found on page 163.) Also, as you go through the exercises and think about your traumatic experience(s), remember that you survived them! That alone, dear reader, is a great thing.

Why DBT for PTSD?

Dialectical behavior therapy (DBT) was initially developed to help people with borderline personality disorder (BPD). So, why is DBT a good treatment method for PTSD? It's because many people with BPD also have PTSD, and vice versa.[102,103]

Now, even though people with BPD and PTSD show different symptoms, they also share similar indicators, such as:

- Inability to tolerate distress
- Difficulty regulating emotions
- Trouble forming and maintaining healthy relationships
- Engaging in self-destructive activities (e.g., self-harm, substance abuse, unhealthy eating habits, etc.)

Because of this, it is believed that DBT could also help people with PTSD; over the years, multiple studies have shown this was true.[104,105,106,107]

Avoidance and Radical Acceptance

Avoidance is a primary symptom of PTSD. There are two types of avoidance: *emotional avoidance* and *behavioral avoidance*.

- **Emotional avoidance** is when we try to stop ourselves from having thoughts or feelings about a traumatic event. This happens to us internally, and even people who know us well might not notice it at all. For example, a person who has been sexually assaulted may try to avoid unpleasant emotions like fear when they are reminded of the trauma.

- **Behavioral avoidance** is when we stay away from places, people, sounds, or smells that remind us of the traumatic event. For example, suppose you survived a major natural disaster (e.g., hurricane, tornado, earthquake, etc.). In that case, you might not want to go back to the place where it happened.

I think DBT's **Radical Acceptance** significantly addresses the PTSD symptom of avoidance. Studies show that *avoidance coping* is linked to anxiety and depression and makes people even more prone to stress[108,109,110,111], underlining Dr. Linehan's belief that *to avoid is to prolong suffering*.

I'm going to get a bit personal here. You see, I did A LOT of *avoidance coping* myself.

In high school, I would eat lunch in the library even though I wasn't allowed to. I did this because it hurt more to be seen eating alone in the cafeteria. In college, right in the middle of my loneliness and depression, I would every now and then get asked by my roommate about how things were going. I always replied, *"Great!"* When there was a party or event, I would act like I had "other plans." If I said yes to something, I would cancel at the last minute because my anxiety was so bad. (I'd get so worried about all the "bad" and "wrong" things that could happen if people saw me in a social setting.)

During therapy, I learned that *avoiding* doesn't mean I was fooling anybody. I can say, *"Great! I'm all good,"* till I was blue in the face, but that doesn't mean they believed me.

Yes, avoidance makes us feel better because it keeps us from facing our traumas, but a big part of that, at least for me, was about hiding. I tried to hide what I was going through. I didn't want anyone to find out. But here's the ugly truth I discovered—everyone close to me already knew.

I'm sharing this, so you'll know that if someone in your life asks you how you're doing or notices how you act and asks about it, it's not an attack. It's highly likely to be a sign of concern. This is why I found Radical Acceptance to be so freeing. Accepting my reality relieved me of the burden of hiding and denying.

So, are you ready to try Radically Acceptance? Let's clarify a few misunderstandings about this concept before you do.

Radical Acceptance IS NOT:

- **Agreement, approval, or consent.** The only thing you accept here is that something traumatic happened to you. You're not agreeing that it should have happened, not approving the event, and not saying you're "okay" with what happened.

- **Giving up or giving in.** When you radically accept reality, this does not mean that you don't want things to improve. It's the opposite. Acceptance is acknowledging where you are now because you know it's the first step to getting better.

- **Inaction.** Acceptance of reality doesn't mean you surrender to whatever life throws at you. You're not a hopeless observer of your own life; you're its creator. So you accept what happened and then work to make your life better.

- **About Others.** Radical acceptance is about your thoughts, emotions, and behavior concerning the traumatic event—no one else's. It may be that the trauma you experienced or witnessed was caused by someone. Still, it's not about understanding them, letting go of them, or even forgiving them. It's all about you.

Think of avoidance as a closed door. You stay away from that door because it reminds you of the trauma you experienced or witnessed. But healing is on the other side of that door. So, if you don't open that door and walk through it, you slow down or prevent your own healing and stay in your current misery (*prolonging your suffering*).

Now, **think of radical acceptance as a key**. It's what can give you the courage to open that door, walk through it, and start walking toward recovery.

> *"You can't move forward with anything in your life until there is radical acceptance."* –Lady Gaga

Worksheet: Radical Acceptance of Trauma

Radical acceptance of trauma is like saying, *"Something terrible happened, and it hurts. But it already happened. I cannot go back and change any part of it. I have no control over the past. The only thing I can affect is the future."*

Take a minute and reflect on the above statement. When ready, write down your Radical Acceptance statement(s) regarding the traumatic event you experienced or witnessed.

Example:
Trauma: Losing your home and all your possessions in a hurricane.
Radical Acceptance Statement: Something so unexpected and painful happened that it's making me feel so hopeless and scared for the future. But it already happened, and it cannot be undone. Focusing on the past just prevents me from making the present better. So I accept what happened. It's no one's fault. I accept it.

Your turn:

_____
_____
_____
_____
_____
_____
_____
_____
_____
_____
_____
_____
_____
_____

Desire to Change

Many mental health problems stem from our inability to "move on" from where we are. We feel stuck and don't know what to do about it. In my opinion, willingness is NOT the issue. Often, the lack of skill (i.e., how to do it) stumps us.

Radical Acceptance of the trauma that happened is just one part of the equation. The rest is taking the necessary steps to CHANGE. It's only when we change that our life becomes better.

> *"You're not stuck. You're just committed to certain patterns of behavior because they helped you in the past. Now those behaviors have become more harmful than helpful.*
> *The reason why you can't move forward is because you keep applying an old formula to a new level in your life.*
> *Change the formula to get a different result."*
> *– Emily Maroutian*

The following DBT skills are the "change steps" or actions you need to take. We already discussed these skills in Chapter 3 (page 198). However, here, we'll discuss how you can apply them specifically for PTSD.

> *"Mindfulness is a pause. The space between stimulus and response: that's where choice lies. –Tara Brach"*

Mindfulness is the PAUSE you need when PTSD symptoms occur. It may seem like things are happening too fast, and you have no control over your actions, but you do.

You see, what's happening is that you're reacting on instinct. You're not giving yourself time—a pause—to enable your brain to take stock of the situation before you act.

This is what Chito[****], a reader, had to say: *"One Friday night, I was driving home from work when a yellow SUV cab ran a red light and hit my car full-on on the driver's side. They say it's a miracle I came out of the accident alive, and I know that's true, but I just couldn't bring myself back into a car after that. Each time I try, I feel the impact on my side all over again. I hear screeching metal that hurts my ears. My heart starts to pound uncontrollably, and I have a panic attack.*

I didn't drive for about three years. Since I was one of five brothers, all that machismo made the fact that I didn't drive a bit of a family joke, but I didn't care... until my wife got pregnant. I thought I really needed to get a grip on this because I won't be able to forgive myself if something happened, and I couldn't drive to get help or bring her to the hospital.

One night, I just said to my wife that I thought I needed help. This is the first time I have talked about the car accident in three years and what I feel whenever I'm around a car. An uncle of hers was a psychotherapist, and it was he who introduced me to DBT.

[****] *Name changed for privacy.*

I'll admit that I wasn't sure DBT was right for me. The minute he said "mindfulness," I think I did a mental eye roll. But I was already there, so I might as well listen to what he had to say, right? To make a long story short, I kept coming back, learned the skills, put them into practice, and got brave enough to drive the day my son was born. Today, I can fully drive again. I still have my moments, though. I don't think they'll ever be gone. Sometimes I think I can still hear metal screeching, and when I'm in a big group, I still worry that someone will trip, fall, or do whatever and ram me on the side, but I can handle these moments now."

When you are mindful, you are not in your past, nor are you in your future. You are simply in NOW. And **when you are in NOW,** the area of the brain that processes **emotions become less active,** and the area that aids in **rational thought and decision-making become more active**. This helps us learn how to control our emotions, including strong emotions like fear, anger, grief, and others.

In the following pages are numerous exercises to help you become more mindful. I recommend making at least one of them part of your daily routine.

Worksheet: 1:2 Breathing

Every time we breathe in, our cells get oxygen to make energy and eliminate toxins. Every time we breathe out, we get rid of the waste gas carbon dioxide. In addition to this exchange of gases, breathing is linked to our nervous system.

Depending on the speed and depth of our breathing, the inhales and exhales trigger either the "fight or flight" or "rest and digest" systems of the nervous system. We trigger the latter—rest and digest—with 1:2 breathing. By making our exhalations twice as long, we calm our nervous system.

1. Sit up straight on a chair, lie on a mat or on your bed, or just stand, whatever is most comfortable for you.

2. Inhale through your nose for a count of four (4), inviting your abdomen to inflate gently like a balloon as you breathe in.

3. Exhale through your nose for an eight (8) count, inviting your abdomen to deflate as you breathe out gently.

4. Do this for 3-5 rounds.

Worksheet: Nadi Shodhana (Alternate Nostril Breathing)

Anyone who has tried mindful breathing knows that "quieting the mind" is a very hard thing to do! This breathing exercise calms your nervous system and mind and helps you focus so that your mind doesn't wander off.

1. Sit up straight on a chair, lie on a mat or your bed, or just stand, whatever is most comfortable for you.

2. Put your right thumb over your right nostril to block the airflow.

3. Slowly *exhale* through your left nostril for a count of four (4).

4. When you're done exhaling, let go of your right nostril and put your ring finger on your left nostril.

5. Take a breath through the right nostril for a count of four (4). After you've taken a full breath in, let it out through your right nostril.

6. Let go of your ring finger and use your thumb to close your right nostril again.

7. Take a full breath in and let out a full breath from your left nose.

8. Repeat the whole process at least twice.

Worksheet: Wise Mind

Wise Mind (WM) is where *Emotional Mind* and *Reasoning Mind* intersect. WM is not something we create. We all have an emotional side and a logical side inside us. It's just that when faced with strong unpleasant emotions, we tend to react or behave based on these emotions[112]. During these moments, we fail to pause and consult our Reasoning Mind on what to do.

Note that acting based only on "logic" isn't a good idea because it means ignoring your or someone else's feelings. So what should you do? **Feel your emotions, but use reason before you do anything.** In other words, always act with Wise Mind.

EMOTIONAL MIND: **REASONING MIND:**

WISE MIND

Emotion + Reason

What you <u>want</u> to do   What you <u>should</u> do

The following reflective exercise will help you make consulting your Reasoning Mind a habit when faced with difficult emotions. This way, you can feel your emotions but don't necessarily have to behave according to them.

1. Think of a time when you did or said something you later regretted. Write down as much as you can about the event.

    Example: I pushed and shouted at my partner for asking me questions about my nightmares.
    Your turn:

    _____
    _____
    _____

2. Why did you do what you did?

    Example: I didn't want to talk about it. My partner's questions were making me angry.
    Your turn:

    _____
    _____
    _____

3. Why do you regret what you did?

    Example: Shouting was already bad, but to get physical? There's no excuse for that.
    Your turn:

    _____
    _____
    _____

4. How would you change things right now?

    Example: Instead of getting angry, I would tell my partner that I'm not ready to talk about my nightmares. I don't fully understand them myself and don't know how to deal with them.
    Your turn:

    _____
    _____
    _____

Notes: Your response to Question #1 refers to an instance of *Emotional Mind*. Your response to Question #3 is you consulting your *Reasoning Mind*. Your answer to Question #4 points to *Wise Mind*.

You are constantly refining your use of Wise Mind through introspection so consider additional circumstances in the past where you acted emotionally and what you would do differently today.

In the present, when you find yourself in a stressful situation, ask yourself, *"What would Wise Mind do?"*

Worksheet: Mindful Body Scanning

This exercise helps you calm down, organize your thoughts, and find your center.

1. Lie on a mat, on your bed, or just stand whatever is most comfortable for you.

2. Box Breathe (page 58) for two cycles.

3. Imagine subjecting yourself to a body scan. Start by focusing on your scalp. Is it feeling "tight"? If so, take a deep breath in and relax your head as you let it out. Move your head side to side if that helps. Imagine this movement making your scalp "loose."

4. Move on to your forehead. Are you frowning? If so, take a deep breath and relax your forehead as you let it out. Release any tension.

5. Notice your eyebrows next. Are they meeting in the middle? If so, take a deep breath and relax your eyebrows as you exhale. Imagine them falling to the sides of your face.

6. Next, focus on your cheekbones. Are they warm? If so, breathe in and imagine a cool breeze touching your cheeks as you breathe out.

7. After checking all the aspects of your face, check your shoulders. Are they flat on the floor/mat/bed? If not, breathe in and out as you've done above.

8. Keep going until you've scanned and relaxed your whole body.

Distress Tolerance Skills for PTSD

> *"You can't calm the storm, so stop trying. You can calm yourself. The storm will pass."* – Timber Hawkeye

If Mindfulness is taking a pause, then Distress Tolerance is like standing still and bearing the distress unpleasant emotions are causing. You do this NOT because you're okay with the situation but because you accept that you can't do anything about it.

The distress is already here. It cannot un-happen. But if you act according to your pain, it will worsen the situation, so the best you can do right now is to tolerate the distress.

My Distress Tolerance level was very low when I was dealing with OCD, GAD (General Anxiety Disorder), and depression. This meant that whenever I was upset, I showed my emotions right away by getting *angry*. This emotional impulse of mine did not help at all and made so many things in my life worse.

Thanks to DBT, I've increased my distress tolerance levels. I no longer act out and have learned the virtue of mentally and physically standing still for a moment.

The following DBT Distress Tolerance exercises will assist you in developing the necessary skills you need to tolerate high-stress situations. I hope they help you as much as they have helped me.

Worksheet: Into the Cold

Cold temperatures activate the *Mammalian Dive Response*, which triggers our parasympathetic nervous system, the network of nerves that tells the body to **slow down and relax**.[113]

Use this technique whenever you are experiencing a very distressing emotion (e.g., panic, fear, anger, anxiety, etc.) or have a strong urge to engage in dangerous behavior (e.g., violence, self-harm, use drugs, etc.).

CAUTION: Subjecting your face to cold water lowers your heart rate. If you have a heart condition or are allergic to freezing temperatures, please consult your physician before doing any of these exercises.

Because PTSD symptoms can happen at any time, you should have a plan for when you are at home or in public. I've started the table with a few ideas. If you like any of them, check them off. Of course, feel free to add your own ideas too.

AT HOME/ALONE	ELSEWHERE/WITH OTHERS
o Go to the bathroom and splash cold water on your face.	o Go to the bathroom and splash cold water on your face.
o Go to the freezer, get a couple of ice cubes and hold them in your hand.	o If it's winter, go outside and face the cold.
o Fill a zip-lock bag with cold water and put it over your eyes and upper cheeks while holding your breath. (This tricks your brain into thinking you are underwater.)	o If you have access to a refrigerator, bring a filled water bottle and put it in there. Grab it and pour the cold water over your face when in distress.
o Take a VERY COLD shower.	o If you have access to a refrigerator, keep a face gel mask cold pack in there and use it when necessary.
o Fill a basin with cold water and submerge your face in it.	

Others:

Worksheet: STOP

When you're in distress, it's likely that you act rashly or impulsively without thinking. This is because you're in search of instant relief from the distress. But people often make things worse when they act without thinking, right? So, you have to stop yourself from (emotionally) reacting. The STOP exercise below will help you keep your cool (as opposed to being controlled by your emotions).

S	**S**top
T	**T**ake a step back.
O	**O**bserve.
P	**P**roceed mindfully.

Following is an explanation of each acronym with some exercises where applicable.

S	**S**top.

Stop! Imagine being "frozen" in time and place for a moment. Just exist. There's NO NEED to say or do anything at all. Stay in control by "freezing." This will prevent you from acting on your emotional impulses.

Example: It's New Year's Eve, but your trauma is related to gunshots. As a result, you can't bear to hear fireworks. However, your family doesn't understand this, and everyone is nagging you to join them outside. You're feeling stressed by all their coaxing. You're holding a drink in your hand, and you have this urge to throw it at someone's face, bang your fists on the table, and scream, "No!" But instead... you freeze in your tracks and do none of the above.

| **T** | **T**ake a step back. |

Take a figurative and literal step back from the situation. Remove yourself from the circumstances until you feel calmer and more in control. Remember that no rule or code demands you reply at this exact moment. You are entitled to take a break from the situation.

Example: Imagine the New Year's Eve situation above. After freezing in your tracks, take a mental step back from whoever is trying to persuade you to check out the fireworks. Imagine "leaving the scene." Take a small (or big) physical step back, too, and say something like, "No, but thanks" or "Stop. I already said No to [family member]."

| **O** | **O**bserve. |

Pay attention to what's going on inside and outside of you. Do this mindfully and without judgment. Observe facts. Observe only what's happening, not why or how things are happening.

Example of observing yourself: I am standing. I'm gripping the drink I have in my hand. My breathing is erratic.
Example of observing your surroundings: [Family member] said something and is looking at me, waiting for a reply. They're holding a drink and half-eaten pizza. My niece is trying to stay awake behind them.

What are you observing?

_____
_____

| **P** | **P**roceed mindfully. |

The previous steps have all been about getting the PAUSE your mind needs to calm down and assess the situation. Now, it's time to move forward and decide what you need to do.

To proceed mindfully, consult [Wise Mind](#) (page 60) and ask yourself, *"What do I want to happen?"*, *"How can I prevent this situation from worsening for me and others?"*

Example: Your Aunt Lily is physically dragging you to join the fireworks activities outside. You're angry and feeling panicked at the same time. Your impulse is to roughly pull your arm from her and shove her away from you. But you don't want to make the situation worse, so you **stop** *(freeze) and take a mental and physical* **step back** *from your aunt. You* **observe** *that she's tipsy. Her face is red, and her speech is slightly slurred. You know that when Aunt Lily is drunk, there's no point arguing. She's likely not even going to remember this event tomorrow. So you* **proceed mindfully** *by slowly extricating your arm while helping her not to lose balance, telling her that you don't like fireworks, and leaving the room.*

Worksheet: ACCEPTS

Distraction is a great way to pull your attention *away* from distressful situations.

The following distracting skills will help you divert your thoughts and emotions so that you don't act impulsively when in distress.

A	Activities.
C	Contributing.
C	Comparisons.
E	Emotions.
P	Push away.
T	Thoughts.
S	Sensations.

Following is an explanation of each acronym with some exercises where applicable.

A	Activities.

Make a list of activities you enjoy that demand your full attention. The objective is to completely lose yourself (be "in the zone") in any of these activities, diverting your attention from whatever or whoever is causing your distress.

Examples: go on a run, swim laps, solve a Sudoku puzzle, etc.

List down as many focus-grabbing activities as you like below.

1. _____
2. _____
3. _____
4. _____
5. _____
6. _____

7. _____
8. _____
9. _____
10. _____

| **C** | **C**ontributing. |

When we are in distress, we become very self-absorbed (e.g., *What's happening to me?*, *Why is this happening to me?*, *Why am I feeling this way?* etc.) A great way to distract yourself is to divert your attention from yourself to others. Studies show that considering others' needs and contributing not only helps the people you are helping but also helps you mentally and physically, making you healthier and extending your life span.[114]

Examples: go through your closet and find clothes to donate, arrange a food drive, donate your time (e.g., volunteer visiting the elderly at a local senior home), create a care package for a friend or family member in need, etc.

What do you want to contribute? List as many ideas that come to mind.

1. _____
2. _____
3. _____
4. _____
5. _____
6. _____
7. _____
8. _____
9. _____
10. _____

| **C** | Comparisons. |

Comparisons are also a way to take your mind off of yourself but in a slightly different way. Here, you're trying to see your situation more positively by comparing it to something worse that happened to you in the past.

Example: Two years ago, I had a panic attack that made me run to my car, leave my wife and toddler in the park, and drive dangerously into traffic. I side-swiped another vehicle and can't forget the fear I had inside at the thought that I might have killed someone. What I'm feeling now is nothing compared to that.

Your turn:

_____

_____

| **E** | Emotions. |

When you're in distress, what are you feeling? Anger? Fear? Frustration? Whatever it is, distract yourself by trying to provoke a completely different emotion from yourself.

Example: If you're afraid, read a feel-good book to feel happy. If you're angry, read a love letter or card you previously received to feel love.

Your turn:

_____

_____

| **P** | Push away. |

When in distress, negative emotional urges arise. For example, if you're mad, you might want to throw something or hit someone. You might want to stand up and run away if you're panicking. PUSH AWAY these impulses by blocking any further thoughts about them. (**Important:** This activity should only be done to avoid making a situation worse.

Please do not use it as your go-to technique when in distress because that can lead to *avoidance coping*, which is unhealthy.)

"Pushing away" is not about denying your emotions. It's about radically accepting your emotions (e.g., *I'm very uncomfortable with this group of people*) and then pushing away any emotional impulse you may have about it (e.g., *I will NOT shove the person next to me away*.)

Here are a few examples of "pushing away" activities you can adopt. Feel free to include your ideas as well.

- ☐ Find a quiet area where you can be alone, then shout "STOP!" (to any negative thoughts and emotional impulses you may have).
- ☐ Stay exactly where you are (freeze), and then build an imaginary wall between yourself and others in your mind.
- ☐ Snip it. Mentally place your urges in a box and then put that box in a far, far away place. Imagine the box going further and further each time you exhale.
- ☐ Others:

_____
_____

T	**T**houghts.

Distract yourself with happy thoughts. *Examples: sing your favorite song in your head, imagine your favorite cartoon character, think about your favorite movie and what "role" you can play, etc.*

Your turn:

_____
_____

| **S** | **S**ensations. |

Distract yourself by submitting your body to various physical sensations. Here are a few examples. Feel free to include your ideas as well.

- ☐ Chew sour gum.
- ☐ Drink annoyingly sweet, sugary drinks.
- ☐ Open the freezer door and cool your face.
- ☐ Bite a chili pepper or throw a few pepper flakes in your mouth.
- ☐ Take a cold shower.
- ☐ Swim in an icy pool.
- ☐ Others:

_____
_____

Worksheet: PASS Kit (Panic Anxiety Stress Support Kit)

The PASS kit is a collection of calming and anti-stress objects developed by University of Waterloo students *Tina Chan* and *Alaaddin Sidahmed*. It's a mental health first aid kit that includes a stress ball, an eye mask, earplugs, flash cards (tips and exercises to decrease stress and anxiety), and a card listing various mental health crisis hotlines if you need help beyond what the kit can provide.

You can purchase the PASS kit online on their website. However, I would suggest creating your own to customize it to your needs. Your trauma is personal to you, and it's you who knows best what items can quickly ease your distress.

Here are a few sample items to put in your PASS kit to jumpstart ideas. As always, don't hesitate to add your own thoughts. **Important**: Don't make your PASS kit big. The kit should be something you can carry with you at all times.

- ☐ Cooling face gel mask.
- ☐ A miniature picture of _____ (someone you love, admire, gives you strength, etc.)
- ☐ Chewing gum.
- ☐ Small stress ball.
- ☐ Small bottle of a scent that calms you.
- ☐ A rosary.
- ☐ Worry beads. (You can wear these at all times if this works for you.)
- ☐ Others:

_____
_____
_____

Worksheet: TIPP

Distract yourself from distressing emotions by changing your body's chemistry. Each skill below causes your body's response patterns to change quickly, making you feel less emotionally agitated. Note that you don't need to do them all. For example, I usually do the *Intense Exercise* skill, and that's enough to calm me down.

T	Temperature.
I	Intense Exercise.
P	Paced Breathing.
P	Paired Muscle Relaxation.

Following is an explanation of each acronym with some exercises where applicable.

T	Temperature.

Calm down by subjecting yourself to cold temperatures. (See Into the Cold, page 249).

I	Intense Exercise.

Distract your mind (and ergo your emotions) by engaging in intense physical activities. Don't have much time? Use apps like the *5 Minute Home Workouts* by Olson Applications or *Seven – 7 Minute Workout* by Perigree AB to get in some quick workouts throughout the day.

P	Paced Breathing.

When we're in distress, we tend to breathe fast and erratically. Calm yourself by pacing your breath. You can try Box Breathing (page 58), 1:2 Breathing (page 242), or Alternate Nostril Breathing (page 243).

P	Paired Muscle Relaxation.

While doing Paced Breathing above, you can combine this with paired muscle relaxation. Here's what to do: When you take a deep breath in, slowly tighten your muscles, but not so much that they cramp. When you take a deep breath out, let all that tension go while telling yourself to relax.

Tip: Do this muscle flexing and relaxing as if you're doing a body scan. For example, flex and release your face muscles, then move on to your neck and shoulders. Next, flex and release your arms and hands, then move on to your core muscles. Continue until you reach your legs and feet.

> *"Feel the feeling but don't become the emotion.
> Witness it. Allow it. Release it."* –Cristal Andrus

Remember this image?

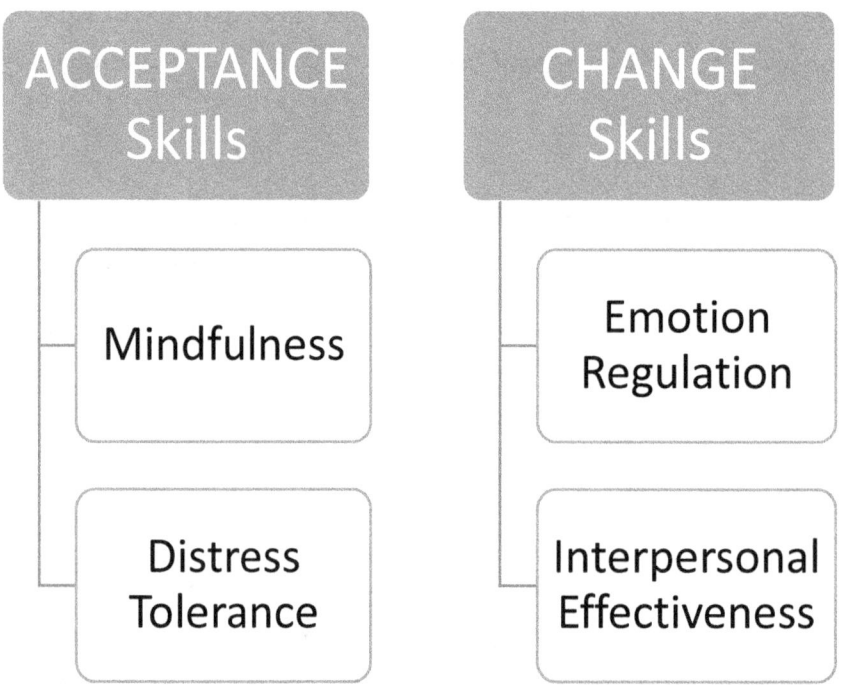

If Mindfulness is the pause we need (time to think), and Distress Tolerance is like standing still for a moment (to stop ourselves from acting out), then Emotion Regulation is where we start to change and learn new behaviors.

Note that Emotion Regulation is NOT emotion suppression. You're not denying or "putting a lid" on your distress or feelings here. You're going to Wise Mind (Emotional Mind + Reasoning Mind) so that you can control your emotions instead of your emotions controlling you.

Worksheet: Check the Facts

Check the Facts is an exercise where you stop, think, and check your feelings against the facts. This helps you understand what's happening instead of what you feel is happening.

First, let's do a reflective exercise. Think back on a few times when you acted too quickly (impulsively). It can also be something you thought was a big deal at the time but turned out not to be.

Question: What emotion do you want to verify?
Example: my fear
Your answer:

Question: What happened? What caused this emotion?
Example: I went inside the living room and saw my son lying face down on the floor.
Your answer:

Question: What presumptions did you have regarding the situation? What was your immediate thought?
Example: My son was dead.
Your answer:

Question: What did you do?

Example: I screamed his name, ran to him, grabbed him up off the floor, and started to check him out.

Your answer:

Question: What happened afterward? What was the consequence of your actions?

Example: My son was crying because he got scared and hurt when I grabbed him. My wife ran from the kitchen to the living room, and she looked frightened and confused at what she saw.

Your answer:

CHECK THE FACTS:

You listed your assumptions above, but <u>WHAT ELSE</u> happened? What was the reality of the situation?

Example: My son was perfectly fine. He was just lying on his belly, playing with a toy I didn't see.

Your answer:

Question: Why do you believe you reacted the way you did? What were you scared of?

Example: My time in Afghanistan was rough, to say the least. I saw dead people, including children, on the ground every single day. When I saw my son like that, I immediately saw dead bodies in my head, and I felt an intense fear come over me.

Your answer:

Question: Looking back, on a scale of 0-5, did your emotion fit the facts? (0 = not at all, 5 = yes):

Example: 0, not at all

Your answer:

Question: What do you believe you could have done differently to avoid reacting impulsively (without thinking)?

Example: I should have taken a step back and looked around, really looked around, to realize where I was, which was in my own living room—not in Afghanistan.

Your answer:

Question: Since your emotion DID NOT fit the facts, what would you do differently?

Example: I would calmly call out to my son and say something like, "Hey bud, what are you doing on the floor?"

Your answer:

Question: Would you do anything differently if your emotion fit or partially fit the facts?

Example: I'm not sure. If my son groaned in pain, I would run to him and lift him off the floor, but I probably would not have been so rough.

Your answer:

IMPORTANT: **Check the Facts** is not limited to past events. You should apply this technique whenever you feel intense, unpleasant emotions. However, I recommend repeating the preceding practice at least two (2) more times. Consider previous incidents in which you may have overreacted and, as a result, made the situation worse. This is to acquaint you with the process of fact-checking your emotions.

Worksheet: Opposite to Emotion

Sometimes, we still have difficulty controlling our behaviour even when we fact-check our emotions and discover that they do not fit the facts. That is, we still want to do what we want, even though we know we may be overreacting!

To help stop yourself, an **Opposite to Emotion** table is provided below. **Column A** covers unhealthy feelings, **Column B** shows what you might ordinarily want to do when you experience these emotions, and **Column C** lists a counter-action to your natural inclination.

The next time you find yourself in a highly stressful situation, consult this table and do what you wrote in Column C. (I've done the first emotion as an example.)

A	B	C
Emotion	**Emotion-Driven Action**	**Opposite to Emotion**
What are you feeling?	*What you would ordinarily do in this situation. (If you have a natural desire to perform something other than what is described below, please write it down on a separate sheet.)*	*Make a list of actions that go entirely against how you feel.*
Fear	Run away, avoid, get mad	*Stay and talk; do some mindful breathing exercises; think happy thoughts*
Sadness	Binge-eat, drink alcohol	
Guilt	Shut down, self-criticize, or even blame others (deflect)	

A	B	C
Emotion	**Emotion-Driven Action**	**Opposite to Emotion**
What are you feeling?	*What you would ordinarily do in this situation.* *(If you have a natural desire to perform something other than what is described below, please write it down on a separate sheet.)*	*Make a list of actions that go entirely against how you feel.*
Anger	Scream, sulk, or do something aggressive, such as slamming the door or breaking something	
Emptiness	Call and hook up with an ex	
Loneliness	Please people around me so they don't leave	
Frustration	Break something	
Helplessness	Cry, scream, punch someone or something, cut myself	
Resentment	Spread stories about someone	
Feel free to add more emotions and scenarios in the extra rows below.		

A	B	C
Emotion	**Emotion-Driven Action**	**Opposite to Emotion**
What are you feeling?	*What you would ordinarily do in this situation.* *(If you have a natural desire to perform something other than what is described below, please write it down on a separate sheet.)*	*Make a list of actions that go entirely against how you feel.*

Worksheet: Problem Solving

You have fact-checked your emotions, and the situation fits the facts. You are justified in feeling what you're feeling. However, that does not mean you should still give in to your emotional impulses. For example, you start to talk to your partner about your PTSD. But instead of being understanding and supportive, they're invalidating or dismissing your experience. *"Oh, surely, it wasn't that bad?", "But that was years ago!"*

Their response hurts and angers you. You fact-checked your emotions, and yes, they are justified. Your instinct is to go over and slap your partner across the face. But... will that make things better? In all likelihood, it won't. So what do you do?

Now's the time to problem-solve the situation itself. The goal here is to **change the situation as a way to change your emotions**.

Question: What's the problem? Describe the situation that's causing your intense, painful, or unpleasant emotions. *Example: After finally getting the courage to open up about my PTSD, my partner is not taking me seriously.*
Your answer:
Question: Did you Check the Facts (page 263)? Y/ N If not, please do the Check the Facts exercise before proceeding.)
Question: What's the short-term goal here? What do you want to happen to feel that you've made progress in this situation? *Example: I want my partner to take this discussion seriously.*
Your answer:
TO-DO: List as many steps or solutions as possible to achieve your goal! Don't evaluate or judge your ideas. List anything that comes to mind that will help you improve this situation.

Example: (1) My partner's multi-tasking, so I have to ask them to sit and focus on what I say. (2) Repeat what I said, but be more direct. (e.g., This is very important to me. I need help.) (3) I probably picked the wrong time to talk to them about this because they just got home from work. I will take a break and talk about this again later when there are no distractions.

Your answers: (Use extra sheets if necessary.)

1. _____

2. _____

3. _____

4. _____

5. _____

6. _____

7. _____

8. _____

9. _____

10. _____

> *"Life is meant to be shared. We need each other."*
> *– Lailah Gifty Akita*

As mentioned, Mindfulness is the pause we need to be fully present in the moment. Distress Tolerance is the skill of bearing distress so that we don't act based purely on emotions. Emotion Regulation is taking steps to control our feelings instead of letting them control us. The last skill, Interpersonal Effectiveness, is finding, building, and keeping healthy relationships because we need these to lead fulfilling lives.

Now, relationships are not just about you. It's also about the other people in the relationship with you. However, we don't control other people, and we're not responsible for their behaviors. The only actions we're responsible for are our own. For this purpose, the Interpersonal Effectiveness skills you're about to learn in the following pages focus on YOU. Specifically, your needs and how you communicate them so that you find your needs met in the relationship.

Living with PTSD can be overwhelming, and it would help if you had the understanding, help, and support of others. Interpersonal Effectiveness enables you to achieve this while considering *their* wants and needs at the same time.

Recovering from Invalidation

In my own mental recovery journey, I've experienced three groups of people: those who (1) focus on you, (2) ignore you, or (3) invalidate you. I found the latter to be the most damaging.

There I was, finally having the courage to talk and seek help for my mental health problems, and some people would tell me things like, *"There's no such thing," "Get over it,"* or *"It can't be THAT bad."*

With PTSD, **traumatic invalidation** occurs when you're constantly being deliberately misunderstood, misread, or misinterpreted, when important facts regarding your trauma are being ignored or denied, or when your experiences (during and after the trauma) are being trivialized or denied.

So, what did I do?

Firstly, I radically accepted that invalidation hurts. Secondly, to deal with the pain I was feeling from being invalidated, I used Distress Tolerance techniques like 5-4-3-2-1 Grounding (page 209) and STOP (page 251). DBT also taught me that "invalidation is rarely a catastrophe" and that my truths and experiences are valid regardless of what others think or say.

And know too that you have influence in your relationships. Suppose someone invalidates you, but you still want to try to have a relationship with that person. In that case, you have nothing to lose by trying any of the skills below.

Worksheet: DEARMAN[††††]

You want your needs met in a relationship. However, there is an "art" to making your request(s) without damaging your relationships. **DEARMAN** is the skill to apply to achieve this goal.

D	Describe the situation.
E	Express how you feel.
A	Assert yourself.
R	Reinforce your request.
M	Mindfulness.
A	Appear confident.
N	Negotiate.

Following is an explanation of each acronym with some exercises where applicable.

D	Describe the situation.

What's going on? What do you want? Discuss the situation using clear and concise words. Don't say what you think or feel; stick to the facts.

Example: I am having a tough time right now, and the last thing I need is a 2-week vacation with my in-laws.

What's the situation?

_____

_____

_____

[††††] *We already did this exercise on page 79. However, it's very good relationship exercise so I'm featuring it again here with PTSD-related examples.*

| **E** | Express how you feel. |

Use "**I**" statements. Remember that what you're describing are *your* thoughts and emotions. **"You"** statements can be taken as accusations by the other person, increasing the chance for conflict. *Example: I get very stressed there with everyone around. It's not their fault. I just need time.*

Your turn:

_____
_____
_____

| **A** | Assert yourself. |

Clearly express what you want to happen without being confrontational. The other person will understand you better as a result of this. *Example: So I don't want to accompany you and the kids when you go.*

Your turn:

_____
_____
_____

| **R** | Reinforce your request. |

Make sure the other person knows how important your request is. So tell them how grateful you will be if they give you what you want or need. *Example: I know it's a big ask, but I would really appreciate the time alone to work on my issues. I would really appreciate your support.*

Your turn:

_____
_____
_____

| **M** | **M**indfulness. |

Keep your words and feelings in check, and no matter what the other person says, stay on topic. *Example: So, I hope you understand me. I need the time away on my own.*
Your turn:

_____
_____
_____

| **A** | **A**ppear confident. |

Convey confidence through your words and body language. Be sure of your request but don't be intimidating. For instance, do not stare other people down. Be consistent with your attitude too. For example, do not sit up straight while making your request and slouch afterward.

I had very low self-esteem, so appearing confident was something I had to practice a lot. For example, I walked looking down for years and had a bad "slouching posture." So I started practicing in front of the mirror, and I would stand and watch myself square my shoulders back. I also imagined a string on the top of my head that was pulling it upwards to prevent myself from looking down all the time. Next, I practiced what I wanted to say in front of the mirror. I slowly learned to use *fewer words* and be as direct (but polite!) as possible.

How do you want to show confidence?

_____
_____
_____

| **N** | Negotiate. |

If the person you're speaking to is unwilling to accommodate your request, try negotiating. This will give you both a chance to devise a workable solution. You can suggest a course of action or inquire about what the other person believes should be done moving forward.

Example: How about I join you guys the last weekend, and then we can all go home together? What do you think?

Your turn:

_____
_____
_____

Worksheet: GIVE

You need to **G.I.V.E.** to get. This exercise is all about effective communication. It teaches us how to say what we want in a way that makes others want to give us what we want.

G	Be Gentle.
I	Act Interested.
V	Validate.
E	Show an Easy Manner.

Following is an explanation of each acronym with some exercises where applicable.

G	Be Gentle.

When making your request, be gentle with your ways. Do not demand or be disrespectful. Also, avoid saying or doing anything that might offend the other person. In short, be nice!

List 5 ways you can ask for something in a ***gentle*** way. *Example: use a soft voice, start your sentence with "Would you do me a favor and..." or "Do you mind if..."*

1. _____
2. _____
3. _____
4. _____
5. _____

I	Act Interested.

If you want the other person to listen and consider your request(s), then you must show an interest in their response.

List 5 things you can do to show that you are **interested** and care about what the other person is saying. *Example: face the person speaking, maintain eye contact, respond to what was said, etc.*

1. _____
2. _____
3. _____
4. _____
5. _____

V	**V**alidate.

Recognize the other person's emotions and opinions with WORDS and ACTIONS. This way, you show that this is not a one-sided conversation.

List 5 things you can do to show **validation** to others. *Examples: say, "I understand this is difficult for you..." or "Let me see if I understand you correctly. You mean..."*

1. _____
2. _____
3. _____
4. _____
5. _____

E	Show an **E**asy Manner.

Display an easy manner so that the other person feels you're making a *request*, not a demand. When you have a friendly attitude, people will feel more at ease and be more open to what you want.

List 5 things you can do to display an *easy manner* to others. *Examples: use a little humor, smile, adopt a non-threatening demeanor (e.g., don't block the other person's way), etc.*

1. _____
2. _____
3. _____
4. _____
5. _____

Worksheet: FAST

This exercise is all about maintaining your self-respect during any interpersonal interaction. Remember, you're not the only one with needs in this relationship, and there will be times when the other person will also assert what they want. So how do you ask for what you want or say no to a request in a way that won't make you feel bad about yourself later? You apply the FAST technique.

F	Be Fair.
A	No Apologies.
S	Stick to your Values.
T	Be Truthful.

Following is an explanation of each acronym with some exercises where applicable.

F	Be Fair.

Be fair to yourself and the other person during the conversation. When you make your request, be sure it's not something above and beyond the other person's capability to grant such a request.

What's your request? Are you sure it's fair to ask this of the other party?

_____
_____
_____

When someone asks you for something, ensure you're actively listening and genuinely considering their request.

How are you validating the other person in this conversation? (See <u>V</u> in <u>GIVE</u> for an example, page 278.)

_____
_____
_____

A	No <u>A</u>pologies.

Don't apologize or over-apologize for anything. Don't say sorry for making a request, and don't say sorry if you say no to a request made of you.

Practice stating your request without apologizing:
Example: I would like to take Friday off.

_____
_____
_____

Practice saying "No" to a request without apologizing:
Example: As much as I want to, I can't give you Friday off because of all our backlog.

_____
_____
_____

S	Stick to your <u>V</u>alues.

Don't give in just because the other person doesn't like or want to do what you want. Repeat your request assertively (but not rudely or threateningly). On the other hand, don't give in and say "Yes" to a request when you know it goes against your values.

Practice sticking to your values when making a request:

Example: I'd need Friday off anyway because I have a very important appointment with my therapist.

___

Practice sticking to your values and say "No" despite the other person's persuasion, nagging, convincing tactics, etc.

Example: I can't stay. I want to help, but this appointment is significant for my mental health.

___

| **T** | Be Truthful. |

Don't tell lies or overstate things to get what you want. Neither should you make false excuses just because you have difficulty turning down a request.

Practice being truthful when making a request:

Example: I've been very stressed at work and at home. Honestly, I don't feel like myself lately. That's why I need the day off.

___

Practice being truthful when saying "No:

Example: I won't be in Friday. I want to help with the backlog, but I've been very stressed at work and at home. Honestly, I don't feel like myself lately. That's why I need the day off.

Chapter Highlights:

- **Dialectical Behaviour Therapy** is a great way to help people with PTSD.
- **Radical Acceptance** addresses avoidance, which is a primary symptom of PTSD.
- **Change** in DBT begins when you understand and put into practice its four primary skills. For this purpose, **Mindfulness**, **Distress Tolerance**, **Emotion Regulation** and **Interpersonal Effectiveness** worksheets are provided.
- **Invalidation**: why it's hurtful, damaging to your mental health, and what you can do about it.

Chapter 5: Continuing the Road to Coping and Healing

"Your present circumstances don't determine where you go. They merely determine where you start."
– Dr. Lauren Fogel Mersy

We covered many things in this book. The first thing I hope you take away from it is that you DO NOT have to suffer indefinitely from the trauma you experienced or witnessed. I promise you, life can be good!

I've shared many DBT exercises to help you with your journey, and the following are a few more tips I'd like to share. They have helped me so much in my healing process, and I hope they do the same for you.

1. **Volunteer (contradict helplessness by helping!).** While going through my mental health problems, I would often be overcome by a feeling of helplessness, as if there's nothing I can do or say to improve things. I found volunteering to be very therapeutic. It gave me a purpose. It made me think of others instead of spending hours wallowing in my own misery.

    Volunteering doesn't have to be a BIG gesture. For example, you can volunteer to rake the leaves for an elderly neighbor or cook a pot of soup for a homeless shelter. For more ideas, you can visit sites like Idealist.org or VolunteerMatch.org

2. **Embrace Nature.** I never considered myself to be the "outdoorsy" type. Self-isolating indoors was my thing. Well, we already know that that didn't work, so I did the exact opposite—I went outside. Before long, I was hooked on nature. Being in nature helped me calm down, slow down, and be more mindful. It helped de-clutter my chaotic thoughts.

If you live in the city, check local parks or visit community gardens nearby. You can also bring nature indoors. For example, add more plants inside your home, plant an herb garden on your balcony, etc.

3. **Get Moving.** Engaging in physical activities is underrated. The mind-body connection is real[115], and I've discovered that if I'm physically exhausted, my mind has no choice but to "de-activate." By the time I have the energy to think, I often realize that what I was so anxious about wasn't as bad as I initially thought they were.

   But don't over-exert and injure yourself. Start slow (but sure!) if you're currently leading a sedentary lifestyle or have not been active for a while. For example, if walking 10,000 steps a day is your goal, buy an inexpensive pedometer or use apps like Pacer or GoogleFit and work up to 3,000-5,000 steps per day. Once you've consistently reached that, add another 1,000 steps until you reach 10,000 steps.

   I aim to walk at least 6,000 steps daily, then I supplement that with resistance band training a few times a week and yoga on the days I don't weight train.

4. **Select and Protect Your Inner Circle.** In the space below, write down the people closest to you. Use more sheets if necessary. If you can only write down a few names, that's okay too.

   My Current Inner Circle:
   1) _____
   2) _____
   3) _____
   4) _____
   5) _____
   6) _____
   7) _____
   8) _____

9) _____
10) _____

Now, take a long and hard look at the list you made. Do you trust these people completely? (*For example, can you confide in them about your PTSD?*) Do they really support you? Do they have your back? Are they loyal to you?

Chances are, not all are. And since social psychologists believe that we are the average of the five individuals we spend the most time with, choose your inner circle wisely.

Part of any mental healing journey is identifying your inner circle because it's best to have support. Yes, the changes must be your choice, and you're the one who needs to do the work, but support from others is essential. They help ease the load and can be your shield against pain, disappointments, vulnerabilities, and others.

Once you find these people, uphold them. Earn your right in their inner circle too.

5. **Learn to Say "Goodbye."** After doing tip #4 above, you might realize that there are people around you who are not positive influences at this time (or at all). In this case, be brave and end that relationship. Remember that you need all the positive energy you can get right now.

   Yes, this is easier said than done. It can be tough to cut people from your life, especially if they are family, but "goodbye" doesn't necessarily mean forever. You can re-evaluate the relationship later on if you feel there have been improvements.

   Here's what my friend Denise**** had to say: *"My oldest brother doesn't believe I have PTSD. He thinks I'm a drama queen and sneers during family events when I discuss therapy. I got tired of defending myself. So one day, I wrote him an email. I said I love*

**** *Name changed for privacy.*

him and always will, but I will be disengaging for now. I want to get better, and maybe later, we can reconnect."

6. **Adopt a Pet.** Studies have shown that having a pet can help with mental health and well-being.[116,117] If your lifestyle situation permits it, consider adopting one. Dogs are known to be great pet choices because they read people well, are sympathetic, and make you go outside!

7. **Keep an Open Mind.** Despite today's awareness concerning mental health problems, many types of therapies people find dubious. My opinion is this: don't discount it until you've tried it. You never know what will work for you. Some alternative therapies are yoga, aromatherapy, music therapy, art therapy, journaling, acupuncture, etc. In addition to DBT, I do yoga each morning.

8. **Self-Monitor.** The DBT exercises in this book are roads to self-discovery. In addition, keep a journal where you can record anything and everything concerning your PTSD. For example, suppose you find yourself always nervous Friday nights. In that case, you can explore that further and take the necessary steps to ensure you don't feel that way (e.g., ensure you're not alone Friday nights, buy extra door locks, etc.).

9. **Find a Support Group.** Family and friends don't have to be your only source of support. Go online and offline and find PTSD support groups. Sometimes, the best people to help are those who know exactly what you're going through. Online, you can look for PTSD support groups on [Facebook](#) or [reddit](#). Offline, you can consult with a doctor or psychotherapist and ask for PTSD support groups you can attend near you.

10. **Be kind and patient with yourself.** Everyone reacts to trauma in their own way, so it's important to go at your own pace. Years ago, I came across this advice: talk to yourself like you would to a dear friend, and I've been practicing it since.

11. **Seek Professional Help If You Need It.** Never shy away from professional help. If you feel like you're not progressing in your journey, then it's time to talk to a

professional. If you find face-to-face therapy to be unavailable in your area or too costly for you, then consider online individual or group sessions like the ones provided by BetterHealth or ReGain as they can be more affordable.

Please go ahead and add your own ideas.
_____
_____
_____
_____
_____
_____
_____
_____
_____
_____
_____

Chapter 6: Conclusion

Living with PTSD can be overwhelming. That's why I'm incredibly thankful to you for choosing this book to help you live a less stressful life and be less influenced by the trauma you've gone through.

Mental healing recovery is never a linear process. Life happens. We might hit a rough patch, and our mental health takes a step back—but that's okay. Remember, you are already a survivor! The next seconds, minutes, hours, and days are new, and it's up to you to determine how great they should be.

Here's a quick recap of what we covered in this book:

- Post-Traumatic Stress Disorder (PTSD): what it is, causes and symptoms, and currently known treatments.
- Living with PTSD: Understand how trauma affects the brain and how PTSD negatively affects your daily life.
- Dialectic Behavior Therapy (DBT) and its main fundamentals (Acceptance and Change) and its core skills (Mindfulness, Distress Tolerance, Emotion Regulation, and Interpersonal Effectiveness).
- DBT for PTSD: An in-depth presentation of DBT exercises you can use for PTSD.
- Additional self-care tips for living a less stressed life due to trauma.

Traumatic experiences change us; for some of us, those changes mean living unhappy lives—sometimes for years. But I want you to know that THERE IS HOPE.

Peace, happiness, safety, security, and other words you might not associate with your life now are within reach. You just need to decide now that you're willing to do the work to achieve them.

Appendix A – Trauma Resiliency[§§§§]

Check the boxes next to the ones that you think describe you best.

- ☐ I like to socialize, and I'm comfortable spending a lot of time with others.
- ☐ I like trying new things.
- ☐ I get along with everyone. (I'm not "difficult.")
- ☐ I have confidence in myself.
- ☐ I try to understand why things happen to me.
- ☐ I try to understand and break down bad situations into parts I can handle.
- ☐ I try to figure out how to deal with problems in my life.
- ☐ I'm an optimist, and I see more good than bad in everything and everyone.
- ☐ I like a good challenge, and when the time comes, I'm up to it.
- ☐ I can adjust to difficult situations easily.
- ☐ I have a good group of friends and people I can turn to for help.
- ☐ After a setback, I can quickly bounce back and pick up where I left off.
- ☐ I can laugh at myself.
- ☐ I appreciate myself.
- ☐ I feel like there is hope.
- ☐ I like to try new things and see things from different angles.
- ☐ I can handle a lot of things at the same time.
- ☐ I care about how other people feel.
- ☐ I'm not easily discouraged.
- ☐ I do my best to plan and structure my own life.

[§§§§] *Adapted from* van der Meer, C. A., te Brake, H., van der Aa, N., Dashtgard, P., Bakker, A., & Olff, M. (2018). Assessing psychological resilience: Development and psychometric properties of the English and Dutch version of the Resilience Evaluation Scale (RES). *Frontiers in Psychiatry, 9*. https://doi.org/10.3389/fpsyt.2018.00169

Question: What do you notice about yourself when you read these statements? Do you feel good? Do you get agitated? Do you reflect?
Answer:
_____
_____

Question: As you went through the list, did you notice any pattern about the items checked and not checked?
Answer:
_____
_____

The more you check, the more likely you are to do something about the trauma you experienced or witnessed and get through it.

Please note that the above scale just provides an indication of your resilience to trauma. It should not be taken as a replacement for a healthcare professional's official evaluation.

Appendix B – PTSD Self-Evaluation

Following is a list of difficulties adapted from the DSM-5 symptom criteria for PTSD[*****] that some people experience after a traumatic event.

Please read each one carefully. Are you experiencing or doing any of these? If yes, please rate how much it has bothered you <u>in the last month</u>.

1) Do you keep having disturbing, unwanted thoughts about the stressful event?

   ☐ Never   ☐ Rarely   ☐ Somewhat   ☐ Often   ☐ Very Often

2) Do you keep having disturbing, unwanted dreams about the stressful event?

   ☐ Never   ☐ Rarely   ☐ Somewhat   ☐ Often   ☐ Very Often

3) Do you have moments when you feel or behave as if the stressful event were repeatedly happening (*re-living* or *re-experiencing*)?

   ☐ Never   ☐ Rarely   ☐ Somewhat   ☐ Often   ☐ Very Often

4) Do you get very upset when something reminds you of your trauma?

   ☐ Never   ☐ Rarely   ☐ Somewhat   ☐ Often   ☐ Very Often

5) Are you experiencing severe bodily reactions (such as a racing heart, difficulty breathing, or sweating) when something brings up the stressful memory?

   ☐ Never   ☐ Rarely   ☐ Somewhat   ☐ Often   ☐ Very Often

[*****] *Adapted from* Weather, F. W., Litz, B. T., Keane, T. M., Palmieri, P. A., Marx, B. P., & Schnurr, P. P. (2013). The PTSD Checklist for DSM-5 (PCL-5). Retrieved November 2, 2022. Scale available from the National Center for PTSD at www.ptsd.va.gov.

6) Are you trying to avoid memories, thoughts, or emotions related to the trauma you experienced?

☐ Never ☐ Rarely ☐ Somewhat ☐ Often ☐ Very Often

7) Do you try hard to avoid people, places, conversations, activities, or situations that remind you of the traumatic event?

☐ Never ☐ Rarely ☐ Somewhat ☐ Often ☐ Very Often

8) Do you have problems recollecting vital parts of the traumatic experience?

☐ Never ☐ Rarely ☐ Somewhat ☐ Often ☐ Very Often

9) Do you look negatively at yourself, others, or the world? For example, do you think things like, *"I am terrible," "I'm not loveable," "I trust no one,"* or *"There's no hope in this world"*?

☐ Never ☐ Rarely ☐ Somewhat ☐ Often ☐ Very Often

10) Do you blame yourself or others for the trauma you experienced?

☐ Never ☐ Rarely ☐ Somewhat ☐ Often ☐ Very Often

11) Do you often suffer from negative emotions such as anxiety, disgust, anger, remorse, or shame?

☐ Never ☐ Rarely ☐ Somewhat ☐ Often ☐ Very Often

12) Have you lost interest in activities you formerly found enjoyable?

☐ Never ☐ Rarely ☐ Somewhat ☐ Often ☐ Very Often

13) Do you feel distant or disconnected from others?

☐ Never   ☐ Rarely   ☐ Somewhat   ☐ Often   ☐ Very Often

14) Do you find it challenging to feel positive emotions such as *happiness* or *love* for others?

☐ Never   ☐ Rarely   ☐ Somewhat   ☐ Often   ☐ Very Often

15) Do you exhibit irritability, impulsivity, or violent behavior?

☐ Never   ☐ Rarely   ☐ Somewhat   ☐ Often   ☐ Very Often

16) Do you engage in excessive risk-taking or dangerous behavior?

☐ Never   ☐ Rarely   ☐ Somewhat   ☐ Often   ☐ Very Often

17) Do you feel "on edge" or "super alert"?

☐ Never   ☐ Rarely   ☐ Somewhat   ☐ Often   ☐ Very Often

18) Are you easily startled or feel "jumpy"?

☐ Never   ☐ Rarely   ☐ Somewhat   ☐ Often   ☐ Very Often

19) Do you have difficulty concentrating or focusing?

☐ Never   ☐ Rarely   ☐ Somewhat   ☐ Often   ☐ Very Often

20) Do you find it difficult to fall or remain asleep?

☐ Never   ☐ Rarely   ☐ Somewhat   ☐ Often   ☐ Very Often

Scoring:

0 = Not at all | **1** = A little bit | **2** = Moderately | **3** = Quite a bit | **4** = Extremely

Using the above scale, please tally up your score.

Your Score: _____

Interpretation:

A score of 31–33 or higher suggests you might have PTSD and need treatment. A score between 31 and 33 *indicates* you don't meet the criteria for PTSD or are at the subthreshold of PTSD symptoms.

Important:

This 20-item **questionnaire does not replace a doctor or licensed mental health provider diagnosis.** However, the reality is that people don't get help because they're afraid their problems aren't real or "bad enough" to warrant professional help. After your self-assessment, if you believe you might have PTSD, please don't hesitate to talk about it with someone, a doctor, or a licensed mental health professional.

Appendix C – Establishing a Sleep Routine

Quality sleep can be elusive. Concerns, worries, and responsibilities often interfere with much-needed respite. Science shows, though, that a consistent sleep routine is critical for good physical, mental, and emotional well-being.[118] So here are some tips for you to do just that.

But before you establish a sleep routine, check your bedroom. Is it conducive to sleep? Is it a place that promotes relaxation and calmness? If not, make some changes. For example:

- Change bedroom curtains and bedsheets to a calming, non-stimulating color such as blue, green, or light yellow. (If necessary, repaint your room too.)
- Go for simple patterns or simple block colors. Bold designs and prints stimulate the mind, keeping you awake.
- Ensure that your pillows and mattress are comfortable. If not, now's the time to invest in new ones.
- De-clutter your bedroom. A messy bedroom can be distracting.
- Remove all electronic devices. These emit blue light, negatively affecting melatonin production (the "sleep hormone").[119]
- Keep the temperature cool. The best temperature for Rapid Eye Movement (REM) sleep, which is when you dream, learn, remember, deal with your emotions, and develop a healthy brain, is between 60 and 67°F. If your room is too hot or too cold, you'll keep waking up, preventing you from reaching this sleep stage.

Now that your bedroom is conducive to sleep, let's establish that sleep routine!

Top 3 Tips to Set a Sleep Routine

A sleep routine is a set of things you do every night in the same order, 30 to 60 minutes before bedtime. The following is what works best for me but feel free to create your own.

1. Based on your lifestyle, **set a specific bedtime** that you can adhere to most days of the week. *Example: 11:00 PM*

   The best time for me to go to bed is: _____

2. What should you be doing **60 minutes before bedtime**? This might be the best time to start wrapping up your day. *Example: plan and prep breakfast for tomorrow, put things in the dishwasher, drink a calming tea, etc.*

   My 60-minute before-bedtime routine:

   # 1. _____
   # 2. _____
   # 3. _____
   # 4. _____
   # 5. _____
   # 6. _____
   # 7. _____
   # 8. _____
   # 9. _____
   # 10. _____

3. What should you be doing **30 minutes before bedtime**? For me, this is the stage when I really plan for sleep. *Example: brush teeth and do other bathroom rituals, put on sleeping pajamas, put a glass of water by the bedside, do 10-minute mindfulness meditation or stretching routine, spray pillows with lavender scent, turn off all the lights, and go to bed.*

My 30-minute before-bedtime routine:

1. _____
2. _____
3. _____
4. _____
5. _____
6. _____
7. _____
8. _____
9. _____
10. _____

Trauma-Related Worksheet: Better Sleep Using Your 5 Senses

In her book *Post-Traumatic Stress Disorder: A Clinician's Guide*, psychologist Matsakis states that *"sleeping problems are perhaps the most persistent of PTSD symptoms."*[120]

Suppose you were traumatized while you were sleeping or in a bedroom. In that case, in addition to the above tips, you must figure out what about that bedroom or about sleeping is contributing to your sleeping problems today.

In this activity, you will use your five senses to help you find possible triggers in your bedroom or about sleeping. You don't have to be sure whether or not something is a trigger. Find the best way to sleep by observing and trying different things.

👁 Use your sense of SIGHT. Is there anything you see in your bedroom triggering your trauma? *Example 1: If you sleep now in a room that's the same color as the room you experienced trauma in, you must change your current room's color. Change it even if that color is known to be "calming."*

Example 2: Look at the items in your bedroom. Is there anything at all that you think is triggering you? If so, remove it or make changes.

Here's what Frank[†††††], a reader, had to say: "I was 6 years old when a fire broke out in the middle of the night and engulfed our whole house. Mom and I lost my dad and baby brother that night. I've had sleeping problems since. During therapy as an adult, I discovered that one of my triggers was the alarm clock on my bedside table. When my dad woke me up and told me to run out of the house, I looked at the time on my alarm clock before I ran.

I have since then removed any clocks on my bedside table and anything else that would remind me of my childhood room."

[†††††] *Name changed for privacy.*

Your turn:

_____
_____
_____
_____

Use your sense of HEARING. Are there sounds in your bedroom or around bedtime that may be triggering your trauma? *Example: If you're a war veteran and live in the city center, the loud sounds at night may trigger you. In this case, wearing earplugs or playing soothing music until you fall asleep might be ideal.*

Your turn:

_____
_____
_____
_____

Use your sense of SMELL. Are there scents in your bedroom that may be causing your sleep problems? *Example: Many people use lavender-scented soaps for bedsheets or spray a lavender mist in the bedroom since lavender enhances good, quality sleep.[121] However, if this was the scent in your bedroom when your trauma occurred, you should experiment with changing the scent or trying to sleep without any scent.*

Your turn:

_____
_____
_____
_____

 **Use your sense of TOUCH. Is there anything touching you while you sleep that may trigger trauma?** *Example: If silk sheets play a role in your trauma, switch to another sheet fabric.*

Your turn:

_____
_____
_____
_____

Use your sense of TASTE. You may not be eating or drinking while you sleep, but what you consume or taste before bedtime can still affect you. *Example: What's the flavor of your toothpaste or mouthwash? A friend of mine related childhood sexual abuse to the minty scent and taste of her attacker. Part of her recovery was to eliminate all minty or citrusy aromas in her bedroom. She then switched her toothpaste and mouthwash to unflavored ones.*

Your turn:

_____
_____
_____
_____

Review Request

If you enjoyed this book or found it useful...

I'd like to ask you for a quick favor:

Please share your thoughts and **leave a quick REVIEW**. Your feedback matters and helps me make improvements to provide the best books possible.

Reviews are so helpful to both readers and authors, so any help would be greatly appreciated! You can leave a review here:

https://tinyurl.com/complete-dbt-review

Or by scanning the QR code below:

Also, please join my ARC team to get early access to my releases.

https://barretthuang.com/arc-team/

THANK YOU!

Further Reading

Be sure to check out my other bestselling DBT books in the Mental Health Therapy series. Here are some of the titles you can find:

- DBT Workbook for Adults
- DBT Workbook for Kids
- DBT Workbook for Teens
- The DBT Anger Management Workbook
- DBT Workbook for PTSD
- DBT Workbook for BPD
- DBT Workbook for Depression

You can get them here:

https://tinyurl.com/mental-health-therapy

DBT Workbook For Emotional Eating

Stop Compulsive Overeating & Quit Your Food Addiction with Proven Dialectical Behavior Therapy Skills for Men & Women |
Stop Binge Eating & Embrace a Healthy Diet

By Barrett Huang

https://barretthuang.com/

FREE Guide: Mastering DBT Essentials

FREE DOWNLOAD ALERT!

Master Dialectical Behavior Therapy Skills in 5 Simple Steps with my Free DBT Quick Guide. Access the 'Mastering DBT Essentials' quick guide at:

https://barretthuang.com/dbt-quick-guide/

Or scan the code below:

Contents

FREE Guide: Mastering DBT Essentials 306
Introduction 311
    Who Should Read This Book 315
    Goals of This Book 315
    Be Patient and Kind to Yourself 315
Chapter 1: Understanding Emotional Eating 316
    What is Emotional Eating? 316
    Emotional Eating vs. Stress Eating vs. Binge Eating 317
    Emotional Hunger vs. Physical Hunger 318
    It's NOT About Food 319
    It's NOT All About Willpower 321
    Emotional Eating: Causes and Triggers 322
    Impact of Emotional Eating on Your Mental and Physical Health 324
        Mental Health 324
        Physical Health 325
Chapter 2: Dialectical Behavior Therapy 101 328
    What is DBT? 328
    How DBT Can Be Used to Treat Emotional Eating 328
    DBT Primary Concepts: Acceptance and Change 329
        Radical Acceptance 329
        Worksheet: Radical Acceptance 331
        Desire to Change 332
        Worksheet: Desire to Change 333
        Worksheet: Radical Acceptance + Desire to Change 334
    DBT Primary Skills: Mindfulness, Distress Tolerance, Emotion Regulation, Interpersonal Effectiveness 335
Chapter 3: Mindfulness Skills for Emotional Eating 337
    Introduction to Mindfulness 337
        Worksheet: Belly Breathing 338

Worksheet: Take 5 339

Worksheet: 4-7-8 Breathing 340

Mindful Eating 341

Principles of Mindful Eating 341

Benefits of Mindful Eating 343

Worksheet: Mindful Eating 345

Worksheet: TASTE 348

Worksheet: Wise Mind 349

Chapter 4: Distress Tolerance Skills for Emotional Eating 352

Introduction to Distress Tolerance 352

Stress and Emotional Eating 352

Stress vs. Distress 352

Importance of Distress Tolerance Skills for Emotional Eating 353

Worksheet: Self-Soothe Using Your Five Senses 355

Worksheet: The Grounding Grid 357

Worksheet: STOP 359

Worksheet: TIPP 362

Chapter 5: Emotion-Regulating Skills for Emotional Eating 364

Introduction to Emotion Regulation 364

Practicing Self-Compassion, Self-Forgiveness, and Self-Validation 365

Worksheet: Self-Compassion 367

Worksheet: Self-Forgiveness 369

Worksheet: Self-Validation 371

Identifying the Emotions That Trigger Your Emotional Eating 373

Worksheet: Identifying Your Emotional Triggers 374

Worksheet: The Happiness Habit 378

Worksheet: Opposite Action 381

Worksheet: PLEASE 386

Chapter 6: Interpersonal Effectiveness Skills for Emotional Eating 388

Introduction to Interpersonal Effectiveness 388

Importance of Healthy Relationships in Recovering from Emotional Eating 389

Worksheet: Communicating Boundaries 391

- Worksheet: DEARMAN 394
- Worksheet: GIVE 397
- Worksheet: FAST 399

Chapter 7: Developing Healthy Habits 402
- Top 10 Healthy Food and Eating Habits 402
- Quick Guide to Meal Planning and Prepping 405
  - What is Meal Planning? 406
  - What is Meal Prepping? 407
- Incorporate Physical Activity into Your Routine 408
- Manage Daily Stress through Healthy Coping Mechanisms 410

Chapter 8: Building a Support System 413
- Cultivate a Supportive Inner Voice (Self) 413
  - Self-Sabotage – What You May Be THINKING 413
  - Self-Sabotage – What You May Be DOING 414
- Build Your Support Circle (Others) 415

Chapter 9: Dealing with Setbacks and Relapses 418
- How to Prevent Setbacks 418
- How to Recover from a Setback 421

Chapter 10: Maintaining Long-Term Success 424
- Top 10 Strategies for Maintaining Healthy Eating Habits 424
- Celebrate Progress and Achievements with Non-Food Related Rewards 426
- Reflection and Gratitude Practice 428
  - Worksheet: Reflection and Gratitude 429

Conclusion 432

Appendix 434
- Emotional Eating Self-Assessment Quiz 434
- The Clean Your Plate Syndrome 438
  - Top 10 Tips to Stop Cleaning Your Plate 438
- How to Establish a Sleep Routine 440
- How to Support an Emotional Eater 442

Review Request 445

Further Reading 446

About the Author 447
Index 448

Introduction

*"Emotional eating is like trying to put out a fire with gasoline.
It only makes things worse." - Unknown*

The bell rings, signifying the end of the school day, and everyone noisily leaves the room. I sense our teacher, *Mr. M*, looking at me, but I avoid eye contact. I walk out of school to a nearby internet café. I buy a bag of chips and a big soda and settle into my favorite corner, where I would stay alone for a few hours. It is getting dark, so I get up and walk home.

As I reach home, I am as quiet as possible because I do not want my family to know I am back. I go straight to my room, close the door and go online to play games (yes, again) or listen to music to pass the time. I reach for my stash of junk food, usually potato chips, and eat until the bag is empty. Often, I am surprised when it IS empty because I do not recall eating so much.

At one point, I hear my dad calling me for dinner. I go down, but since I stuffed myself already, I barely eat. Dinner is unpleasant because my parents are in the middle of a divorce. My sister and I are trying to avoid anything that might trigger my mom or dad to fight. Finally, dinner is over, and I go up to my room.

I listen to music, watch TV, play online, or do whatever homework I need to do. At this point, I would now switch to eating the Chinese pastries and buns my father had brought home from the bakery where he works. I have sleep problems, so I stay up all night and eat. Throughout this time, junk food and pastries are beside me... my constant companion on another day of loneliness.

This is how I spent the majority of my adolescent years. I often felt like I was in a never-ending cycle of despair, boredom, and loneliness. I truly did not have much hope for the future and did not even think about it. Every day, my only goal was to make it through.

Back then, I did not think I was emotionally eating. I was not focused on *how* I was coping. My thoughts were preoccupied with *what* I was coping with.

My parents emigrated from China to Canada in the 1980s to provide a better future for their children to come. (My sister and I were born in Toronto.) Unfortunately, they could not escape their personal mental issues.

My father was a hoarder with undiagnosed Obsessive-Compulsive Disorder (OCD). My mother was constantly worried about something and always expected some disaster to strike at any moment. She had undiagnosed General Anxiety Disorder (GAD). With both parents emotionally absent, I was understandably often anxious and confused. There was just nothing "stable" in my world. This, of course, greatly impacted my everyday behavior and approach to life.

It also did not help that my parents were going through a messy divorce when I was around 11 years old. I was not talking to my mom and sister since I was on my dad's side, and my sister was not talking to our dad and me because she was on our mom's side. My family was torn apart just at the time my sister and I needed a stable and loving environment to help us through our adolescent years.

Unsurprisingly, by the time I was in my teens, I already had signs of OCD and GAD (later, as an adult, I would be officially diagnosed with these mental health disorders by a professional).

My mental health problems wreaked havoc on my social skills. So much so that when I was in high school, I would not have a single friend in a school with nearly 5,000 students. This loneliness made me self-isolate and turn to food to cope. I did not know it then, but I used food to self-medicate.

They say it is better to be mad (show anger) than sad (admit pain). I guess I was doing this because I would rather hide and eat than be seen not having any friends. That would just be too humiliating and painful.

Did things get better for me? Fortunately, they did—for a while.

When I graduated from high school, I went to college and traveled to Asian countries. I spent time in China, South Korea, Hong Kong, Thailand, and the Philippines. I spent three years teaching English as a Second Language (ESL) in South Korea. To this day, I consider it one of the best decisions I have ever made. Living on my own made me independent, and teaching gave me a sense of fulfillment I had never had before.

People say that traveling opens your mind, and I agree. Traveling to different parts of the world and seeing how other people dealt with their challenges (I visited some underprivileged areas) helped me see things from more than just my point of view.

My years away from home also opened my mind to the possibility of "better," something I never thought was possible for me before. Unfortunately, I resorted to my old ways when I returned home to my family.

I did not know what to do with my life when I returned from Asia. So, I stayed with my sister and hibernated on her couch for a year. And guess who my constant companion was during this time? Food, of course.

I ate because I was bored.
I ate because I was lonely.
I ate because I could not deal with all the "family drama" I had left behind for nearly four years.
I ate because my OCD, GAD, and depression were getting worse.
I ate because I was uncertain about the next chapter of my life.
I ate and ate... but nothing became better.

Did things change for me? Fortunately, they did—this time for good.

I always had poor eyesight, and the years spent playing online and watching TV caught up with me. My vision got so bad that I got myself off that couch and got an eye exam, which revealed I had a retina tear. Fortunately, it got repaired, but I got an increase in eye floaters, which affected my vision and quality of life. I became depressed and self-isolated again, with nothing but food as my "friend."

After some time, I started to adapt. I realized that I could do nothing about my eye floaters and that I should start being more mindful about what I eat and put in my body since food affects one's health. Also, I was already 30 at this stage. I was not in my teens or twenties anymore and did not want to spend the rest of my life on my sister's couch. So, I decided to get better.

I contacted a mental health professional who prescribed anti-anxiety medication for my GAD, which jumpstarted my healing process. In addition, I went through psychotherapy, specifically Cognitive Behavior Therapy (CBT). I also dived into many self-help books to learn more about happiness, philosophy, and how to improve myself.

After a while, I felt well enough to ask my doctor to reduce my dosage. (For the record, I continue to take anti-anxiety medication, which helps me manage my GAD.) I also realized that I needed something other than CBT, so I began to look into different psychotherapy methods. I discovered Dialectical Behavior Therapy (DBT), which enables me to finally break free from my unhealthy coping strategies and live the life I never even dared to dream of before.

I still experience bouts of OCD, GAD, and depression occasionally, but these disorders no longer cripple me. **I no longer use food to feel better, either.** I have found the tools to help me deal with my emotions more positively. I earnestly hope you will accomplish the same with this book.

Who Should Read This Book

This book is for anyone who wants to be free from emotional eating. Whether you use food for comfort or reward, this book aims to give you better, healthier ways to cope with life. This book is also for you if you find that your emotional eating has led to food addiction, weight problems, eating disorders, mental or health issues, or if you want to prevent these adverse effects. Finally, this book is for you if you want to control your emotions instead of having them control you.

Goals of This Book

The purpose of this book is to help you get a better understanding of emotional eating and to give you real-life tools to help you better cope with unpleasant emotions.

Emotional eating is very complex, so I sincerely hope this book gives you clarity. Awareness and understanding are critical when dealing with any unhealthy coping mechanism. However, understanding emotional eating is only half the battle; the other half is learning how to cope. This is when the book's second section comes in.

Dialectical Behavior Therapy (DBT) taught me NOT to use food to cope with negative emotions. I will go through DBT in-depth and provide plenty of exercises to help you properly use these approaches.

Be Patient and Kind to Yourself

Wherever you are right now, it did not happen overnight. So have patience and understanding with yourself. Remember that, for the most part, emotional eating is a learned behavior, and it can be difficult to break the cycle. So refrain from criticizing and judging yourself for your struggles. And whenever setbacks happen, as they always do, keep moving forward. Remember, each positive step is one taken in the right direction.

Chapter 1: Understanding Emotional Eating

"Eating your emotions won't make them go away."
—Karen Salmansohn

What is Emotional Eating?

Emotional eating is turning to food in response to emotions instead of eating to satisfy physical hunger or nutritional demands.

When you are experiencing unpleasant feelings, this is usually accompanied by feelings of emptiness. In this instance, you may use food to temporarily fill that emptiness, so food becomes a source of comfort.

Food can also be used in response to positive emotions. In fact, using food as a reward is a common practice in our society. Many of us use food as a way to celebrate milestones or as a way to reward ourselves for accomplishing a task. However, when you do this, it reinforces the idea that food is more than just nourishment for your body. Food is linked to moments of happiness.

Furthermore, using food as a reward can lead to a cycle of restriction and bingeing. For example, you may restrict your food intake during the week, only to indulge in high-calorie foods as a reward on the weekend. This cycle can lead to feelings of guilt and shame, which can further perpetuate the emotional eating cycle.

So, emotional eating is a way for us to deal with emotions rather than fill a hungry stomach.

Emotional eating is different from physical hunger in several ways. When you eat emotionally, you often crave specific foods high in sugar, fat, or salt rather than healthy and nutritious foods your body needs. Emotional eating can also make you eat quickly without paying attention to your body's natural signals of fullness and hunger. You may eat until you feel uncomfortably full, then experience guilt, shame, or regret.

Technically, emotional eating is not classified as an eating disorder in the Diagnostic and Statistical Manual of Mental Disorders (DSM-5).[122] However, emotional eating can be a symptom of an eating disorder. It is important to note that emotional eating is a behavior, not a diagnosis, and should be addressed in the context of your overall mental health and well-being.

Emotional Eating vs. Stress Eating vs. Binge Eating

Emotional eating, stress eating, and binge eating are often interchanged phrases. Although there can be some overlap between them, there are distinct differences too.

Emotional eating is the practice of eating in response to an emotional state. Emotional eaters use food to soothe negative emotions or as a reward for positive emotions and often eat more than they need to feel full or satisfied.

Stress eating, or stress-induced eating, is emotional eating **specifically triggered by stress**. When under stress, people often turn to food for comfort, which can lead to overeating and weight gain over time. However, not all emotional eating is related to stress, and not all stress eating is related to negative emotions.

Binge eating disorder (BED) is defined by recurrent eating sprees, which entails quickly eating enormous amounts of food while feeling out of control. Binge-eating episodes are often accompanied by guilt, shame, and distress. Unlike emotional eating, which can occur sporadically, binge eating is a consistent pattern of behavior that can interfere with daily life.

Emotional Hunger vs. Physical Hunger

You may confuse emotional hunger with physical hunger because the sensations in the body can be very similar. Both physical and emotional hunger can cause a grumbling stomach, headaches, and feelings of weakness or lightheadedness.

Additionally, you may have been taught to use food as a coping mechanism for uncomfortable emotions, leading you to *automatically* rely on food when feeling stressed, anxious, or upset. This, in turn, can make it difficult for you to distinguish between true physical hunger and the desire to eat as a way of soothing emotional discomfort.

Finally, if you are not in touch with your emotions or struggle with identifying and expressing your feelings, you may find it hard to recognize the difference between emotional and physical hunger.

Following are more telltale signs that what you are feeling is emotional hunger, not physical hunger:

- **Unexpected.** Emotional hunger hits you all at once, making you feel rushed and overwhelmed. On the other hand, physical hunger comes on more slowly. Unless you haven't eaten in a long time, the desire to eat does not feel as strong or needs to be satisfied immediately.

- **Cravings.** When you're emotionally hungry, you want certain "comfort foods." You most likely want junk food or sweet snacks that can give you an immediate rush. Healthy foods, like an apple or carrot sticks, simply will not suffice.

- **Mindless**. Emotional hunger often makes people eat without thinking. Before you know it, you have eaten a whole bag of chips or several slices of cake without really paying attention or fully enjoying it. Eating to satisfy physical hunger makes you usually more aware of what you put in your mouth.

- **Unsatisfied**. Emotional hunger is never really satisfied. You eat for temporary relief, but the "hunger" does not disappear, so you want more and more. As a result, you often eat until you are too full to move. On the other hand, physical hunger doesn't need to be filled. When your stomach is full, you feel good about yourself.

- **Not related to your stomach.** Emotional hunger is not felt in your stomach. That is, you usually do not experience rumbling or even pain in your stomach. Instead, you strongly desire to eat that will not go away. Your attention is riveted on how certain foods feel, taste, and smell.

- **Leads to sorrow, guilt, or shame.** After giving in to your emotional hunger, you feel bad after eating. Deep down, you know you are not eating because you need nutrients; you are eating to fill an emotional void.

It's NOT About Food

Emotional eating is not about food but about eating in response to feelings. In fact, when you emotionally eat, you may not even be (physically) hungry at all! The problem is that you are trying to apply a food solution to an emotional problem.

Although you may be eating to cope with certain emotions, it is important to note that emotions and food influence each other. That is, emotions can influence your food choices, and food can, in turn, influence your emotions.

For example, you may turn to junk food when dealing with negative emotions because it provides temporary comfort or pleasure. The high fat and sugar content in junk food triggers the release of feel-good chemicals in your brain, such as dopamine, which can make you feel better in the short term. Additionally, you may associate certain junk foods with positive memories or emotions from your past, such as eating ice cream when you pleased your parents as a child. So, when you experience negative emotions, you may turn to these familiar foods to self-soothe and escape from your current distress.

Unfortunately, consuming unhealthy foods to feel better in the short term exacerbates negative emotions in the long term.

Junk foods and processed foods have been shown to harm our emotions and mood.[123] These foods are often high in refined carbohydrates, sugar, and unhealthy fats, which can lead to a rapid spike and subsequent drop in blood sugar levels. This can cause feelings of fatigue, irritability, and mood swings. Additionally, regularly consuming these foods can lead to chronic inflammation in the body, which has been linked to an increased risk of depression and anxiety.[124]

Additionally, junk foods and processed foods are often high in additives and preservatives that can negatively affect your brain chemistry. For example, some artificial sweeteners have been linked to changes in brain activity that can lead to increased hunger and overeating.[125] Further, some food additives and preservatives have been shown to disrupt the balance of neurotransmitters in the brain, leading to mood disturbances and other emotional imbalances.

So, by eating to soothe your feelings, you are, in turn, making those emotions worse. You are now caught in a harmful emotional eating cycle.

The Emotional Eating Cycle

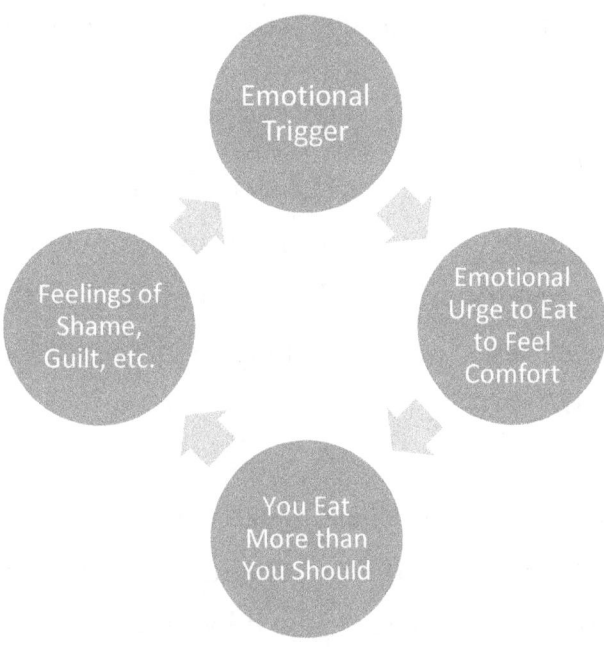

It's NOT All About Willpower

In my own healing journey, one of the things that truly put me down was when people said that I should "*get over it,*" "*move on,*" or "*just commit.*" I felt bad after each unsupportive comment. This would, of course, send me into another emotional eating frenzy. After which, I would spend every free thought beating myself up for my food choices and how I looked and felt.

Many people looked at me and thought I was weak and lacked willpower. Deep inside, I did not believe this. For one, I knew my co-morbid mental health issues hampered me. Second, I did well in school and was determined to finish high school with the best grades possible so I could go to a good college. So, I thought to myself, "*If I have that determination and am willing to do what it takes to achieve it, I do have willpower!*"

So, why did I not have the same willpower regarding food? It's because **emotional eating is more than just willpower**.

As kids, most of us are taught to use food to make ourselves feel better. So, as adults, we eat when we are sad and want to feel better, not because we are hungry. So, emotional eating is a very strong learned behavior.[126]

Additionally, these "reward foods" or "pleasure foods" we were given as children were usually high in sugar and fat (e.g., candy, ice cream, cake, donuts, etc.). According to research, eating high-fat, high-calorie, and high-sugar foods changes the brain's reward centers.[127,128] We have trained our brains to react more positively when we eat the "bad stuff" than the "good stuff."

Research has also shown that emotional eating is a behavior that may become more linked to the trigger than the relief itself.[129] For example, if you reach for a bag of Doritos each time you are stressed, you are most likely to eat it because that is what your brain has been conditioned to do. That is, reaching for chips and eating them is an automatic habit linked to stress, not to any relief that may result from eating them.

The above situations have nothing to do with willpower. So, willpower alone is insufficient to overcome the underlying emotional triggers and habits that lead to emotional eating. What you need to do is to *replace* this coping mechanism. You need to learn new ways to deal with your emotions.

In Chapter 2: Dialectical Behavior Therapy 101, you will learn all these new ways. And here is the best part: as you discover healthier ways to deal with unpleasant emotions, your "willpower" will naturally grow. But first, let us learn what causes emotional eating.

Emotional Eating: Causes and Triggers

Emotional eating is a complex behavior that various factors can cause. Still, understanding its possible causes is important in developing effective strategies to manage your emotional eating and develop a healthy relationship with food.

Emotional eating can have various underlying causes, including the following:

1) **Stress**. When stressed, the body releases the hormone *cortisol*, which increases appetite and cravings for high-calorie foods. Additionally, stress can trigger negative emotions, leading to emotional eating to cope with these feelings.[130,131,132]

2) **Trauma**. Individuals who have experienced trauma, such as physical, emotional, or sexual abuse, may turn to food to cope with their emotional pain.[133,134] Additionally, trauma can alter the brain's reward system, making individuals more likely to seek high-calorie foods to regulate emotions.

3) **Low self-esteem**. Individuals with low self-esteem may use food to cope with negative emotions or seek comfort and pleasure. Although food may temporarily relieve negative feelings, it can also reinforce a negative self-image. Furthermore, chronic emotional eating can lead to weight gain, further damaging self-esteem and perpetuating the cycle of emotional eating.[135,136,137]

4) **Depression and anxiety**. Individuals with depression or anxiety may use food as a coping mechanism to deal with negative emotions, stress or overwhelm, or seek comfort and pleasure. Emotional eating can temporarily relieve these negative feelings. Still, it can reinforce guilt or shame and lead to other negative emotions.[138,139,140]

5) **Boredom**. People may eat when bored to distract themselves from their boredom or to add excitement to their day. Eating can also serve as a way to pass the time or fill a void.[141,142]

6) **Social and cultural factors**. Social norms, family customs, peer pressure, and cultural beliefs can all influence your relationship with food and eating habits.[143,144] For example, social gatherings that involve food may encourage overeating or consuming unhealthy foods. Cultural beliefs that promote the "clean your plate" mentality can also contribute to emotional eating.[145] (See also The Clean Your Plate Syndrome, page 438.)

7) **Dieting history**. When you follow a strict diet plan to lose weight, you may become obsessed with food, leading to feelings of deprivation and intense cravings. This can result in binge eating episodes, becoming a habit and a coping mechanism for dealing with negative emotions. Dieting can also disrupt the body's hunger and fullness cues, making distinguishing between emotional and physical hunger harder.[146,147]

8) **Genetics**. Some evidence suggests that genetics may play a role in emotional eating. Studies have shown that certain genes can affect a person's appetite, cravings, and response to stress and emotions.[148,149]

Impact of Emotional Eating on Your Mental and Physical Health

Mental Health

Emotional eating can greatly affect your mental health. When you use food to cope with your emotions, it can lead to feelings of guilt, shame, and regret. It can also lead to a disconnection from your emotions. You may find it difficult to identify and process your feelings if you use food to suppress or avoid uncomfortable emotions. This can ultimately lead to a sense of numbness or emotional exhaustion.

Although emotional eating is not a disorder, it can be a symptom of a mental health disorder. For instance, someone with Major Depressive Disorder (MDD) may turn to food to cope with their depression. In contrast, someone with General Anxiety Disorder (GAD) may use food to calm their nerves or distract themselves from their worries.

People with Post-Traumatic Stress Disorder (PTSD) may use food to cope with trauma-related emotions and memories. At the same time, those with Borderline Personality Disorder (BPD) may turn to food to regulate their moods or deal with feelings of emptiness.

Emotional eating can also be a sign of binge eating disorder, in which people repeatedly eat large amounts of food, often in secret and while feeling out of control.

Important: Emotional eating alone does not mean you have a mental health disorder. However, when it becomes a persistent pattern of behavior and begins to impact your quality of life, it may be a sign of an underlying issue that needs to be addressed.

Physical Health

Emotional hunger cannot be satisfied with food. As such, you tend to want to it more and more, which can lead to negative impacts on your physical health, such as the following:

1. **Weight gain**. Emotional eaters usually consume more food than they need. These foods are also often high-calorie, high-fat, and high-sugar. As such, weight gain and obesity are common side effects. Additionally, emotional eating often involves mindless eating, where you do not pay attention to portion sizes or fullness cues, leading to overeating. Emotional eating can also disrupt normal hunger and satiety signals, leading to a cycle of eating whether you are hungry or not. Over time, emotional eating can contribute to weight gain and difficulty maintaining a healthy weight.

2. **Poor digestion**. Mindless eating usually means not chewing your food properly, leading to larger particles that are more difficult to digest. The stress hormones released during emotional eating, such as cortisol, can also disrupt digestion by slowing the digestive process and reducing the production of digestive enzymes. The unhealthy foods consumed can also lead to gut inflammation, causing digestive issues such as bloating, gas, constipation, and diarrhea.

3. **Fatigue**. Unhealthy foods can cause a sudden spike in blood sugar, followed almost immediately by a crash. This drastic up and down of your blood sugar levels can lead to feelings of fatigue and lethargy. Additionally, emotional eating can disrupt sleep patterns, which can also contribute to feelings of fatigue. For example, if you eat a

large amount of food or eat late at night, your body is still working to digest the food while trying to sleep, leading to less restful sleep.

Emotional eating can also lead to "emotional fatigue." Feelings of guilt, shame, and regret associated with emotional eating can lead to another bout of emotional eating. This roller coaster of negative feelings-eating to feeling better-negative feelings can leave you emotionally exhausted.

4. **Skin problems**. Eating a diet high in sugar and processed foods can cause inflammation and lead to skin problems such as acne, eczema, and premature aging. The resulting fatigue and low-quality sleep from emotional eating can also affect skin health and contribute to dark circles and puffiness under the eyes. Further, any resulting weight gain can stretch the skin and cause stretch marks.

5. **Insomnia**. When you eat large amounts of food, particularly sugary or high-fat foods, your body must work harder to digest them. This can cause discomfort, bloating, and indigestion, making falling or staying asleep difficult. Additionally, emotional eating can cause a surge of energy, making it harder to feel tired and ready for sleep.

6. **Increased risk of chronic diseases**. Consistently engaging in emotional eating can increase the risk of developing chronic diseases such as high blood pressure, high cholesterol levels, diabetes, heart disease, stroke, and certain types of cancer.

7. **Nutrient deficiencies**. Eating processed and unhealthy foods can lead to nutrient deficiencies, as these foods often lack essential vitamins and minerals for optimal health. Emotional eating may also disrupt the body's ability to absorb and utilize nutrients, further exacerbating the problem of nutrient deficiencies.

8. **Weakened immune system.** An unhealthy diet can weaken the immune system, making you prone to various infections and illnesses such as colds, flus, and pneumonia.

9. **Increased inflammation.** Eating processed and high-fat foods can cause inflammation in the body, increasing the risk of several chronic diseases such as arthritis, asthma, diabetes, and even Alzheimer's disease[150].

10. **Poor physical performance.** A diet high in processed foods and sugar can lead to poor physical performance, affecting your fitness levels. These foods can make you feel sluggish, bloated, and tired, making engaging in physical activities like exercise or even simple daily tasks harder. Additional weight gained from emotional eating can further reduce physical performance by putting more strain on your joints and muscles.

Emotional eating can have serious, damaging consequences on your physical and mental health. This coping mechanism may provide short-term relief, but it is actually causing long-term damage to your mind and body.

To live the life you deserve, you must develop healthier coping mechanisms for unpleasant emotions. The next chapters will assist you in doing so.

Chapter 2: Dialectical Behavior Therapy 101

"Healing is about breaking the cycle of bad habits and patterns."—Unknown

What is DBT?

Dialectical Behavior Therapy, or DBT, is a type of therapy that helps people learn new ways of managing intense emotions and improving relationships with others. It was developed in the 1980s by Dr. Marsha M. Linehan[151] due to her and her colleagues' work with individuals suffering from Borderline Personality Disorder (BPD). Today, however, DBT treats various conditions, such as depression, anxiety, and eating disorders.

DBT is a form of CBT. However, while CBT focuses on identifying and converting negative thought patterns into positive ones (change-focused), DBT applies two opposing (dialectical) tactics: **Acceptance** and **Change**.

How DBT Can Be Used to Treat Emotional Eating

DBT was primarily developed for people suffering from BPD, which involves *difficulty regulating emotions* as one of its primary symptoms. Emotional eating is the propensity to use food in response to positive or negative emotions. As such, DBT is a great technique to address the issues associated with emotional eating and other eating problems.[152,153,154]

DBT Primary Concepts: Acceptance and Change

Dr. Linehan states that when she first started to work with individuals with BPD, she applied traditional behavior therapy techniques, which were change-focused. Clients would then question this method and say something like, "*What?! You mean I am the problem?*"

This prompted Dr. Linehan to change tactics and use acceptance strategies. She would listen to patients and urge them to be open and accepting of their feelings and experiences. However, these prompted clients to say, "*You mean you are not going to help me?*"

At this point, Dr. Linehan realized that she needed to find a way to bring acceptance and change strategies together. Fortunately, she was able to do so, resulting in a new type of therapy called DBT.

Radical Acceptance

Acceptance is reality acceptance in DBT. You are encouraged to accept your current reality AS IS. There is no need to question, evaluate or judge your past or the circumstances leading you to emotional eating. You cannot change what has happened, so spending time on it is futile.

This may appear simple or easy, but as someone who has struggled with mental health issues and emotional eating for many years, I am the first to say it is not.

When you experience emotional pain, your brain interprets it as threatening your well-being. Your natural response is to try to ignore, avoid or escape it. However, when you cannot immediately escape the source of the pain, your brain is likely to continue to focus on it, analyzing and meditating on the experience in an attempt to find a solution or relief.

So you either try to avoid the emotional pain or focus on it. Either way, you are prolonging your suffering because neither avoiding the problem nor ruminating on it fixes it.

So the first step to moving on involves accepting your reality rather than fighting against it or trying to change it. It means acknowledging and accepting the present moment, even if it is painful or difficult, rather than trying to deny or escape it. Acceptance must also be complete, not just lip service. You must accept with your whole heart, mind, and body. In DBT, this is called **Radical Acceptance**.

Worksheet: Radical Acceptance

Radical Acceptance is a freeing concept; it involves nothing but accepting your current reality. There is no need to assess, question, or judge anything; there is also no room for doubt, blame, or fear. Just acceptance.

Inside the circle, write down your thoughts about your current reality. There are no right or wrong answers. Just write whatever comes to mind.

Examples: (1) I accept that I use food to cope with my emotions. (2) I accept that my emotional eating has led to weight gain and health problems. (3) I eat when I am lonely. (4) I eat when I am bored. (5) I do not know why I eat even when I am not hungry.

Desire to Change

If Radical Acceptance is half of the equation, **Change** is the other half. Why? Because whatever it is you are doing is not working for you. Continuing down the road of emotional eating is not in your best interest. But the good news is there are *other* roads to take, and you just need to discover them.

Change is not easy, and that is true. The human brain does not like change[155]. One of the primary reasons is that humans are creatures of habit and routine, and change disrupts our established patterns and comfort zones. Additionally, change often involves uncertainty and unpredictability, which can be uncomfortable. We also have a natural aversion to risk and loss, making change seem daunting and intimidating. Lastly, change is often seen as a "problem" or "challenge" instead of a chance to learn, grow, and improve. However, as American entrepreneur, author, and motivational speaker Jim Rohn said, "*Your life doesn't get better by chance. It gets better by change.*"

So if you want to live healthier and be happier, change is what you need to do. You can only break the chains of emotional eating by learning new habits and skills.

Worksheet: Desire to Change

This exercise will assist you in welcoming change in your life. There is no need to make any plans here. Just write down your thoughts about change in the circle below. Remember, there are no right or wrong answers. Just write whatever comes to mind.

Examples: *(1) I am willing to learn new ways to manage my feelings. (2) I am ready for "better." (3) I am willing to make positive changes. (4) I am ready to stop using food to numb my pain. (5) I am ready to stop using food to feel loved.*

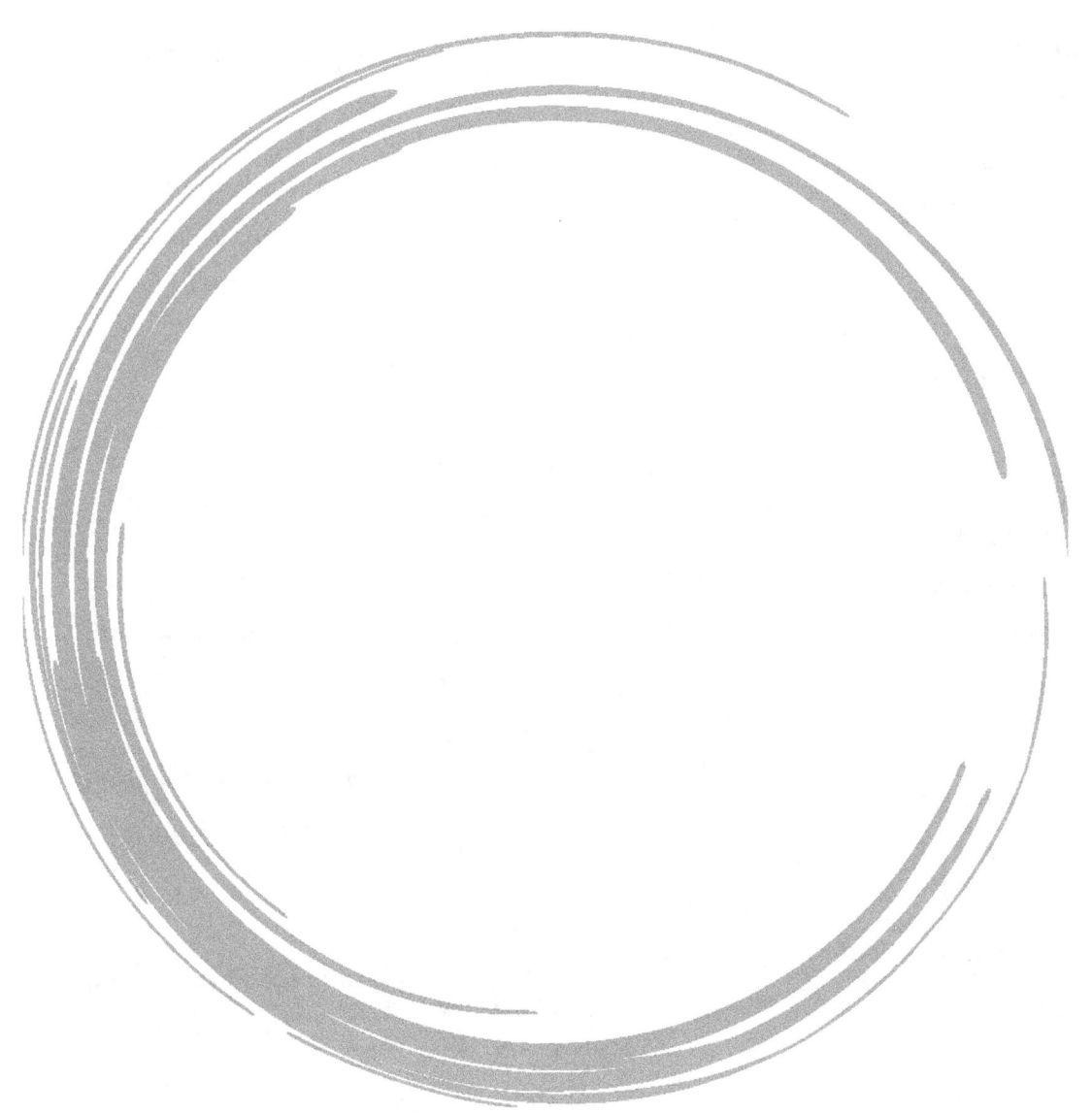

Worksheet: Radical Acceptance + Desire to Change

It is time to bring Radical Acceptance and Desire to Change together.

RADICAL ACCEPTANCE: Write statements accepting your current situation.

DESIRE TO CHANGE: Write statements expressing your desire to change or how change can benefit your life.

DECLARATION: Be kind to yourself as you acknowledge today and your wants and needs for tomorrow.

RADICAL ACCEPTANCE:	DECLARATION:	DESIRE TO CHANGE:
I accept that I use food to cope with my emotions.	"I accept who I am today. I am tired of fighting myself, and others. Life is full of ups and downs, and I can't control everything. So I've decided not to struggle against things I can't change.	I am willing to learn new ways to manage my feelings.
I eat when I am lonely.		I'm ready for "better."
I accept that my emotional eating has led to weight gain and health problems.	I may not have caused all my problems but I accept that I have to solve them anyway—for my own benefit.	I am willing to make positive changes.
I eat when I am bored.		I am ready to stop using food to numb my pain.
I do not know why I eat even when I am not hungry.	I also accept that I'm not living my best life now. So I am opening that door to change. I am going to give myself the opportunity to be "better." I deserve it.	I am ready to stop using food to feel loved.

DBT Primary Skills: Mindfulness, Distress Tolerance, Emotion Regulation, Interpersonal Effectiveness

In addition to the application of dialectics (Acceptance + Change), DBT is also unique because it is skill-based therapy. As Dr. Linehan says, *"DBT uses skills intentionally and wisely. Everyone who comes into DBT gets skills."*

At the time, most traditional therapies were focused on *behavioral change*. However, the HOW is often missing. For example, emotional eaters are often encouraged to practice "mindful eating," but how exactly do you do that? What are the steps?

Dr. Linehan ensured that people who took her program developed new skills that produced the desired behavioral change. And this change of behavior will then produce the outcomes you want out of life.

DBT SKILLS -> BEHAVIORAL CHANGE -> DESIRED OUTCOME IN LIFE

In DBT, the four primary skills to master are Mindfulness, Distress Tolerance, Emotion Regulation, and Interpersonal Effectiveness.

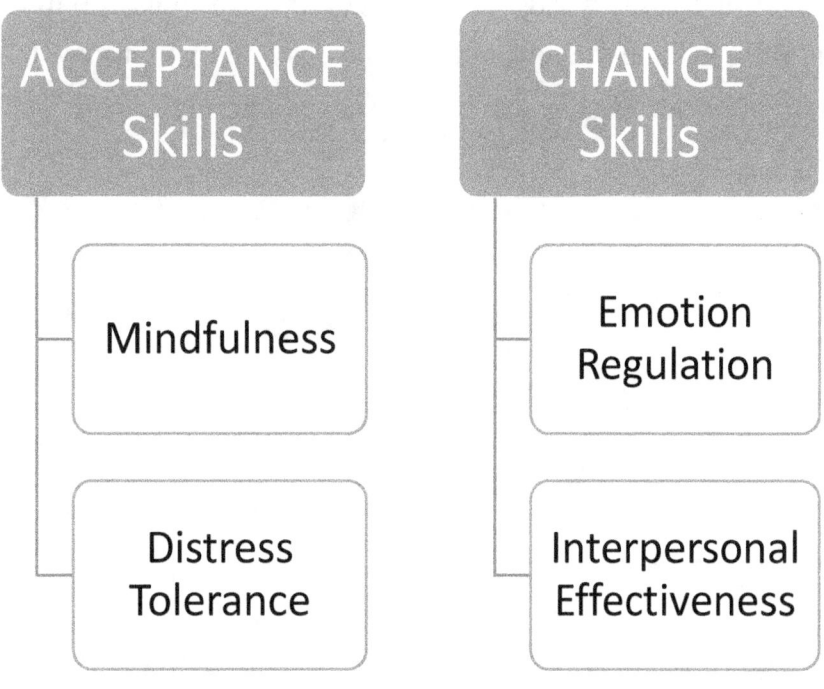

As you can see in the figure above, Acceptance is achieved by learning Mindfulness and Distress Tolerance skills. At the same time, Change is realized by learning Emotion Regulation and Interpersonal Effectiveness skills.

The succeeding chapters will explain each DBT skill in detail. Numerous exercises will be provided for each skill. Why? Because learning involves both knowing and doing.

Reading and understanding DBT skills is one thing, but to genuinely effect positive change in your life, you must practice these skills in real-world settings. In short, learning entails obtaining theoretical knowledge AND putting that knowledge into practice! The exercises provided are how you will accomplish this.

Important: The exercises are NOT intended to be one-time activities. I encourage you to apply what you learn in your daily life regularly. To be honest, this is actually easier than you think.

For example, remember when you first learned how to ride a bicycle? You had to practice balancing, pedaling, steering, and maybe even memorize biking regulations in your area. However, over time and with consistent practice, you simply... biked. Today, you do not even think about many things when you ride your bike; you just do it. Remember this as you learn the DBT skills in the next pages. They may be "new" today, but over time, and with consistent application, they will become second nature to you.

Chapter 3: Mindfulness Skills for Emotional Eating

"Mindfulness can help people of any age reshape their relationship with food and eating."— Dr. Susan Albers

Introduction to Mindfulness

Mindfulness is the practice of paying attention to the present moment without judgment. It involves being aware of your thoughts, feelings, and surroundings and accepting them without trying to change or resist them. Practicing mindfulness teaches you to be more present, focused, and calm.

Why is mindfulness important? In many ways, emotional eating is a knee-jerk reaction to emotions. Emotional eaters reach for food out of habit and often do not take the time to think about the consequences of this habit. Mindfulness helps improve your mental control. With this skill, you will learn to become more aware of your emotions rather than reacting to them with food.

For starters, let us begin your mindfulness practice by using your breath. Just like eating, breathing is so basic, so mundane, no? So much so that you do not really think about how you are breathing. For example, have you ever thought of how short or long you take each breath? Have you ever noticed how your breath reacts to a specific event, place, or person?

Also, did you know that most people are shallow breathers? These are fast and short breaths that only fill a tiny area of the lungs. Shallow breathing does not stimulate mindfulness. So, let us begin your mindfulness practice by learning how to breathe deeper and with more intention.

Worksheet: Belly Breathing

Belly breathing, or diaphragmatic breathing, aids in relaxation and stress relief. It's an excellent first-time workout for shallow breathers. The steps for belly breathing are as follows.

1. Take a seat or lie down on your bed.
2. Place one hand on your tummy and one on your chest.
3. Gently inhale through your nose, allowing your stomach to expand like a balloon. (Your chest should be quite motionless.)
4. Slowly exhale through your lips, allowing your belly to shrink like a balloon. (Try to expel all of the air from your lungs.)
5. Continue to breathe in this manner, focusing on the sensation of your abdomen rising and falling with each breath, like gentle ocean waves.

Ensure you breathe deeply from your diaphragm, not shallowly from your chest. You can also use this technique with your eyes closed, envisioning a peaceful landscape to help you relax. As you become more familiar with this method, gradually lengthen your belly breaths.

Worksheet: Take 5

This five-minute breathing exercise gives your mind and body time to relax.

1. Set a timer for five minutes.
2. Find a comfortable and quiet place where you will not be interrupted.
3. Take a seat or lie down on your bed.
4. Close your eyes and take a deep breath through your nose, counting to five as you inhale.
5. Hold your breath for a count of five.
6. Slowly exhale through your mouth, counting to five as you release your breath.
7. Repeat this process until the timer sounds.

Notes:
- As you do the above exercise, focus on the sensation of air moving in and out of your body, and let go of any distracting thoughts.
- When you are finished, take a moment to notice how you feel, and then slowly open your eyes.

Worksheet: 4-7-8 Breathing

4-7-8 Breathing is an advanced breathing technique that encourages deep relaxation. In this workout, you will exhale and hold your breath for longer than you inhale.

1. Find a comfortable and quiet place where you will not be interrupted.
2. Take a seat or lie down on your bed.
3. Close your eyes and take a few deep breaths to relax your body.
4. INHALE for 4 counts through your nose.

   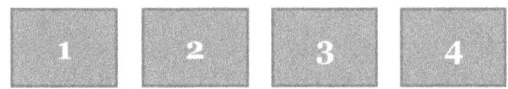

5. HOLD YOUR BREATH for 7 counts...

6. EXHALE for 8 counts through your mouth.

7. Do steps 4-6 for at least four cycles.

Mindful Eating

Mindful eating is being present at the moment and paying attention to the experience of eating without judgment or distraction. It is to develop a healthier relationship with food and to become more attuned to your body's needs and signals.

Principles of Mindful Eating

Here are some of the principles of mindful eating:

1. **Engage all of your senses while eating.** When you eat, interact with the food with all your senses. For example, use your eyes to notice the colors of food, your nose to register its smells, your tongue to notice the textures and tastes of the food, etc.

2. **Eat slowly and savor your food.** When you eat slowly, you give yourself time to fully taste and enjoy your food, increasing your satisfaction and making you less likely to overeat.

3. **Pay attention to your hunger and fullness cues.** Mindful eating is also observing your hunger and fullness cues. For example, is your stomach growling? If so, you may still be hungry. However, if you feel a sense of fullness or pressure in your stomach, that is a fullness cue, and you should stop eating.

    It is believed that it takes about 20 to 30 minutes for your brain to receive fullness signals from your stomach. So, you may think you are still hungry, but you already have enough. This is also why eating slowly (tip #2 above) is important. In short, do not rush your meals. Give your body time to tell you that you are full.

4. **Notice and acknowledge the thoughts and emotions that arise while eating.** Taking note of what you are thinking and feeling during a meal is important. It encourages you to be aware of your internal experiences and how they may affect your eating behavior. For instance, when you reach for and eat cookies in front of the TV, ask

yourself, *"Why did I do that when I just had dinner,"* or *"Why do I want cookies now?"* This will help you identify why you use food as a coping mechanism.

5. **Cultivate a non-judgmental attitude towards your eating habits.** Mindful eating involves noticing and observing your thoughts and emotions around food without judging or criticizing yourself. For example, if you notice that you reach for cookies each time you are bored, there is no need to feel ashamed, guilty, or judge yourself. Radically accept what you have done and your reason(s) for it, and work on learning new ways to change.

6. **Make conscious and intentional food choices.** Remember that food is meant to *nourish* your body. As a result, choose foods that keep your body healthy and performing at its best rather than unhealthy foods that negatively affect your mood and make your body sick.

7. **Practice gratitude and appreciation for the food you eat.** We often forget to be thankful for what we eat. However, expressing appreciation can help you build a more positive relationship with food and make you attentive to the nourishing advantages of the food you eat. Additionally, practicing gratitude during meals will help you slow down and taste your food more.

   In Japan, saying thanks before and after a meal is a habit. They say *Itadakimasu*, which means *Let us eat* or *Bon Appétit*, then at the end of the meal, they say *Gochisosama*, which means they are grateful for the sumptuous meal they just had. These words demonstrate the Japanese enthusiasm for not only the food itself but also for all that went into putting the meal in front of them.

8. **Be mindful of the environmental and social impact of your food choices.** You are not living alone on this planet; your food choices affect your family, friends, the environment, the community, and the world. This principle encourages you to choose healthy foods for yourself, others, and the planet, such as locally sourced and sustainably grown produce, grass-fed meat, and wild-caught fish.

Benefits of Mindful Eating

Mindful eating is not just a way to develop a healthier relationship with food and to prevent using food as a coping mechanism. Here are some of its other benefits.

1. **Helps with weight management.** Mindful eating can help you regulate your eating habits, increasing awareness of hunger and fullness cues. It can also reduce overeating, which can aid in weight management.[156,157]

2. **Improves digestion.** Eating slowly and mindfully helps your body digest food more effectively and reduces digestive discomfort.

3. **Reduces stress**. Mindful eating encourages relaxation and helps you become more aware of your body, reducing stress and promoting a sense of well-being.

4. **Increases enjoyment of food.** By savoring each bite and fully experiencing the taste, texture, and smell of your food, you can increase your enjoyment of meals and find greater satisfaction in eating.

5. **Promotes healthier food choices.** Mindful eating can help you become more aware of the impact of your food choices on your emotions, body, and the environment. As such, it will encourage you to choose healthier, more nutritious foods.

6. **Enhances mindful awareness.** Mindful eating can enhance your overall mindfulness practice by increasing awareness of your thoughts, emotions, and physical sensations during eating.

7. **Improves overall health.** By reducing stress, improving digestion, promoting healthier food choices, and enhancing mindful awareness, mindful eating can contribute to overall health and well-being. For instance, research shows better food choices and intake may lead to better sleep.[158,159]

Now that you understand how mindful eating can help you avoid emotional eating, try some of the mindful eating exercises on the following pages.

Worksheet: Mindful Eating

1. If you have time, do the <u>Take 5</u> breathing exercise (page 339). It will destress your nervous system and improve your digestion and metabolism.
2. **Choose a food item.** Select a food item you want to eat mindfully, such as fruit or a small snack.

   What food item did you choose?
   Example: tangerine, lunch salad, etc.

   _____
   _____

3. **Settle in.** Sit down at a table or in a quiet place to focus on your food without distractions.
4. **Observe and engage all your senses.** Take a moment to observe the food in front of you. Use all of your senses as you interact with the food.

   What do you see?
   Example: the dark orange color of my tangerine

   _____
   _____

   What sounds do you associate with this food?
   Example: a soft ripping sound as I peel the tangerine

   _____
   _____

What do you smell?

Example: the distinct citrusy smell of tangerines

_____
_____
_____

What is the texture of the food?

Example: the tangerine is firm but soft

_____
_____
_____

What does your food taste like?

Example: the tangerine is very sweet

_____
_____
_____

5. **Take small bites**. Take a small bite of the food and chew it slowly, paying attention to its taste and texture.

6. **Pause**. Put down the food and take a deep breath. Notice how the food feels in your mouth and how your body responds to it.

7. **Repeat**. Repeat steps 5 and 6 until you have finished the food item.

8. **Reflect**. Take a moment to reflect on the experience.

    How did it feel to eat mindfully?

    Example: It was weird at first. I didn't realize I was eating so fast before. The first time I tried this, it felt like I was eating forever.

What did you notice about the food?

Example: Now that I was taking time to eat the tangerine, I realized there were so many "steps" before I put the fruit in my mouth. I never really thought about those steps before.

How did you feel using all your senses while eating?

Example: It felt like I was "tasting" the food more!

Worksheet: TASTE

TASTE[160] is a great technique to remember when trying to eat mindfully.

T	**Think** Before you reach out for food and put anything in your mouth, take a moment to think if you want food due to physical hunger or because you are reacting to emotion.
A	**Appreciate** Take the time to think about what happened before the food was brought to you. Think about how much energy and resources went into making your meal.
S	**Eat Slowly** Eat slowly. Chew multiple times until the food is properly broken down before you swallow. Doing this will improve digestion and give your stomach enough time to signal to your brain that you are reaching satiety. **Tip:** Put down your fork between bites to force yourself to eat slower.
T	**Take the Time to enjoy your meal** As you chew, take the time to enjoy the flavors of the meal in your mouth. **Tip:** See if you can tell which flavor comes from which ingredient!
E	**End your meal when satisfied** Finish eating when you feel satisfied, not when you are stuffed. You will derive more pleasure from your meal this way.

Worksheet: Wise Mind

Wise Mind is our inner wisdom. It is the union of our emotional and rational selves. Emotional eaters usually let their emotions take complete control of the situation. Emotion prompts eating; ergo, we eat.

However, as you know, emotional eating brings in a lot of feelings of guilt, shame, and remorse. So you should not let your emotions rule. On the other hand, making decisions or taking actions based 100% on logic is also not a good idea. This is because it implies ignoring the feelings *behind* your emotional eating.

My sadness and the fact that I felt very alone at school led to my emotional eating. (At this point, I was listening to my Emotional Mind.) If I had just stopped eating junk food because I was gaining weight, I would have been using my Reasonable Mind, but I wouldn't have understood that I was eating to avoid being alone. I wouldn't have realized that food was a self-soothing strategy substituting for friends.

So, the best way to proceed is to learn to consult Emotional Mind and Rational Mind (to enter Wise Mind).

EMOTIONAL MIND: **REASONABLE MIND:**

WISE MIND

loneliness

boredom

sadness

anger

Wise Mind is the middle ground between feeling and thinking.

facts

statistics

data

acting 100% on my emotions

It takes feelings into account, but it also thinks about what makes sense before moving or reacting.

acting 100% using reason

guilt

shame

focused

organized

reactive or defensive

non-judgmental

Now, it is your turn to practice Wise Mind.

1. Think about the last time you emotionally ate.

2. Under **Emotional Mind**, please write down how you felt or your mood when you started thinking about food.
   Example: *I was feeling sad and lonely.*

3. Under **Reasonable Mind**, write down facts about the situation. (What do you KNOW for sure?)

Example: *I just had dinner. I should not have been thinking or wanting food.*

4. Under **Wise Mind,** write down any conclusions you reach after combining emotions and logic.

   Example: *I am feeling sad and lonely right now. That is okay; my feelings are valid. But I know I do not need to eat right now. I am not physically hungry. So I'll call my best friend and chat for a few mins.*

Chapter 4: Distress Tolerance Skills for Emotional Eating

"The more you tolerate, the more you can change."
— Dr. Marsha Linehan

Introduction to Distress Tolerance

Distress tolerance is crisis survival. In terms of emotional eating, distress tolerance is your ability to withstand your cravings or urge to reach for food in response to emotions.

Stress and Emotional Eating

Stress and emotional eating are closely related.[161,162] Many people use food to cope with stress, anxiety, and other negative emotions. When we experience stress, our bodies release hormones like *cortisol* and *adrenaline*, increasing our appetite and cravings for high-calorie, high-fat foods.

Unfortunately, the relationship between stress and emotional eating can become a vicious cycle. Emotional eating can lead to weight gain and other health problems, which can cause additional stress and negative emotions. This can lead to further emotional eating, creating a cycle of negative thoughts, emotions, and behaviors.

Stress vs. Distress

Stress is a typical reaction to the demands and pressures of everyday life. It can be positive or negative, motivating us to take action and perform well.

Positive stress, also known as *eustress*, can enhance our performance, increase our focus and alertness, and help us achieve our goals. For example, say you are preparing to give a presentation at work. Eustress can drive you to be more focused and to work harder to ensure a successful presentation.

Distress is a negative form of stress that can lead to physical, emotional, and psychological problems. Distress is often the result of chronic or overwhelming stress that is not managed effectively. For example, say you are preparing to give a presentation at work. Distress can make you chaotic, procrastinate and turn to emotional eating.

Importance of Distress Tolerance Skills for Emotional Eating

It is not only stress that may prompt a person to eat emotionally. Practically ANY emotion can trigger emotional eating because, as mentioned before, but emotional eating can also be a reaction to both negative (loneliness, sadness, boredom, etc.) and positive emotions (a.k.a. happy eating[163]).

As such, distress tolerance skills are not just about tolerating or surviving stress per se. It is about giving you the tools so that you DO NOT reach for food due to your emotions, whether positive or negative.

Here are some of the potential benefits of increasing your distress tolerance:

1. **Eliminates or reduces emotional eating.** Distress tolerance skills can help you tolerate and manage your emotions without resorting to food. This can reduce the frequency and intensity of emotional eating episodes or eliminate them altogether.

2. **Improves emotional regulation.** Developing distress tolerance skills can help you better manage and regulate your emotions, reducing the likelihood of emotional eating in the future.

3. **Increases resilience**. Increasing distress tolerance, levels can help you become more resilient in the face of stress and adversity. You may feel more confident handling difficult situations without relying on food as a coping mechanism.

4. **Enhances problem-solving skills**. As you become better at managing distress (i.e., your need to reach out for food), you will develop stronger problem-solving skills and become more adept at finding solutions to the underlying issues causing your emotional eating.

5. **Improved overall well-being**. Developing distress tolerance skills can help reduce stress, improve your emotional well-being, and enhance your overall quality of life.

Let us now work on increasing your distress tolerance using the exercises below.

Worksheet: Self-Soothe Using Your Five Senses

Grounding strategies bring you back to the present moment, giving you time to disconnect from your desire to reach for food. You will use your five senses—sight, smell, sound, touch, and taste—for this grounding practice to help you stay centered and focused and reduce feelings of (emotional) hunger.

List FIVE (5) things you can see right now.

Example: water bottle, fern plant, pear tree outside, neighbor's window, post-it notes

1.
2.
3.
4.
5.

List FOUR (4) things you can touch right now.

Example: my sweater, keyboard, mouse, PC monitor

1.
2.
3.
4.

List THREE (3) things you can hear right now.

Example: birds chirping, passing cars, co-workers typing on their keyboard

1.
2.
3.

List TWO (2) things you can smell right now.

Example: office room deodorizer, my hand lotion

1.
2.

List ONE (1) thing you can taste right now.

Example: coffee

1.

If you are still thinking of food after this exercise, do this practice again or write down as many things as possible per sense.

Worksheet: The Grounding Grid

Choose an activity from the **Grounding Grid** below whenever you feel the need to eat in response to your feelings. I have jumpstarted the list per grid to give you ideas. Please feel free to add more to the list.

THE GROUNDING GRID
What do you want to do?

SELF-CARE	PHYSICAL ACTIVITY
1. Relaxing bath	1. Walk outside
2. Massage	2. 5- minute stretch
3. 15-minute digital break	3. Climb up and down the stairs
4.	4.
5.	5.
6.	6.
7.	7.
CREATIVE PURSUITS	**MINDFULNESS**
1. Painting	1. Belly breathing (338)
2. Drawing	2. Take 5 (page 339)
3. Writing	3. 10-minute quiet meditation
4.	4.
5.	5.
6.	6.
7.	7.

SOCIAL CONNECTION

1. Call a family member
2. Message a friend
3. Go over to a colleague and invite them to a quick break
4.
5.

6.
7.

Worksheet: STOP

STOP is another great exercise to keep yourself from acting impulsively based on your emotions.

S	**Stop** Stop in your tracks! Literally, freeze in place and be motionless. Imagine a big STOP sign right in front of you. Stopping physically prevents you from doing what your emotions urge you to do. For example, suppose you are a boredom grazer and have a habit of going to the kitchen to find something to nibble on when bored. In this case, physically freeze, stay in place, and imagine the kitchen as "closed."
T	**Take a step back** When emotional hunger strikes, "thinking straight" can be difficult. So, give yourself time to process by mentally or even physically stepping back. Here is an example of mentally stepping back: close your eyes and take deep breaths until you feel the urge slipping away. Here is an example of physically stepping back: suppose you are at a party with many unhealthy snacks and drinks. However, you just had a meal. In this situation, physically step out of the room.

Observe

Pay attention to what is going on inside and outside of you. Take notes as if you were making a list. Observing distracts your attention from your urges by occupying your mind with something else.

Examples of self-observation:
I am standing between a door and a weird-looking chair.
As I look down, I notice that my shoes need dusting.

What are you observing about yourself? (List down as many as you can.)

_____
_____
_____
_____
_____
_____

Examples of observing your environment:
Mom's plants need watering.
Dad is somewhere in the garden.

What are you observing about your environment?

_____
_____
_____
_____
_____
_____

Proceed mindfully

Kudos! You have distracted yourself successfully. Now it is time to move on—mindfully. You do not want to be in the same emotional situation, so ensure you move forward in the right direction. Ask yourself questions like, "What is the best course of action to do right now?" or "What can I do to prevent myself form being in this situation?

What is the best course of action to do right now?
Example: (1) Get up from the sofa. (2) Brush my teeth. (3) Go to bed.

_____
_____
_____

What can I do to prevent myself from being in this situation?
Example: Remove all the "nibbles" I have in front of the TV.

_____
_____
_____

Worksheet: TIPP

Did you know you can change how you feel by changing your body chemistry?[164] The **TIPP** techniques listed below are simple to implement and work quickly to relieve you of any food thoughts.

|  | **Temperature**

Emotions occur in the body. Rapidly changing your body's temperature will help you lower the strength of your emotions.

Splash your face with cold water or wear a gel mask to feel better. This helps drop your blood pressure quickly, which aids in lowering the intensity of your feelings.

Other ideas: pour cold water on your wrists and forearms, hold ice cubes, chew ice chips, stand in front of the fridge or freezer with the door open, etc.

Even though cold temperatures have long been believed to assist in changing emotions, some people find hot temperatures work best for them. For example, a hot shower might be more soothing.

Other ideas: drink a cup of hot tea or coffee, fill a hot water bottle and hug it, rub your hands together to generate heat and place them over your eyes, etc.

See what works best for you and choose accordingly. |

Intense Exercise

Divert your thoughts by subjecting your body to rigorous exercise! The intensity of your desire to emotionally eat dictates how long you should be exercising.

For example, if a sudden craving hits, perhaps a 5- or 7-minute routine is all you need. You can use apps like the *5 Minute Home Workouts* app by Olson Applications or the 7 Minute Workout by Johnson & Johnson.

However, if you are going through very unpleasant emotions and have been battling your emotional hunger for a while, then intensely exercise for at least 20 minutes. Go for a quick jug or run, climb up and down the stairs, or use apps like FitOn to find full workouts from 5 minutes to 30+ minutes.

Paced Breathing

Slowing your inhalations and exhalations and breathing deeply from your belly will help you reduce the emotional intensity of what you are feeling. If you are new to paced breathing, do Take 5 (page 339) but omit holding your breath, just focus on inhaling and exhaling. Once you are used to this, do the exercise with the step where you hold your breath for five counts. If you are ready to progress, do 4-7-8 Breathing (page 99).

Paired Muscle Relaxation

You can combine your breathing practice above with Paired Muscle Relaxation. Slowly tense your muscles (but not so much that they cramp) as you take a deep breath. And then, as you take a deep breath out, let all that tension in your muscles go.

Chapter 5: Emotion-Regulating Skills for Emotional Eating

"It's not what you're eating, it's what's eating you."
— Janet Greeson

Introduction to Emotion Regulation

Emotion regulation refers to your ability to recognize and manage emotions effectively. It involves developing skills to help you identify and label your emotions, understand what triggers them, and respond to them effectively.

As mentioned, emotional eating is a maladaptive coping mechanism. The word *maladaptive* is derived from the combination of two Latin words: *malus*, which means "bad," and *adaptare*, which means "to adjust or fit." Together, they form *maladaptare*, which means "to adjust poorly." From here, the word *maladaptive* is derived to describe behaviors or responses that are ineffective or counterproductive in helping individuals cope with or adjust to their environment. (In the case of emotional eaters, it is difficult to cope with their *emotional environment*.)

Many emotional eaters know what they are doing. They know they are reaching for food not because they are hungry but because of "something else." Other people do not know, or at least do not want to accept, they are emotional eaters. A friend once said, *"Oh, I'm not an emotional eater. I'm really not. I just tend to graze excessively during moments of boredom or downtime. I don't finish a whole bag of Cheetos! Just handfuls of nuts, pretzels, cheese, and a couple spoons of peanut butter. You know..."*

The point is: emotional eaters reach for food because of their emotions. But by continually doing this, you are only making things worse for yourself (emotionally, mentally, physically, financially, etc.). What you need to do is BREAK THE CYCLE of emotional eating. How? By learning emotion regulation skills. If you increase your ability to manage your emotions better, you decrease (and potentially remove) the likelihood of emotional eating.

Practicing Self-Compassion, Self-Forgiveness, and Self-Validation

Before you go ahead and learn the skills to manage your emotions (instead of letting them manage you), let us first go over three important things: *self-compassion*, *self-forgiveness*, and *self-validation*. A lot of guilt and shame surround emotional eating. So much so that emotional eaters cannot heal because they find it difficult to practice these three concepts. But, as I have learned, these three beliefs are important for developing a healthy relationship with food... and yourself.

Self-compassion entails being kind and understanding to oneself, especially during difficulties, failure, or self-doubt. It means being gentle and supportive towards oneself rather than harshly self-critical. Self-compassion involves recognizing your suffering and offering yourself the same empathy, understanding, and support a good friend offers.

Examples:
I am doing my best, and that's all I can ask of myself.
I am not alone in my struggles. Many people go through similar experiences, and reaching out for help and support is okay.

Self-forgiveness involves letting go of self-blame and negative self-judgment after a mistake or failure. It involves acknowledging your mistakes, taking responsibility for them, and then working towards repairing any harm caused. Self-forgiveness involves releasing yourself from the burden of guilt and shame and finding a way to move forward with a sense of self-acceptance and self-worth.

Examples:
I forgive myself for my past mistakes and shortcomings.

I recognize that forgiveness is a process, and I choose to be patient and gentle with myself as I work through it.

Self-validation involves recognizing and accepting your thoughts, feelings, and experiences without seeking external validation or approval. It means acknowledging and accepting one's emotions, opinions, and experiences as valid and important, regardless of whether others agree.

Examples:
I'm doing my best to manage my emotional eating and deserve credit for my efforts.
I know that healing from emotional eating is what's best for me. I deserve understanding and respect for my choices.

Do you practice these views? If not, the following worksheets should help you.

Worksheet: Self-Compassion

1. Find a quiet and comfortable place to be alone with your thoughts. Take a few deep breaths and settle yourself by sitting or lying down in a comfortable position.

2. Close your eyes and visualize a recent situation where you felt stressed, anxious, or overwhelmed. While remembering, allow yourself to experience the emotions without judging or trying to change them.
   Example: I was very lonely last Friday. The silence was deafening in my small apartment. I ended up giving in and reaching for a tub of ice cream. Remembering it now, I feel disgusted with myself.

3. Now, imagine that you are speaking to yourself as you would to a good friend going through a similar situation. What would you say to offer support, kindness, and compassion? What words of encouragement or understanding would you offer to help your friend feel better?
   Example: It's okay; no one is perfect, so don't be so hard on yourself. Everyone finds it hard to change habits they have formed over time. Just keep going, and you'll get there.

   Your turn:
   _____
   _____
   _____

4. Repeat those words silently or out loud. Use a kind and gentle tone, and offer yourself the same support and compassion you would offer a good friend.

5. As you continue to offer yourself compassion, notice how your body feels. Do you feel more relaxed, calm, or at ease? Take a few deep breaths and let yourself fully feel the good feelings of being kind to yourself.

6. Slowly open your eyes and reflect on your experience. Use this exercise anytime to offer kindness and support or to practice cultivating self-compassion daily.

Worksheet: Self-Forgiveness

1. Find a quiet and comfortable place to be alone with your thoughts. Take a few deep breaths and sit or lie down in a comfortable position to calm down.

2. Think of a situation where you gave in to your feelings, emotionally ate, and then felt a great deal of regret. Allow yourself to fully acknowledge and feel your emotions without trying to change them or judge them. (Remember, this already happened, you cannot change it.)

Example: I was doing so well. For nearly a month, I could stay away from emotional eating. But last week, my dog Buster died. I was devastated, and before I knew it, I finished half a box of donuts. I regret that action so much because I felt that I undid my health efforts.

3. Acknowledge that everyone makes mistakes and that you are not alone in your experience. Take a deep breath and imagine releasing any self-blame or negative self-talk you may be holding onto. Visualize releasing them like letting go of a balloon.

4. Now, offer yourself forgiveness and understanding for the situation.

Example: I forgive myself for any mistakes that I made. I am human, and I am allowed to make mistakes. I understand that I did my best at that moment and am willing to learn and grow from this experience.

Your turn:

_____
_____
_____

5. As you continue offering forgiveness and understanding, notice how your body feels. Do you feel lighter, more at ease, or less burdened by guilt or shame? Take a few deep breaths and fully allow yourself to experience the positive feelings of self-forgiveness.

6. When you are ready, slowly open your eyes and take a moment to reflect on your experience. Use this exercise anytime to offer yourself forgiveness or to practice cultivating self-forgiveness in your daily life. Remember, self-forgiveness is a process. Be patient and kind as you work through any difficult emotions or experiences.

Worksheet: Self-Validation

1. Begin by finding a quiet, comfortable place to sit or lie down and relax. Take a few deep breaths and become present in the moment.

2. Take a moment to reflect on the last time you emotionally ate. As you recollect what happened, allow yourself to fully experience and acknowledge the emotions that come up for you. However, do not judge or criticize yourself for feeling this way.

3. Once you have identified the emotions you are experiencing, explore the thoughts or beliefs that may be driving them. Ask questions like "What am I telling myself about this situation?" "What beliefs or assumptions do I have that might contribute to these feelings?"

    What are you telling yourself about this situation?
    Example: I don't have any willpower against food.

    _____
    _____
    _____

    What beliefs or assumptions do I have that might be contributing to these feelings?
    Example: I'm just a weak person.

    _____
    _____
    _____

4. Challenge negative or self-critical thoughts by asking yourself, "Is this thought or belief true?" "What evidence do I have to support it?" "Is there a different way to interpret this situation?"

    Is this thought or belief really true?
    Example: I guess...

What evidence do I have to support it?
Example: It doesn't take me long to give in to food. I feel like I don't even fight the urge to eat and eat.

Are you the same in other aspects of your life?
Example: Hmmm, not really. I'm pretty good at work and don't consider myself "weak" there.

5. Once you have challenged negative thoughts or beliefs, practice self-compassion by acknowledging your difficulties and offering yourself words of kindness and encouragement.

   Examples:
   I am doing the best I can.
   I am worthy of love and acceptance, no matter what.
   I wasn't born an emotional eater; I learned to be one. So this means I can unlearn it.

6. Finally, take a few moments to reflect on any insights or learnings that have come up during this exercise. Consider how you can apply these insights to future situations and continue to practice self-validation in your daily life.

Identifying the Emotions That Trigger Your Emotional Eating

We all have different reasons for our emotional eating. For me, it was because of the extreme isolation and loneliness I experienced in my teens. It is very hard to describe the pain I felt going through days when no one even said "Hi" to me at school. So, *loneliness* is my trigger. I have been triggered by other emotions, such as stress, boredom, and anxiety as well. But the main trigger for me is loneliness. What is yours?

Worksheet: Identifying Your Emotional Triggers

Following is a step-by-step exercise to help you identify your emotional eating triggers.

1. **Start a food journal.** Begin by recording everything you eat (e.g., when, where, what) and how you feel before, during, and after. It is important to be as specific as possible with your entries, including the time of day, location, and other relevant details.

2. **Identify patterns.** After keeping your food journal for a few days, review your entries to identify patterns or trends. Look for commonalities in the types of foods you eat, the time of day you eat them, and the emotions you experience before, during, and after eating.

   Example: After writing in my food journal for two weeks, I noticed I mindlessly snack in front of my computer while working, specifically in the afternoons.

   _____
   _____

3. **Reflect on your emotions.** Take some time to reflect on the emotions you experience throughout the day. Are there certain times of day or situations that trigger strong emotions? Are there specific emotions that you find particularly challenging to manage?

   Example: I'm not bored or stressed while working, so at first, I wasn't sure why I ate so much. Then I realized I'm not really close to any of my colleagues, so maybe that's why I eat at work—to fill that gap (lack of social connection). Also, because I over-snack in the afternoon, I don't snack too much at home. I have a very fit partner, so I think I'm hiding my snacking so I don't overeat at home. Is this shame?

   _____
   _____

4. **Identify your emotional eating triggers.** Based on the data you have gathered from your food journal and reflecting on your emotions, identify specific triggers that lead you to engage in emotional eating.

    Example: I tend to emotionally eat when I am alone, like when I'm not talking to anyone at work. I also tend to emotionally eat out of shame because I don't want my partner to see me making unhealthy choices.

5. **Develop a plan.** Once you have identified your emotional eating triggers, develop a management plan.

    Example:
    (1) I'll get rid of my "snack stash" at work. (My partner doesn't know about these snacks. I grocery shop for them alone and bring them straight to work.)
    (2) I'll invite a colleague tomorrow for a walk after lunch.
    (3) I'll talk to my partner and ask them to help me make better choices.

Remember, identifying emotional eating triggers is an ongoing process that takes time and practice. By developing greater self-awareness and using the tools and resources available, you can learn to manage your emotions to reduce the likelihood of emotional eating.

But what if your trigger is not an emotion but a specific person (or group of people)? People are still emotional triggers.

I have noticed that being around family members makes me tremendously nervous and anxious because of my terrible childhood and the numerous arguments I still have with them. When this happens, I sometimes feel the urge to eat until I am stuffed and cannot feel anything.

Please note I love my family and know they love me. We just do not love each other the same way, or perhaps not in the ways we want to be loved. When I realized this, I developed a plan.

(1) I would visit preferably in the afternoons, not during lunch or dinner. Chinese lunches and dinners usually involve a lot of rice and carb-heavy foods. Also, my parents would insist I eat every morsel of food (Clean Your Plate mentality), and refusing would often lead to arguments. The fights would upset me, making me want to eat when I returned home emotionally!

(2) I would visit when I am in the right mindset. I have since learned that being "obligated" to visit on specific days (i.e., Sundays) was unhealthy. For example, if I had a deadline at work and were still required to go to my parent's house, I would arrive already short-tempered and thus emotionally eaten. But I also respect my parents, so I don't just drop by. I call ahead and ask if it is convenient for them if I visit.

(3) When a visit triggers me, and I want to emotionally eat when I get back home, I stand up, grab my gear and work out at my local club to release my emotional tension. (**Tip:** If you have a go-to move like this, always have your "gear" ready. Prepare them on weekends or during your downtime. It should always be ready for you to grab and use.)

Is a specific person(s) triggering your emotional eating? If so, who?
Example: my ultra-endurance athlete twin brother

What emotions do you normally feel when you are around them?

Example: I've always felt "less" compared to him; less successful, less healthy, etc. I laugh it off during family occasions, but it gets to me. When I get home, I would experience feelings of anger and eat.

If you cannot avoid these people, develop a plan to manage situations when you are with them.

Example: see my 3-step plan above on how I handle being with family

Now that you have identified your trigger(s), it is time to develop ways to regulate your emotions instead of letting them control your actions.

Worksheet: The Happiness Habit

Although negative and positive emotions can trigger emotional eating, some studies suggest that negative emotions such as stress, anxiety, loneliness, and depression are more likely to lead to emotional eating.[165,166] As such, it makes sense to increase the happiness level in your life to improve your emotional eating resilience. (Note: If you are a "happy eater," someone who emotionally eats when experiencing positive emotions, please see a list of Non-Food Related Rewards on page 426.)

As part of my healing journey, I found a book called *The Happiness Advantage*[167] by *Shawn Achor*. In the book, an activity helped me make it a habit to remember good things and build happy memories. By doing so, I could gradually reframe my thoughts to focus on the positives in life. I hope this activity is also beneficial to you.

Write down five (5) things that you are grateful for today.

Example: my perfectly hot cup of coffee, the sweater I'm wearing my grandma knitted, the green plants that surround me at home, the watch I have been wearing for over 10 years, the 30-minute walk in the woods I took this morning

1. _____
2. _____
3. _____
4. _____
5. _____

Important: Do this gratitude habit for at least 30 consecutive days. By doing this daily, you train yourself to switch from focusing on the negative (as most people do) to the positive.

–OR–

Write down one (1) positive event that has happened to you in the last 24 hours.
Example: the call I got from an old friend I have not heard from in a while

NEXT...

Think of an activity that makes you happy and commit to doing this for 30 consecutive days.
Joyful Activity: _____
Example: Pilates
Commitment Statement:
I will _____ for 30 days.
Example: I will start my day with a short Pilates routine for 30 days.

ALSO...

Be Mindful of Positive Experiences
Pay full attention as you do your Joyful Activity. Do not multitask or think about what you must do *after* the activity. Do not make plans; just be.
After you have completed your chosen Joyful Activity, make a list of everything you noticed. Describe your emotions, thoughts, and physical reactions as thoroughly as possible.
Example: I could not fully focus on my Pilates routine this morning. I was bothered by the construction noise outside. Still, I powered through and finished the session and do not regret it!

Be Mindful of Positive Experiences

Looking forward to tomorrow.

_____
_____
_____
_____
_____
_____

Worksheet: Opposite Action

Opposite Action is exactly what it means: doing the exact opposite whenever you feel you want to emotionally eat. It is a neat "life hack" to treat emotional eating. But first, a few things:

First, <u>Radically Accept</u> (page 48) that you want to eat. (**Tip**: If you have problems accepting, consult <u>Wise Mind</u>, page 60.)
Second, do any of the <u>Distress Tolerance</u> exercises in this book (page 64) if you feel overwhelmed by the desire to eat.
Lastly, do your preferred **Opposite Action**.

Opposite Action is effective because it is not a delaying or avoiding tactic. Doing the opposite of what you want influences how you feel about the situation. For example, say you want to eat because you are bored. But instead of eating, you do something that eliminates boredom, such as calling a friend, walking outside and seeing and greeting other people, playing an online game with others, etc. After a while, chances are you are not bored anymore, right?

In the table below, **Column A** lists unpleasant emotions that may be the reason behind your emotional eating. **Column B** shows what you would ordinarily want to do. **Column C** lists a counter-action to what you wrote under the previous column. I have put in some examples to jumpstart ideas. Please fill out the rest of the table.

OPPOSITE ACTION

A Emotion *What you are feeling.*	B Emotional Eating Impulse *What you would usually do when you feel this way.*	C Opposite Action *Write down a counter-action.*
Boredom	*Example: get some "nibbles" from the kitchen and watch something on Netflix*	*Example: start a 1,000-piece puzzle*
Emptiness	*Example: get a tub of ice cream*	*Example: go through my photos and see a lot of happy memories with friends and family*
Guilt		
Anger		
Fear		
Sadness		

OPPOSITE ACTION

A	B	C
Emotion	**Emotional Eating Impulse**	**Opposite Action**
What you are feeling.	*What you would usually do when you feel this way.*	*Write down a counter-action.*
Loneliness		
Frustration		
Helplessness		
Resentment		
Feel free to add more emotions and scenarios in the extra rows below.		

OPPOSITE ACTION

A	B	C
Emotion	**Emotional Eating Impulse**	**Opposite Action**
What you are feeling.	*What you would usually do when you feel this way.*	*Write down a counter-action.*

For some people, having ONE go-to activity works better. A colleague of mine, Max[19], turned to running. He said that whenever he felt the urge to eat emotionally, he thinks, "*Oh, it is time to get in some miles.*" When he returns, he no longer feels like eating whatever he wanted before the run. Of course, he may eat for recovery, but then he always chooses healthy food items such as nuts or a hard-boiled egg and always eats in moderation. He says, "*I don't want to undo my running! So when I return, I am truly not even in the mood for what I wanted to emotionally eat.*" And another benefit is that he has no shame, guilt, or regret after running.

One of my friends, Linda[19], shared with me this great hack: "*I have multiple subscriptions to health and fitness magazines. Whenever I feel the urge to emotionally eat, I grab one of them and start reading. All the articles about weight loss success, health tips, fitness routines, etc. inspire me so much that I am motivated to NOT reach for food and stay on track with my health goals.*"

If you prefer having ONE go-to move, great! What do you want to do?
Examples: walk outside, do yoga for at least 20 minutes, start knitting, etc.

_____
_____
_____
_____
_____
_____

---

[19] Name changed for privacy.

Worksheet: PLEASE

Emotional eating negatively affects your physical health and vice versa.[168] As such, it is important that you take care of your body.

PL	**Treat Physical iLlness immediately.** Not feeling well? If you are sick or suffering from an illness, go and seek medical help immediately and take any prescribed medications. I would also advise reaching out to a friend, family member, or loved one so you are not alone during your illness. If you do not want professional medical help, consider a holistic approach to getting well, such as engaging in reiki, acupuncture, aromatherapy, acupressure, yoga, etc. The objective is to improve your health as soon as possible so it does not worsen. **Tip**: Do not skip seeing your doctor for a yearly checkup to avoid physical ailments.
E	**Eat a balanced diet.** What does a "balanced diet" look like? According to the Healthy Eating Plate: ½ of your plate should be made up of fruits and vegetables, ¼ should be whole grains, and the final ¼ should be protein.[169] One way to ensure that you are consuming healthy meals is to develop the habit of meal planning and prepping. If you do not know how, please see <u>Quick Guide to Meal Planning and Prepping</u> on page 405.
A	**Avoid unhealthy substances.** Unhealthy substances such as alcohol and prohibited drugs are considered "mood-altering" and can lower your resistance to negative emotions. For example, when you have had one too many glasses of wine, your resolve to not eat emotionally might be low. So, as you try to unlearn emotional eating, avoid unhealthy substances.

	If you are used to a glass of wine after a meal, switch to a healthier drink such as tea or coffee. Do the same when dining out.
S	**S**leep. Some research shows a link between sleep deprivation and emotional eating.[170] Others show a link between sleep deprivation and the propensity to reach for junk foods,[171] while others indicate that not getting enough sleep makes it harder for people to exercise self-control when it comes to food.[172] All this points to the need to get enough sleep! But how much is enough? According to the American Academy of Sleep Medicine and Sleep Research Society, adults need seven (7) or more hours of quality sleep nightly.[173] **Tip**: Not getting enough quality sleep? See How to Establish a Sleep Routine on page 440.
E	**E**xercise. There are plenty of reasons to engage in physical activities. For instance, it gives one a feeling of mastery. This, in turn, improves self-esteem, which is one of the possible causes of emotional eating. Additionally, being fit makes it easier to remain fit and avoid mindless eating. Also, if you emotionally eat out of boredom or loneliness, exercising can eliminate these. As a general rule of thumb, aim to exercise for at least 30 minutes daily. If you are a beginner or have not worked out in a while, start with shorter, less strenuous activities like walking or power walking for 10 minutes, and work your way up. Keep in mind that consistency is key! So whatever physical activity you choose, make it a habit to keep on doing it!

Chapter 6: Interpersonal Effectiveness Skills for Emotional Eating

"Asking for help isn't giving up, it's refusing to give up."
— Unknown

Introduction to Interpersonal Effectiveness

Emotions make us human, but relationships make life meaningful. As such, learning Interpersonal Effectiveness skills are crucial to your healing journey. Although there are various reasons for emotional eating, for the most part, it is a learned behavior. To unlearn this behavior, you need the help and support of other people.

The people around us greatly affect our thoughts, feelings, and actions. Motivational speaker, author, and entrepreneur Jim Rohn said, "*You are the average of the five people you spend the most time with.*" Some research shows that it goes one connection beyond that.[174] For example, if your mom's sister is an emotional eater, there is also a chance you will become an emotional eater. Dr. Mark Hyman, an American physician and author of books in the nutrition and longevity niche, also said, "*... the social threads that connect us might, in the end, be more important than genetics.*"

So, the people around you influence your relationship with food whether you like it or not. And as you try to step away from emotional eating, it is critical that they understand, accept, and support you. Unfortunately, this is not always easy.

For example, a couple of years back, my mom visited me and basically cleared my kitchen cupboards of all my healthy food items and replaced them with unhealthier options while I was at work. She did this because she was unfamiliar with what I had in stock, which in her mind, meant I was not eating well. (By the way, in Chinese culture, it is common for parents to invade their children's privacy like this.) I had to reiterate my boundaries concerning my kitchen and the food I like to eat repeatedly.

If the British have afternoon tea, the Germans have a strong *Kaffee und kuchen* (coffee and cake) culture. So, my German friend Abigail[20] found it difficult to say "No" and explain to her parents that since she always has late lunches at work, she did not want coffee and cake whenever she made any afternoon visits. She told me her father got upset that she was not respecting a long-standing, beloved tradition. "*I tried cajoling, manipulating, even getting angry, but it didn't work. However, I am a social worker and was exposed to DBT at one point. When I got to the section about Interpersonal Effectiveness, I thought I would apply the techniques I learned, and it worked!*"

Importance of Healthy Relationships in Recovering from Emotional Eating

The importance of healthy relationships in recovery from emotional eating cannot be overstated. Here are a few specific ways that healthy relationships can support you:

1. **Emotional support and comfort**. When we have healthy relationships, we have people we can turn to for emotional support when triggered to emotionally eat. Friends, family, and loved ones can replace food as a source of comfort.

2. **Accountability**. When we have healthy relationships, we have people who can hold us accountable to our goals and commitments. This can be particularly helpful in recovery from emotional eating, as it can help us stay on track to manage our emotions and develop healthier coping mechanisms.

   If you have people in your life that enable your emotional eating, consider removing them from your inner circle, at least for the time being. If this is not possible, as it is

---

[20] Name changed for privacy.

with immediate family members or colleagues, then try to minimize your time with them.

3. **Social connection**. You do not need to go on your healing journey alone. Healthy relationships provide opportunities for social connection, reducing feelings of loneliness and isolation. Supportive social connections also foster a sense of camaraderie. Knowing that others support you is a huge lift, even if they are not fighting the same struggle.

   Keep in mind that starting and establishing social connections start with you. That is, be proactive and seek opportunities to meet people rather than waiting for others to find you. How? Here are a few ideas: do volunteer work, attend online or offline classes or workshops, join online or offline emotional eating support groups, join clubs or groups that cater to your hobbies, etc.

4. **Self-esteem**. Healthy relationships can help improve our self-esteem and sense of self-worth. This can be particularly important for individuals who struggle with emotional eating, as low self-esteem and negative self-talk can be major contributors to emotional eating behaviors. For example, someone saying, "You got this!" is a great moral boost.

   Struggling with self-esteem? Here are a few tips to boost your confidence:
   - Practice self-care (e.g., take mental breaks throughout the day, get enough sleep, meditate, etc.)
   - Set and undertake small, achievable goals (e.g., increase your number of steps per day, say "Hi" to people you don't know, drink more water, etc.)
   - Practice self-compassion (e.g., avoid negative self-talk, practice gratitude, treat yourself like a friend, etc.)
   - Reflect on your accomplishments, big or small.

The Interpersonal Effectiveness exercises on the following pages will help you develop effective communication and relationship skills that will help you have the right support on your journey.

Worksheet: Communicating Boundaries

Do you struggle to communicate your wants and needs for your emotional eating journey? If so, you are not alone. Many people do not tell others about wanting to recover from emotional eating for various reasons. This may include fear of rejection and disapproval, wanting to avoid conflict, or difficulty asserting boundaries. However, if you do not communicate your boundaries, they will keep getting crossed, making your healing journey more difficult.

Here's an example of a step-by-step boundary-setting exercise for emotional eaters:

1. Identify a specific situation in which you tend to engage in emotional eating.

   Example: A few hours after dinner, my partner and I tend to hibernate on the sofa after a long day's work. We might be watching something together or doing different things. Still, there is always an assortment of snacks (e.g., roasted nuts, chips, cheese, crackers, pretzels, etc.) on the coffee table for us to munch on.

   _____
   _____
   _____
   _____

2. Write down how you typically respond in this situation. This could include thoughts, feelings, and behaviors related to emotional eating.

   Example: This is a habit we both developed in our marriage. I don't really associate it with any negative feelings or thoughts. I guess it started as a way to unwind and make our time together cozy or homely.

   _____
   _____
   _____

3. Identify the boundary you would like to set in this situation.

   Example: Since the birth of our second child (five years ago), I have been battling weight and body image issues. I realized that I have been turning more and more to food to cope, which, of course, worsens my situation. So want to limit the amount of junk food we keep in our house. Of course, I want to keep our together time at night, but I don't want to do the mindless late-night munching anymore.

4. Write down your boundary in a clear, specific, and assertive manner.

   Examples:
   I will only keep healthy snacks in the house and avoid buying junk food. But, before I do, I will communicate with my husband what I am feeling and why.
   I will encourage my husband to do the same. But it's okay if he doesn't want to change because this is about me.
   I will say "No" when my husband offers me late-night snacks.

5. Practice communicating your boundary assertively with someone you trust. This will help you feel more sure of yourself and ready to talk about your limits when the time comes.

6. Enact your boundary in the identified situation.

   Examples:
   If my husband offers me late-night snacks, I will always say these words, "No, but thanks, babe."
   If I find the snacks too tempting, I will do <u>Take 5</u> (page 339) or any of the <u>Distress Tolerance</u> exercises (page 64) I've learned.

7. Evaluate the effectiveness of your boundary and adjust as needed. If your boundary was effective, continue to practice it in similar situations. If it was ineffective, re-evaluate your boundary; perhaps there is another way or angle to enforce it. If you are still at a loss, seek the advice of someone you trust or a mental health professional.

Remember that setting boundaries is a process that may take time and practice to find what works best for you. Be patient and compassionate with yourself.

Worksheet: DEARMAN

DEARMAN is about *objective effectiveness*. It is the ability to successfully and clearly explain what you want to get out of a conversation. You see, there is an art to asking. If you demand, you will likely not obtain what you want, possibly harming your relationships. **DEARMAN** will assist you in asking effectively.

D — Describe the situation

What do you want or need to happen? Discuss the situation in simple, straightforward language. Say what you know to be true, not what you believe or feel.

What's the situation?

Example: Mom/dad, please stop questioning my new food choices and eating behavior. I would also appreciate it if you didn't call the whole family and "update" them about what I'm doing.

_____

_____

_____

E — Express how you feel

Begin your sentences with "I." Remember that you are discussing how you feel and what you think. People may interpret "You" remarks as accusations, increasing the likelihood of tension in the conversation.

Example: I want to change my eating habits and relationship with food to live happier and healthier.

_____

_____

_____

A	### Assert yourself

Express your intentions without being confrontational. You do not want to get into an argument. You want to be heard clearly and efficiently.

Example: I know you care about me, but THIS is what is good for me right now.

_____
_____
_____ |
| **R** | ### Reinforce your request

Make it obvious to the other person how important your request is to you. Also, thank them immediately if they give in to what you want.

Example: This is really important to me. I have been struggling for a long time and would appreciate your support.

_____
_____
_____ |
| **M** | ### Mindfulness

Be mindful of what you want out of the conversation. Whatever the other person says, stay on track and keep your viewpoint. Others may object, insist, dismiss, or dispute with you if they disagree. Whatever they do, do not be persuaded, and stick to your guns! |

Example: I hear you, mom/dad. I hope you hear too that the way I was eating before was not beneficial for me; I am now making changes that I know are good for me.

Appear confident

Do not show any sign of weakness in your argument. Demonstrate confidence through verbal and nonverbal signs, but do not be intimidating. Do not raise your voice or "stare down" the people you are talking to. Remember to be consistent as well. For example, do not slouch your shoulders after expressing your request or look nervous.

How do you want to show confidence?

Example: In a confident voice, say, "I hope you understand because I'm not going to change my mind on this."

Negotiate

If the other person(s) still refuses to grant your request, it is time to negotiate. This will give you enough time to come up with a viable answer. You might suggest how to proceed or ask the other person what they think should happen next.

Examples:

How about we avoid the topic of my eating whenever I visit? What do you think?

Worksheet: GIVE

GIVE is about relationship effectiveness. It is the ability to keep great relationships with others by fostering positive interactions. Simply put, you want the other person to feel good about your conversation so that they will be more likely to approve your request.

G	**Be Gentle.** When asking someone to support you in your journey, you should do so with kindness. Demanding to be respected achieves disrespect. Also, do not say or do anything that could make the other person feel bad. Simply put—be nice! List five ways to ask for something in a nice way. *Example: I'm trying to change my eating habits to better manage my emotions. Can you help me by not bringing unhealthy foods into the house?* 1. _____ 2. _____ 3. _____ 4. _____ 5. _____
I	**Act Interested.** If you want the other person to hear you, you must show that you hear them too. When the other person is talking, pay attention and ensure you understand their perspective. List five ways you convey interest. *Examples: maintain eye contact during the conversation, don't interrupt, don't do other things, etc.* 1. _____ 2. _____ 3. _____

V	4. _____ 5. _____
V	**Validate.** Show that you understand what the other person is thinking and feeling. List five ways you validate others. *Examples: repeat what the other person said, look interested (not bored), etc.* 1. _____ 2. _____ 3. _____ 4. _____ 5. _____
E	**Show an Easy Manner.** Be friendly. Remember, you are making a request, not telling others what to do. People will feel more at ease and open to what you want if you maintain a friendly demeanor. List 5 ways you can show friendliness. *Examples: smile, adopt a calm and friendly voice, etc.* 1. _____ 2. _____ 3. _____ 4. _____ 5. _____

Worksheet: FAST

FAST is about maintaining your self-respect during difficult conversations. It is the ability to protect yourself from betraying your values and beliefs to receive approval or get what you want. **FAST** should be applied when you make a request and the other party is not agreeing (at least, not yet) or when someone insists on a request you do not want to grant because it goes against your values.

F	**Be Fair.** When making a request, be fair to yourself and others. For example, as you make your request, ensure it is not something the other person cannot grant. Also, make sure to ask politely. Make no demands or make the other person feel frightened or guilty if they refuse to comply with your request. *Practice making a request fairly and reasonably.* *Example: I've been struggling with emotional eating lately and could use some support. Would you be willing to listen when I feel stressed or upset?* _____ _____ _____ _____ _____
A	**No Apologies.** Don't say sorry or apologize excessively. There is no need to feel apologetic when making a request, and there is no need to apologize if you want to say "No" to someone. *Practice making a request without apologizing:* *Example: I've been struggling with emotional eating lately and could use some support. Would you be willing to listen when I feel stressed or upset?*

NOT: I'm so sorry to ask this of you. I know you're busy. Geez, I feel really bad for asking.

_____
_____
_____
_____

Practice saying "No" without apologizing:
Example: I don't want more food, thank you.
NOT: I am so sorry, I don't mean to offend you, but I am so full and cannot eat anymore. Sorry!

_____
_____
_____
_____

Stick to your **V**alues.

Do not betray your values because the other person does not agree with your request. Also, do not sacrifice your convictions because someone pressures you to say "Yes" to something.

Practice sticking to your values when making a request.
Example: I understand you want to continue bringing junk food to our house. I just wanted to let you know that I plan to stop eating them from now on. And I would appreciate your love and support if you didn't eat them in front of me.

_____
_____
_____
_____

Practice sticking to your values and saying "No" no matter what the other person says, does, or tries to get you to do.

Example: No, I will not make and bring fried chicken wings on your birthday. You know I'm a vegetarian.

_____
_____
_____
_____
_____

Be Truthful.

T

When making a request or denying one, be honest about your reasons. Do not lie, dramatize or exaggerate to get what you want or avoid doing what you do not want to do.

Practice honesty when making a request:

Example: I've been struggling with my relationship with food and want to stop my emotional eating. This is why I don't want junk food in the house.

_____
_____
_____
_____

Practice honesty when saying "No:

Example: [when offered food you don't want to eat] No, thank you.
NOT: [when offered food you don't want to eat] Oh! I really, really want to, but I just had the biggest meal!

_____
_____
_____
_____

Chapter 7: Developing Healthy Habits

*"If you always do what you've always done,
you always get what you've always gotten."— Jessie Potter*

Healthy living helps prevent emotional eating because it promotes physical and emotional wellbeing. As mentioned, emotional eating is usually a coping mechanism for unpleasant or negative emotions. However, life has ups and downs, so you cannot eliminate unpleasant situations and emotions. What you can do, in addition to the DBT skills you have learned, is strengthen your emotional resilience so that you can cope and manage life's obstacles while maintaining a sense of well-being. This chapter explores various effective ways to develop healthy habits. These practices will not only help you overcome emotional eating. They also have the power to impact every aspect of your life positively.

Top 10 Healthy Food and Eating Habits

Emotional eating and unhealthy eating habits reinforce each other. Adopting healthy food and eating habits helps prevent this maladaptive behavior by helping to stabilize your blood sugar levels, improve your mood, reduce cravings, prevent you from undertaking restrictive diets, etc. Following are 10 tips regarding food and meals that can help your journey:

1. **Make <u>mindful eating</u> (page 341) a way of life**. Eating mindfully helps you become more aware of your eating habits and the sensations of hunger and fullness in your body. By paying attention to *what* and *how* you eat, you can develop a healthier relationship with food and reduce the likelihood of emotional eating and overeating. This practice can also help you enjoy your food more fully and appreciate the sensory experience of eating.

2. **Practice portion control**. Switch to smaller plates, bowls, and cups to help control your portions and avoid overeating. You can also try using divided plates to separate your food into different groups. This way, you can get a balanced meal with all the

nutrients your body needs. If you are a "snacker," use divided snack plates. This way, even if you do emotionally eat, you can "trick" your brain by only filling one part with something unhealthy (e.g., chips, mini pretzels, etc.) while filling the rest with healthy snacks such as cut-up vegetables, unsalted and unroasted nuts, etc.

3. **Keep healthy snacks on hand**. Keep healthy snacks like fruits, vegetables, and nuts on hand to help curb cravings. **Tip**: Make reaching for healthy snacks an easy choice by (1) getting rid of unhealthy ones (e.g., cookies, chips, soda, etc.) in your home and (2) pre-cutting fruits and veggies into bite-size portions you can store in your fridge.

    Are you a "junk food snacker?" If your emotions make you crave something sweet, salty, or savory, look for healthier alternatives. For example, switch from potato chips to air-popped popcorn, processed chicken nuggets to homemade ones, ice cream to frozen yogurt with berries, etc.

4. **Drink a lot of water**. Drinking enough water can help you feel full and hydrated, which can help prevent reaching for food. Additionally, research shows that water improves mood![175,176]

    The amount of water that should be consumed depends on various parameters, including age, gender, weight, activity level, and climate. The National Academies of Sciences, Engineering, and Medicine suggests that men strive to drink around 3.7 liters (125 ounces) daily, while women aim for a total daily water intake of around 2.7 liters (91 ounces).[177] It is important to note that this recommendation includes all water sources, including water from beverages and food. So, if you consume plenty of water-rich foods and beverages throughout the day, you may not need to drink as much plain water to meet your daily needs.

    Hate drinking plain water? Try *infused water*. For example, add ginger and mint, watermelon slices, or various citrus fruits and peels to your water.

5. **Avoid skipping meals.** Skipping meals can make you hangry (hungry+angry) and lead to emotional eating AND overeating later in the day. So, make sure to eat regular meals and snacks to help regulate physical hunger. To do this, space out your meals so you can eat every 3-4 hours. For example, have breakfast at 8 AM, a mid-morning snack at 10:30 AM, lunch at 1:00 PM, an after snack at 3:30 PM, dinner at 6:30 PM, and an evening snack at 8:30 PM.

6. **Eat protein-rich foods.** Protein-rich foods like lean meats, eggs, and legumes can help you feel full and satisfied. Further, research suggests that consuming protein-rich foods can help improve mood and reduce symptoms of depression and anxiety.[178,179]

    The suggested daily protein consumption varies depending on age, gender, weight, exercise level, and overall health. However, as a general rule of thumb, the recommended daily protein intake is 56 grams per day for men and 46 grams per day for women.[180] If you are vegan, you can still meet this requirement by consuming protein-rich foods such as pulses, soy products (e.g., tofu, tempeh, etc.), nuts and seeds (e.g., almonds, walnuts, chia seeds, etc.), whole grains (e.g., brown rice, oats, etc.), plant-based protein powders, etc.

7. **Do NOT grocery shop when hungry.** Shopping for groceries while hungry can lead to impulsive purchases of unhealthy snacks or comfort foods that you may regret later. You can make more rational and healthy food choices by avoiding grocery shopping when hungry. Furthermore, shopping while hungry can lead to overbuying, contributing to food waste and raising overall food costs.

8. **Develop a daily eating routine.** A regular eating schedule helps prevent skipping meals, overeating, and the likelihood of impulsive or emotional eating. A routine also helps stabilize your blood sugar levels and reduce cravings for sugary or high-fat foods. Lastly, it can help you establish structure and predictability in your daily life, reducing stress, anxiety, and other unpleasant emotions. (See also Quick Guide to Meal Planning and Prepping below.)

9. **Practice self-compassion (page 365)**. Be kind and compassionate to yourself if you slip up and emotionally eat. Avoid negative self-talk and focus on making healthier choices moving forward.

10. **Keep a food journal**. Starting and maintaining a food journal can help you identify patterns in your eating habits and help you make healthier choices. (See also Identifying Your Emotional Triggers, page 374.)

When changing your food and eating habits, refrain from thinking about what you are "giving up" and focus instead on what you are gaining—a healthier mind and body!

Quick Guide to Meal Planning and Prepping

Meal planning and prepping can be particularly helpful for individuals struggling with emotional eating. Otherwise, there is a risk that you will revert to old eating habits because that is what you know; that is what is easy and comfortable to do. Here are other reasons why meal planning and prepping are advantageous:

1. **Reduces decision fatigue**. Deciding what to eat can feel overwhelming when you are mentally or emotionally exhausted. By having a pre-planned menu, you can avoid decision fatigue and the temptation to turn to unhealthy foods when you feel overwhelmed.

2. **Provides structure and routine**. For many, emotional eating can be triggered by a lack of structure or routine in their daily lives. Meal planning and prepping can provide a sense of structure and routine around meal times, which can help to reduce the likelihood of emotional eating.

3. **Encourages healthy food choices**. Meal planning and prepping can help you make healthier food choices by providing a framework for meal times. By planning and preparing your meals in advance, you can ensure that you incorporate various healthy foods into your diet.

4. **Reduces stress around meal times**. By having pre-prepared meals or components of meals, you can reduce the stress associated with meal times. You do not have to worry about what to cook, missing ingredients, etc., and you can quickly assemble a meal when hungry.

5. **Increases feelings of control**. Emotional eating often feels like you do not have control. Meal planning and prepping can provide that sense of control over food choices, which can be empowering for individuals struggling with emotional eating.

Note: Meal planning and prepping is a broad topic beyond this book's scope. Still, I have added the sections below as a guide to jumpstart this healthy habit for you.

What is Meal Planning?

Meal planning is deciding in advance what meals you will eat for a set period, typically a week or two, and then creating a shopping list based on those meals. Meal planning aims to ensure that you have healthy, nutritious meals available throughout the week while reducing the time, effort, and stress associated with meal preparation.

Meal planning typically involves several steps:

1. **Decide on the meals you want** to prepare for the week, considering your dietary needs and preferences. Do not rush this process. Choose a time when you are calm and comfortable and have enough time to plan at least a week's worth of meals. (**Tip**: Don't meal plan when you are hungry!) Make the plan or menu as detailed as you can. Include what you want to eat for breakfast, lunch, dinner, and snacks and when you should be eating these meals.

2. **Create a grocery list** of the ingredients you will need for your meals. **Tip**: This will most likely require you to review your kitchen cupboards to see what you have. Use the opportunity to get rid of unhealthy and expired food items.

3. **Shop for the groceries on your list**. Do this when you are not hungry so you are not tempted to reach for anything beyond what is on your list.

4. At home, **place your groceries where you can easily see and reach them**. Remember, make healthy food an easy choice for you! For example, put fruits on your table, vegetables at the front of your fridge, nuts and seeds in clear glass jars, and put them at the front of your cupboards, etc.

5. **Stick to your meal plan** throughout the week, adjusting only when necessary for changes in your schedule or unexpected events.

What is Meal Prepping?

Meal prepping is preparing meals or portions of meals in advance, typically for a week's worth of meals at a time. The meals are usually pre-cooked, portioned, and stored in the fridge or freezer until ready to be consumed. Meal prepping can involve cooking entire meals, such as casseroles or stir-fries, or preparing components of meals, such as grilled chicken, roasted vegetables, or cooked grains that can be assembled into a full meal on a later date.

Meal prepping is often done in one batch on a designated day each week, and it can save time, money, and stress around meal times. By having pre-cooked meals or components readily available, you can avoid making impulsive and potentially unhealthy food choices when pressed for time or feeling stressed.

Here are some common components of meal prepping:

1. **Cooking proteins**. This can include grilling chicken breasts, cooking ground turkey or beef, roasting fish, or preparing tofu or tempeh.

2. **Preparing grains**. This can include cooking rice, quinoa, or other grains in advance for various meals throughout the week.

3. **Prepping vegetables**. This can include washing, chopping, and roasting or steaming vegetables to be used in salads, stir-fries, or as side dishes.

4. **Preparing snacks**. This can include cutting up fruits and vegetables, portioning out nuts and seeds, or making energy bites or protein bars to have on hand for quick snacks.

5. **Assembling meals**. This can include putting together salads, stir-fries, or other meals in advance and storing them in containers to be grabbed and eaten or reheated and consumed throughout the week.

If this is the first time you are food planning and prepping, start with easy meals you know how to prepare so you do not get overwhelmed. Also, you do not always have to come up with different meals.

For example, some people are perfectly okay with having the same breakfast for a week. I usually eat the same breakfast each day: oatmeal or granola with whole-wheat toast and a piece of fruit. The routine is easy and calming and ensures I get a healthy breakfast.

Incorporate Physical Activity into Your Routine

Physical activities can help prevent emotional eating by reducing stress, improving mood, and boosting self-esteem.[181,182] Regular exercise can also improve sleep quality[183], which is important for managing appetite, reducing cravings for unhealthy foods, and regulating emotions. Additionally, exercise can *replace* food as a coping mechanism when mentally and emotionally overwhelmed.

Here are 10 tips for incorporating physical activity into your routine:

1. **Make engaging in physical activities an EASY choice.** If you think working out is hard, you might not do it even if you want to. So remove any barriers that might make it

hard to choose to exercise. For example, choose a gym or fitness center near your home or workplace. If you prefer to work at home, invest in some basic equipment, such as resistance bands or dumbbells, so you do not feel limited. If you prefer to exercise first thing in the morning, lay out your workout clothing the night before by your bed. In short, make exercising convenient for yourself.

2. **Start small**. If you are new to exercising, start with small, manageable goals. This could be as simple as taking a 10-minute walk each day and gradually increasing the duration and intensity of your workouts over time.

3. **Set realistic goals**. No one begins mountain climbing by taking on Mount Everest. So, set goals that are achievable for you. For example, walking for 30 minutes three times per week.

4. **Find an activity you enjoy**. This could be anything from walking or jogging to swimming or dancing. When you enjoy the activity, you are more likely to stick with it.

5. **Schedule it in**. Treat exercise as an important appointment and schedule it into your daily routine. This could be first thing in the morning, during your lunch break, or after work.

6. **Create opportunities to move.** One of the primary reasons people cite for not exercising is "lack of time." Many people lead busy lives with work, family, and other commitments, so it can be difficult to find time for exercise. Even so, find "pockets of opportunity" within your day. For example, take breaks throughout the day to stretch or take a short walk, use the stairs instead of the elevator, and park your car further than usual to ensure you walk.

7. **Mix it up**. Incorporate various exercises into your routine to prevent boredom and keep things interesting. For example, start with a 5-min warmup, followed by 20 minutes of cardio, 15 minutes of strength training, and end with a 5-min cooldown.

8. **Make it a family affair or a social activity.** If possible, involve your family in physical activities like walking in nature or riding a bike together. Join a fitness class or find a workout buddy to help keep you motivated.

9. **Use technology.** Use fitness apps like Olson Applications' *5 Minute Home Workouts*, Workout Apps' *7 Minute Workout*, FitOn's *FitOn Workouts*, and others to easily squeeze in quick workouts whenever you have a few spare minutes. Invest in wearable devices, such as inexpensive step counters to FitBit watches, to set exercise goals and track progress.

10. **Focus on the benefits!** Remind yourself of the advantages of exercise, such as increased mood and energy, decreased stress, improved sleep, and less susceptibility to emotional eating. Concentrating on the good consequences will help you to get started.

Manage Daily Stress through Healthy Coping Mechanisms

Stress is one of the leading triggers for emotional eating. As such, stress management techniques can be extremely helpful in reducing this behavior. Here are 12 tips for managing daily stress:

1. **Practice mindfulness (page 55).** Mindful breathing, meditation, mindful eating, hitting "Pause" during the day, sitting still for a few minutes, and other mindfulness practices help reduce stress and improve focus. Make it easy to start this practice by setting reminders throughout the day. You can use your phone and set the alarm every 60 minutes, reminding you to take a quick 5-10 minute break, or you can download and use apps such as Stand Up!. Desktop apps such as BreakTimer and Stretchly can help remind you to take a break when you are always in front of a computer.

2. **Exercise regularly.** Regular physical activity helps reduce cortisol, the stress hormone, in the body. At the same time, it releases endorphins, the feel-good hormone.

3. **Actively relax your muscles**. Stress causes muscle strain, causing tension headaches, backaches, and fatigue. Fight these physical manifestations of stress by stretching, getting a massage or massaging yourself, taking warm baths, etc. (**Tip**: See TIPP on page 102, and do Paced Breathing with Muscle Relaxation.)

4. **Get enough sleep**. Adequate sleep is essential for managing stress and promoting overall health. (See also How to Establish a Sleep Routine, page 440.)

5. **Stay organized**. Keeping a schedule and staying organized can help reduce stress and improve productivity. Use a planner or organization system to create a daily routine to establish structure and reduce decision fatigue. You can use a simple notepad or journal or apps like Microsoft To Do or Trello.

6. **Take multiple mental breaks during the day**. Step away from your normal activities and allow yourself to relax and recharge. Examples: go for a short walk, do Take 5 (page 339), listen to music, do a 5-minute yoga routine, etc.

7. **Take breaks from social media and news consumption**. Constant exposure to negative news stories and social media can be overwhelming, contributing to feelings of stress and anxiety. Take breaks that promote relaxation, such as walking in nature, cuddling your pet, watering your plants, etc.

8. **Say "No."** Protect yourself, your time, and your sanity by learning the power of saying "No." It takes time and effort to heal from emotional eating, so focus on yourself now. If this is hard for you, start by saying "No" to small requests or invitations, and work up to bigger ones. For example, say, "*I can't join you for coffee, but thanks!*" before moving on to something like, "*I can't add any more to my workload.*" (See also Communicating Boundaries, page 391.)

Here are some other tips to help you say "No."

- **Use "I" statements** to explain why you say "No." For example, "*I'm unable to commit to that right now because I have other priorities.*"
- **Be clear and direct** when saying "No." It is important to be clear and direct in your response. Avoid being vague or giving mixed signals. For example, "*I can't accept that new task. I have enough on my plate right now.*"
- **Say "No" without being rude or aggressive**. Be firm but polite in your response, and avoid apologizing excessively or over-explaining yourself. For example, say, "*I can't join you guys for dinner this weekend because I already have plans,*" instead of, "*I'm so sorry! I already have plans this weekend. Oh my, I feel bad. Please don't be mad, guys.*"
- **Offer alternatives.** If you are declining an invitation or request, offer an alternative solution. For example, "*I can't make it to the party, but maybe we can grab coffee next week instead.*"

9. **Give yourself joy**. Engage in hobbies or activities that bring you happiness. Many people forego simple pleasures for various reasons: lack of time, fear of being judged, prioritizing others or other responsibilities, family or societal pressure, etc. However, life is too short not to enjoy it! So, even when your schedule is tight, find ways to do something for yourself (e.g., read a few pages of a book, shower and sing your heart out, dance while cooking, etc.)

10. **Connect with others.** Spend time with family and friends to promote feelings of connection and support. For example, call a friend or family member you have not talked to in a while or message people to say "Hi" and find out how they are doing.

11. **Practice gratitude**. Focus on the things you are grateful to shift your focus away from stress. (See also Reflection and Gratitude Practice, page 428.)

12. **Seek support if needed**. If stress becomes overwhelming, consider seeking support from a mental health professional or support group.

Chapter 8: Building a Support System

"Surround yourself with only people who are going to lift you higher."—Oprah Winfrey

Emotional eating involves using food as a coping mechanism for emotions; breaking that pattern can be very difficult without the help and support of others. Many people like to "carry the load" on their own. However, is it also not true that most people are more than willing to extend a helping hand when asked? So, remember that you do not need to suffer the weight of your healing journey alone. Reach out to others because they have the power to make your recovery easier.

Cultivate a Supportive Inner Voice (Self)

Before you seek support from others, ensure that you support your efforts. Developing a supportive inner voice is practicing self-compassion and learning to speak to yourself in a kind, encouraging, and supportive manner. It also entails treating any self-sabotaging behaviors.

Self-Sabotage – What You May Be THINKING

Several beliefs may be sabotaging your success with emotional eating, including:

All-or-nothing mentality. This is the belief that everything you do must be "perfect" to change your eating habits. This can lead to feelings of failure and frustration, leading to emotional eating.

> **What to do:** Shift your mindset from black or white to shades of gray. Accept that healing is not a linear process and that there will be good and bad moments. Do not worry about being perfect. Just do your best one step at a time.

Negative self-talk. Negative self-talk involves the critical and negative messages you tell yourself. This can include thoughts like "*I'll never be able to control my eating habits,*" "*I'm not good enough to make positive changes in my life,*" or "*I doubt I can do this.*"

> **What to do:** Practice <u>Self-Compassion, Self-Forgiveness, and Self-Validation</u>, page 365.

Believing that food is the ONLY WAY to cope with emotions. The word "comfort foods" exist for a reason, but food is NOT the only thing that can bring comfort and help you deal with your emotions.

> **What to do:** See the chapter on <u>Emotion Regulation</u>, page 364.

"I don't deserve..." mentality. There is a great deal of shame and guilt associated with emotional eating. As a result, you may develop the mindset that you do not deserve to be happy or do not deserve to take care of yourself or make good choices because you believe you are unworthy, flawed, or incompetent.

> **What to do:** Practice self-care, <u>self-compassion</u> (page 365), and building your <u>self-esteem</u> (page 390).

Self-Sabotage – What You May Be DOING

Apart from any self-sabotaging thoughts, you may also be countering your efforts by doing any of the following:

"Holding on" to unhealthy food items. As much as possible, remove all temptations in your home. Think: if you cannot see it, you cannot eat it. If you find it a waste to throw these food items, donate them.

Buying "emergency comfort foods." When grocery shopping, refrain from buying the things that you usually consume when you emotionally eat. Some people like to keep an "emergency stash," but you see, that means you are expecting yourself to fail. Instead, expect yourself to succeed! And if something truly unpleasant happens: practice [Mindfulness](page 55) + [Distress Tolerance](page 64) + [Emotion Regulation](page 364).

Staying around "enablers." Not everyone will be supportive of your journey. Some may not understand you; some may secretly envy you, while others may have unhealthy eating habits and feel uncomfortable or threatened by your healthier choices. Of course, it is unfortunate if the people you love do not support you. Still, it can be damaging if they undermine your efforts. Examples: a family member constantly offering unhealthy food or drinks, friends who encourage you to emotionally eat with them, co-workers who "joke" about you no longer being sociable because of your new eating habits, etc. The best way to handle these people is to steer clear of them. If this is not possible, limit the time you spend with them.

Build Your Support Circle (Others)

Support from others can provide a sense of accountability, encouragement, and motivation. Support from family, friends, or a support group can help you feel less alone in your struggle and provide a safe space to share experiences and emotions. It can also provide practical assistance, such as help with meal planning and preparation or finding alternative coping mechanisms.

Creating a support circle involves identifying people who can offer assistance. Here are some steps to help you create your support circle:

1. **Identify the support you need.** Consider what kind of support you need and what types of people can provide that support. Reflect on the list below to help you figure out what you need.

    ☐ **Moral support.** Do you need people who regularly check in to see how you are doing?

- ☐ **Physical support.** Do you need others' physical presence in your journey, such as a fitness buddy or another person trying to heal from emotional eating or an eating disorder?
- ☐ **Emotional support.** Do you need someone to listen to you, understand your journey, and talk you through your emotions?
- ☐ **Intellectual support.** Do you need someone who knows more than you know? Someone to give you tips and recommendations, or perhaps someone who has studied nutrition or eating behaviors.
- ☐ **Resource support.** Do you need someone who can provide tangible and practical support? Examples: driving you to and from fitness or workout classes, babysitting your kids so you have time for yourself, helping you grocery shop for healthy food, sharing access to exercise equipment, etc.

2. **Reach out to friends and family.** After you identify what kind(s) of support you need, consider reaching out to friends and family members you feel comfortable talking to and who have shown themselves to be supportive. Explain what you are going through and ask if they would be willing to offer their support.

3. **Join a support group.** Look for local support groups or online communities focusing on your specific struggles or interests. These can provide a great source of comfort and understanding as you connect with others with similar experiences. For example, visit the websites of national eating disorder organizations like the National Eating Disorders Association (NEDA) or Eating Disorder Hope and use their search tools to find emotional eating support groups in your area. You can also use apps like MeetUp to look for online support groups in your country.

4. **Be open to new relationships.** Be open to meeting new people and building relationships with those who share your interests or struggles. You never know who may become an important part of your support circle.

5. **Consider a therapist.** A licensed therapist or counselor can provide a safe and supportive environment to work through your challenges and help you build the skills

you need to heal. They can also help you identify additional resources or support that may be helpful.

As you go through the above steps, you may realize that certain people are not helpful (e.g., enables and saboteurs). In this case, you need to evaluate their presence in your life. If they are damaging to your journey, then perhaps it is time to let them go, at least for now.

Letting go of unsupportive people can be a difficult but necessary step to take. If you are struggling with this, here are some tips.

Firstly, **recognize and radically accept their impact** on your journey. Take a moment to reflect on how this unsupportive person affects your mental health, goals, and well-being. And even though it may be painful, acknowledge that their behavior is not conducive to your growth.

Secondly, try and **communicate your needs** if this is someone with whom you cannot or do not want to sever all ties (e.g., a close family member, childhood friend, etc.). Do not ghost these people and "disappear" from their lives. Let them know what you are going through, that their behavior is not helpful, and that you need their support. If communicating with an unsupportive person does not work, **set strong boundaries**. This may mean limiting your contact with them or avoiding certain topics when you are with them.

Lastly, if communicating your needs and setting boundaries do not work, it is time to **let them go with love**. Remember that you deserve to be surrounded by people who uplift and encourage you.
So, tell unsupportive people that you are prioritizing yourself right now, wish them well, and express your hope to possibly reconnect with them in the future.

Building a support system takes time and effort. It is important to be patient and persistent because you can make your healing journey easier with the right attitude and people by your side.

Chapter 9: Dealing with Setbacks and Relapses

"A setback is a setup for a comeback." — T.D. Jakes

Emotional eating can be difficult to break, and setbacks and relapses are common occurrences as you develop a healthier relationship with food. However, instead of feeling "defeated," it is important to recognize that setbacks and relapses are NOT signs of failure but a natural part of the healing process.

How to Prevent Setbacks

Social situations, such as parties, holidays, and family gatherings, can be challenging for those struggling with emotional eating. The abundance of food, pressure to indulge, and emotional triggers can make it difficult to keep up with your healthy eating habits. However, with the right strategies, navigating these situations and avoiding setbacks is possible.

One approach is to **plan ahead**. Before attending a social event, consider the types of foods that will be available and make a plan for what you will eat. Focus on healthy options, such as fruits and vegetables, lean protein, and whole grains. Bring a healthy dish to share, if possible, so you know at least one option will align with your goals.

If you are concerned more about the presence of certain people rather than the presence of certain food, again, plan ahead. Visualize encountering this person and what you are dreading from the conversation. Next, rehearse in your mind what you will say or do.

Who triggers you?

Example:
I always get triggered when my younger siblings ask why I still don't have "someone" in my life.

What is your plan for dealing with this person?

Example: (1) Do <u>STOP</u> (page 251). (2) If my sisters persist in nagging me, I'll say, "I feel ridiculed when you guys always comment about me not having a partner. Why do you do that?" or "When you guys joke about me, it takes the fun out of these gatherings for me. I want to enjoy coming here, so please stop doing that."

Important: When you visualize the conversation, practice your plan over and over in your head or role-play with someone you trust. This will give you the courage to do it when the time comes.

Another approach is to **practice mindfulness** before, during, and after social events. Take the time to savor and enjoy your food rather than mindlessly consuming it. Listen to your body's natural hunger and fullness cues, and take breaks between bites to allow your body to register when satisfied. Mindful eating is not just something to do at home. It is something you can apply all the time whenever you are eating.

Focus on socializing, not avoiding food. Instead of making the event all about food, focus on socializing and spending time with friends and family. Engage in conversation and activities that do not involve food.

Another strategy is to **enlist the support of others**. Tell your friends and family about your goals and ask for their support in sticking to them. If someone offers you food you do not want to eat, politely decline or ask for a smaller portion.

Remember, it is okay to indulge in moderation. If there is a particular food that you love and want to enjoy, allow yourself a small serving. The key is to avoid overindulging and to stay mindful of your choices.

How to Recover from a Setback

Setbacks can happen anytime during your emotional eating journey despite your efforts to avoid them. When they do, keep the following in mind:

1. **Practice radical acceptance (page 329).** If a setback or relapse occurs, accept it. Remember, this already happened; no power on earth can undo it. To think about it over and over only prolongs your suffering.

2. **Reframe your thinking: setbacks are a necessary part of progress.** Do not think of setbacks as a step backward. Think of them as just a momentary pause in your progress. For example, suppose you have not emotionally eaten for months. However, something unexpected and tragic happened, and you spent the previous night emotionally eating. You did not forget all you learned or wasted the efforts of the previous months, right? So, you did not step backward and undo all your hard work. What counts now is what you do next.

3. **Practice self-compassion and self-forgiveness.** Be kind and gentle with yourself when you experience a setback or relapse. Avoid self-blame and negative self-talk. Recognize that it is natural to have challenges and difficulties in recovery.

4. **Do you need a break?** Do not rush to bounce back. You may feel exhausted, disappointed, and unmotivated when a setback occurs. It is okay to take a little break. Note, though, that taking a break does not mean engaging in emotional eating. Give yourself some TLC (tender loving care) and tell yourself that the setback is something you need to experience. Additionally, do not take a break for too long, as this may worsen feelings of guilt or shame over the setback, or you might slip back into unhealthy eating habits.

5. **Reconnect with your motivation.** Reflect on why you started your journey toward emotional eating recovery in the first place. Reconnect with your motivation by reminding yourself of the negative consequences of continued emotional eating. For

example, consider how emotional eating has contributed to your weight gain and how this has negatively affected your ability to join family and friends in various physical activities (e.g., outdoor sports, gardening, etc.).

6. **Reflect on the trigger.** Identify the trigger that caused the setback or relapse. Was it a specific event, emotion, or thought? Understanding the trigger can help you create a plan to prevent future relapses.

    Example: Breaking up with my partner triggered my emotional eating.

7. **Reflect on what may have contributed to the setback apart from the trigger**. A relapse can be caused by a single trigger, but were there additional reasons for your emotional eating? For example, were you ill or under great stress, or do you not have a strong social network? If there are other contributing factors, see how you can address these as well.

    Example: The breakup happened while I had been stressed out about a major assignment at work for months. In the future, I must manage my stress better. I've always enjoyed yoga, but I've fallen out of practice over the years, and I believe I need to pick that up again.

8. **Create a plan**. Develop a plan for how you will get back on track. This might include revisiting the principles of mindful eating, scheduling more self-care time, or seeking professional support.

    Example: (1) I'll visit my family over the weekend. I need to be surrounded by people who are supportive "constants" in my life. (2) I'll revisit my meal planning and prepping efforts because these practices helped me last time.

9. **Learn from the setback.** Use the setback as an opportunity to learn and grow. Reflect on what worked and what did not work. Use this knowledge to make adjustments to your plan so that you can better cope with future challenges.

Example: I realize now that I became dependent on my partner, and our relationship became my only priority. If and when I get into another relationship, I'll make sure I have other people I give time and attention to in my life.

Setbacks and relapses are normal in the journey toward overcoming emotional eating. It is important to plan ahead to avoid them, but if they do occur, do not feel guilty or ashamed. Pick yourself up and carry on with your goals.

Chapter 10: Maintaining Long-Term Success

"Motivation is what gets you started. Habit is what keeps you going."—Jim Ryun

Maintaining a healthy relationship with food requires ongoing effort and commitment. Here we will cover key strategies and practices for sustaining your progress toward a healthier relationship with food.

Top 10 Strategies for Maintaining Healthy Eating Habits

1. **Continuously assess and manage your emotions**. As mentioned, emotions, pleasant and unpleasant, are what make us who we are. So, the goal is never to eliminate our feelings; the objective is how to better manage them. As such, it is important to always be "tuned in" with your emotions and identify any triggers that may lead to emotional eating. Also, whenever you desire to reach for food for comfort, turn to other coping mechanisms, such as journaling, practicing mindfulness, or engaging in stress-relieving activities.

2. **Embrace DBT concepts (Acceptance + Change) and skills (Mindfulness, Distress Tolerance, Emotion Regulation, and Interpersonal Effectiveness).** What you have learned here is not intended for one-time reading. Applying what you have read and practicing them when you do not need them is the key to applying them when necessary.

3. **Establish a healthy routine**. Establish a daily routine that includes healthy habits such as exercise, nutritious meals, and sufficient sleep. A routine can help you stay on track and make healthy choices easier and more automatic.

4. **Continue practicing mindful eating**. Make mindful eating a way of life. Eat with awareness, savor each drink and bite, and recognize hunger and fullness cues—all the time.

5. **Continue prioritizing yourself**. Accept that YOU are valuable and deserve a life free of the mental, emotional, physical, and financial costs associated with emotional eating. As you uplift yourself, it is possible that not everyone will support you, which is okay. Remember, this journey is yours, not theirs. So, establish boundaries, communicate what you need, and be okay with letting unsupportive people go, at least for now.

6. **Set realistic and achievable goals.** Breaking free from emotional eating or any other unhealthy behavior always seems like a mammoth task, leading you to feel overwhelmed. So, break long-term goals into smaller, manageable steps. And enjoy those small steps because each is part of your journey.

7. **Learn from setbacks**. Accept that setbacks and relapses are a normal part of the change process. Instead of feeling shame and regret, or getting mad, use setbacks as an opportunity to learn and grow.

8. **Stay connected with your support system**. Maintain contact with your support system, whether that is family, friends, or a therapist. Regular check-ins can help you stay accountable and motivated.

9. **Stay adaptable**. Be open to adjusting your goals and strategies as needed. Life is unpredictable, and circumstances may change, so it is important to be flexible and adaptable to maintain healthy habits.

10. **Set new goals!** Once you have achieved your initial goals, set new ones to continue growing and evolving in your recovery. For example, suppose your initial goal is to practice mindful eating. Once you are comfortable with it, aim to apply it daily. Now that you have a better appreciation for what you eat, perhaps the next goal is to try meal planning and prepping.

Celebrate Progress and Achievements with Non-Food Related Rewards

It is important to celebrate your progress for various reasons. Firstly, it **reinforces positive behaviors and habits** because it helps to solidify the connection between your efforts and the positive outcomes you have achieved, making it more likely that you will continue engaging in those behaviors. It also **contributes to your self-awareness**. Celebrating your progress is an opportunity to reflect on your journey and better understand your strengths and capabilities.

Celebrating your achievements, big and small, also **helps you maintain your commitment** to freedom from emotional eating. By acknowledging and honoring your progress, you create a positive association with the process of personal growth and transformation, making it more likely that you will continue working towards your goals.

But how do you celebrate? Many grow up associating progress, success, and milestones with food. However, while these associations are deeply ingrained, it is time for you to challenge them to develop healthier habits. Look at the list below, start reshaping your perception of success, and find other meaningful ways to celebrate your achievements.

Following are 35 non-food-related rewards. Check which ones appeal to you or are the easiest for you to do. Please feel free to add other ideas as well in the space provided.

- ☐ Take a bubble bath.
- ☐ Get a massage.
- ☐ Buy a new book.
- ☐ Watch a movie.
- ☐ Take a nap.
- ☐ Listen to music.
- ☐ Buy a new piece of clothing.
- ☐ Go for a walk.
- ☐ Treat yourself to a manicure or pedicure.

- ☐ Go on a weekend getaway.
- ☐ Visit a museum or art gallery.
- ☐ Buy a new plant for your home or office.
- ☐ Attend a concert or live performance.
- ☐ Take a yoga class.
- ☐ Buy yourself a new piece of jewelry.
- ☐ Spend time with a friend.
- ☐ Get a new haircut or style.
- ☐ Take a day trip to a nearby city or attraction.
- ☐ Start planning a vacation.
- ☐ Buy a new piece of art or home décor.
- ☐ Take a cooking class.
- ☐ Sign up for a dance class.
- ☐ Treat yourself to a spa day.
- ☐ Take a photography class.
- ☐ Buy a new journal or planner.
- ☐ Attend a sports game or event.
- ☐ Start meal planning and prepping.
- ☐ Let go of unsupportive people.
- ☐ Go on a hike.
- ☐ Visit a friend living in a different city.
- ☐ Spend a day exploring a new town or city.
- ☐ Try a new hobby or craft.
- ☐ Sign up for a fitness class or program.
- ☐ Buy yourself a new piece of technology or gadget.
- ☐ Spend a day volunteering for a cause you care about.
- ☐ Others:

_____
_____
_____
_____

Reflection and Gratitude Practice

As mentioned, emotional eating is about coping with difficult emotions or situations. By practicing reflection and gratitude, you can learn to identify and acknowledge your feelings more healthily, helping you avoid turning to food for comfort.

Reflection can help you become more aware of your emotional triggers and patterns, helping you develop strategies to manage them. By reflecting on past experiences and emotions, you can gain insight into *why* you turn to food for comfort or distraction and work on developing healthier coping mechanisms.

Gratitude can also be a powerful tool for managing emotional eating. When you focus on the good things in your life and cultivate a sense of gratitude, you are more likely to feel positive and hopeful, reducing your stress levels and making you less likely to turn to food to ease your stress.

Worksheet: Reflection and Gratitude

Here is a simple reflection and gratitude exercise that you can try:

1. Find a quiet and comfortable space where you will not be interrupted. Sit down and take a few deep breaths to center yourself.

2. Reflect on your day or week. Think about the things you accomplished, the challenges you faced, and the people you interacted with. Try to focus on the positive aspects of your experiences.

   Where are your thoughts taking you?
   Example: *I'm proud of myself for changing my eating patterns and how I feel about food.*
   _____
   _____
   _____

3. Take out a notebook or journal and write down three things you are grateful for. These can be big or small things, such as a supportive friend, a sunny day, or a good cup of coffee.

   What are you grateful for?
   Example: *(1) The incredible sense of well-being I felt following a brisk 20-minute walk before breakfast this morning. (2) My mother, who approves wholeheartedly of my recent lifestyle changes. (3) No waiting in line at the grocery store.*
   (1) _____
   (2) _____
   (3) _____

4. Next, write down one thing you could have done differently today or this week. Be honest with yourself, but also be kind and gentle.

What could you have done better?

Example: *I could have prioritized getting enough sleep better this week.*

_____
_____
_____

5. Reflect on what you wrote down in Step 4 above. Next, write down what steps you can take to do better. Remember to break down any goals into small, achievable ones.

How should I improve on what I wrote down in Step 4?

Examples: *I should stop browsing the news and social media sites on my phone when I go to bed.*

_____
_____
_____

6. Finish the exercise by setting an intention for the next day or week. This could be a goal you want to achieve, a habit you want to develop, or a positive attitude you want to cultivate.

What is your intention for tomorrow?

Example: *I will stop browsing the news and social media sites on my phone tonight. Tomorrow, I will buy a puzzle book to take to bed in case I can't sleep right away.*

_____
_____
_____

What is your intention for next week?

Example: *I intend to start a sleep routine.*

Remember, reflection and gratitude are powerful tools for cultivating a positive mindset and reducing stress and anxiety. By taking a few minutes each day to reflect on the good things in your life and set positive intentions, you can improve your overall well-being and increase your resilience in the face of challenges.

Conclusion

""Believe you can, and you're halfway there."
— Theodore Roosevelt

Emotional eating may not be an official "disorder," but that does not mean healing from it is easy. Why? Because it is never easy to face one's emotions and address the reasons—the real reasons—behind them. However, as someone who has relied on food for comfort for many years, I can say from experience that there is hope. Believe in yourself, do the work and you WILL recover from emotional eating and feel better.

In my quest to heal from my mental health difficulties and emotional eating, I have read many books, tried many tips, talked to a few psychotherapists, and even studied psychology. Through it all, I discovered Dr. Marsha Linehan's Dialectical Behavior Therapy (DBT) to be crucial to my recovery. I hope you find it as beneficial as I have.

Here is a quick recap of what we covered in this book:

- Understanding Emotional Eating: emotional eating is coping with emotions or situations and has nearly nothing to do with food or physical hunger.
- Dialectical Behavior Therapy: DBT primary concepts (Acceptance and Change) and its primary skills (Mindfulness, Distress Tolerance, Emotion Regulation, and Interpersonal Effectiveness).
- Mindfulness: the DBT skill that teaches awareness and how mindful eating (eating without judgment or distraction) can help you develop a healthier relationship with food.
- Distress Tolerance: the DBT skill that teaches you how to survive a crisis. This is what you need to overcome moments when you feel a strong impulse or urge to reach for food to cope with your emotions.

- Emotion Regulation: the DBT skill that teaches you how to recognize and manage your emotions effectively. It is what you need to understand WHY you want to reach for food and why doing so is unhelpful in addressing the emotions and situations causing you to emotionally eat.
- Interpersonal Effectiveness: the DBT skill that teaches you how to make conversations and interactions effective. "Effective" means being more successful in getting what you want from a conversation.
- Developing Healthy Habits: this chapter discusses how taking care of your physical and emotional well-being helps prevent emotional eating. It discusses the importance of developing healthier food and eating habits, meal planning and prepping, incorporating exercise into your life, and dealing with everyday stress.
- Building a Support System: this chapter provides important tips on preventing possible self-sabotaging thoughts and actions and building an amazing internal (self) and external (others) support system.
- Dealing with Setbacks and Relapses: this section helps you prevent setbacks and how to bounce back from them when they do happen.
- Maintaining Long-Term Success: this section provides tips on maintaining a healthy relationship with food and recovering from emotional eating for good.

Appendix

Emotional Eating Self-Assessment Quiz

This emotional eating self-assessment quiz is meant to help you determine if you tend to eat in response to emotions rather than physical hunger.

Important: Please note that the results of this quiz are not intended to be a substitute for professional medical advice, diagnosis, or treatment. It is solely for informational and educational purposes. It should not be used as a basis for any decision or action regarding your health. If you are experiencing any symptoms or concerns related to emotional eating, please seek the advice of a qualified healthcare professional.

Please answer the questions below to the best of your ability.

1) **Do you find yourself eating more when you feel stressed, anxious, or upset?**
   a) Yes, all the time
   b) Sometimes
   c) Rarely
   d) Never

2) **Do you tend to eat even when you are not hungry?**
   a) Yes, all the time
   b) Sometimes
   c) Rarely
   d) Never

3) **Do you feel guilty or ashamed after eating emotionally?**
   a) Yes, all the time
   b) Sometimes
   c) Rarely
   d) Never

4) **Do you eat to distract yourself from unpleasant emotions?**
    a) Yes, all the time
    b) Sometimes
    c) Rarely
    d) Never

5) **Do you eat when you are bored?**
    a) Yes, all the time
    b) Sometimes
    c) Rarely
    d) Never

6) **Do you find yourself eating more when you are alone?**
    a) Yes, all the time
    b) Sometimes
    c) Rarely
    d) Never

7) **Do you tend to eat quickly and not really taste your food?**
    a) Yes, all the time
    b) Sometimes
    c) Rarely
    d) Never

8) **Do you crave specific foods when you are feeling emotional?**
    a) Yes, all the time
    b) Sometimes
    c) Rarely
    d) Never

9) **Do you eat to reward yourself?**
   a) Yes, all the time
   b) Sometimes
   c) Rarely
   d) Never

10) **Do you feel like you cannot control your eating when you start?**
    a) Yes, all the time
    b) Sometimes
    c) Rarely
    d) Never

11) **Do you feel like your emotions are driving your eating habits?**
    a) Yes, all the time
    b) Sometimes
    c) Rarely
    d) Never

12) **Do you often eat until you feel uncomfortably full?**
    a) Yes, all the time
    b) Sometimes
    c) Rarely
    d) Never

Scoring:

You can score the quiz by assigning the following point values to each answer:
- Always - 3 points
- Often - 2 points
- Sometimes - 1 point
- Never - 0 points

What your total score indicates:

- 0-5 points: Low likelihood of emotional eating
- 6-11 points: Mild likelihood of emotional eating
- 12-23 points: Moderate likelihood of emotional eating
- 24-36 points: High likelihood of emotional eating

The Clean Your Plate Syndrome

The Clean Your Plate (CYP) mentality refers to the idea that one should eat all the food on their plate, regardless of whether they are still hungry or not. Also called "consumption closure," this mentality is often instilled in individuals from a young age to prevent wasting food and encourage gratitude for having enough to eat.

I can definitely relate to the CYP mentality. We are constantly reminded of the significance of avoiding food waste in China. And because my parents grew up poor, this was a prevalent theme in our household during meals. A Chinese teacher once told me that her mother said every grain of rice she did not eat would turn into a mole on her face!

Unfortunately, the CYP mentality can lead to emotional eating because food is now closely linked to feelings of economy and gratitude rather than fuel for the body. And if you do not comply, feelings of guilt or shame may follow. This, again, promotes the emotional eating cycle. So, if you have a CYP mentality like me, here are some tips to help you stop it.

Top 10 Tips to Stop Cleaning Your Plate

1) **Take 5.** Develop the habit of doing the Take 5 breathing exercise (page 339) before eating. It will relax your nervous system and improve your digestion and metabolism. It will also center you and make you more mindful of what you put on your plate and in your mouth. (If you cannot do the whole five minutes, do five breath cycles before eating.)

2) **Do not feel guilty about not cleaning your plate.** There is no need to finish everything on your plate. If you are concerned about wastage, do not be. Save leftovers for later or compost any excess food.

3) **Consider the consequences.** Remind yourself that overeating leads to discomfort. Also, research shows that the CYP mentality can lead to larger waistlines.[184] By not finishing your plate, you are practicing self-care.

4) **Use smaller plates**. Smaller plates mean less food to put on them. This way, you are "cleaning your plate" without necessarily overeating.

5) **Serve yourself smaller portions**. When serving yourself, start with smaller portions. Avoid returning for seconds until you have given yourself time to assess whether you are still physically hungry. When dining out or ordering in, ask for smaller portions. In Thailand and Japan, asking for less rice or noodles is common. This way, you remove the chance of ending up with more food than you need.

6) **Slow down and savor your food**. Eat slowly and mindfully. (See also [Mindful Eating](), page 345.) Give your brain a chance to tell you that you are full.

7) **Do not eat in front of distractions**. Avoid eating while working on your computer, watching TV, or checking your mobile phone. These activities can distract you from your food and cause you to get second helpings you do not need.

8) **Pay attention to your hunger cues**. Listen to your body and stop eating when you feel full. To avoid CYP guilt, remind yourself that leaving food on your plate is okay if you are already satisfied.

9) **Practice saying, "No, thank you."** Politely decline offers for more food or dessert if you feel full or satisfied. If someone insists and still puts food on your plate, leave it. If they ignore your "no," then feel free to ignore their actions. This is also a sign for them to take your objections seriously next time.

10) **Doggy bag it!** If you are eating out and the serving size is too big, do not feel compelled to finish your food. Ask for a doggy bag instead.

How to Establish a Sleep Routine

Sleep is one of the most underrated components of a healthy lifestyle. We take it for granted, not realizing how much harm we do ourselves by not getting the recommended 7 to 9 hours of sleep we should have each night.

One of the best ways to get the quality sleep we need is to establish a sleep routine. Following are some tips to accomplish this.

1. **Go to bed and wake up at the same time daily** to establish a regular sleep rhythm.

2. **Reserve your bed for sleep and romance.**

3. **Establish a clutter-free, peaceful, tranquil environment that promotes sleep**. Your bedroom should be a haven of peace and tranquility at the end of a long day.

4. Create **complete darkness and silence** (eyeshades and earplugs are useful instruments). Remove or cover any illuminated clocks or digital electronic displays.

5. **Get at least twenty minutes of sunlight exposure daily**, especially first thing in the morning. Sunlight penetrates your eyes and causes your brain to release hormones such as melatonin, which is essential for good sleep cycles and mood balance. If you live somewhere where the sun is scarce at certain times of the year, like I do in Canada, consider investing in a light therapy lamp to help reset your circadian rhythm.

6. **Do not eat within three hours of going to bed.** A large dinner before bedtime will result in a restless night's sleep. Energy will be diverted to digesting your meal rather than the repair and mending that is supposed to occur at night. Eating too late is also a foolproof method to gain weight since your body will store the food (as fat) rather than burn it.

7. **Avoid using bright, stimulating screens before going to bed.** Using electronic gadgets in bed changes the normal sleep molecules in your brain. Do not check your e-mail, read on your iPad, or check your phone. Watching television straight before bed can also greatly disrupt sleep. If you must use it to check something important, ensure your device has a blue light filtering app installed, such as Twilight for your phone or f.lux for your laptop.

8. **Allow an hour (or at least twenty minutes) for total relaxation.** To prepare your thoughts for sleep, listen to quiet music or read something pleasant in bed. You might also try some simple yoga stretches or breathing exercises.

9. **Make a list of your concerns.** Are you ruminating or worried about something? Get up and start writing them down. Mentally unload whatever is disturbing your sleep, and then return to bed. (**Tip**: Keep a notepad or journal beside your bed for such moments.)

10. **Cool down your bedroom.** Room temperatures between 60 and 67°F are ideal for Rapid Eye Movement (REM) sleep, which occurs during the stages of dreaming, learning, memory, emotional processing, and healthy brain growth. If your room is too hot or cold, you'll wake up frequently, preventing you from attaining REM and deep, restorative sleep.

11. **Warm up your core.** This boosts your core temperature and aids in activating the right chemistry for sleep. A hot water bottle, heating pad, or your partner's warm body can help.

12. **Avoid sleep-interfering drugs.** Sedatives such as antihistamines, stimulants, cold medications, steroids, and caffeine-containing headache remedies should be avoided. These medications eventually disrupt natural sleep patterns.

How to Support an Emotional Eater

If you have a friend or loved one trying to heal from emotional eating, know your support is an important factor in their journey. Here are some of the ways you can support them:

1. **Acknowledge how difficult their journey is for them.** Understanding and support come after acknowledgment. Often, it is difficult for people to offer support because they cannot relate to the issue. However, keep in mind that this is *their* story, *their* journey. You need not be an emotional eater to love and support one.

2. **Be non-judgmental and empathetic.** It is essential to be compassionate towards your friend or loved one. Do not judge their previous choices and criticize them, but support their intention to improve.

3. **Listen actively.** Show genuine concern and support by encouraging them to talk about their emotions, what triggers their emotional eating, and what struggles they are going through in their journey. Pay attention to what they are expressing, and avoid interrupting them as they speak. Remember, the goal of active listening is to walk away from the conversation with a complete understanding of the other person's point of view.

4. **Help them identify healthy coping mechanisms.** Emotional eaters may not be aware of alternative ways to deal with their emotions. Help them identify healthy coping mechanisms like exercising, meditating, journaling, starting a new hobby, etc. If possible for you, offer your time. For example, if they are shy or unsure about joining a nearby gym, offer to join and attend classes with them.

5. **Encourage healthy eating habits**. Be a positive influence by suggesting nutritious meals and snacks that are satisfying and healthy. Encourage them to eat slowly, savor their food, and stop when full (mindful eating). If you are not into these things yourself, the best thing you can do is to at least not be an enabler of emotional eating. For

example, avoid consuming unhealthy foods and drinks in front of them; refrain from mentioning people or events that you know trigger them, etc.

6. **Offer the support they need**. Let your friend or loved one know that you are there to support them in the way they want to be supported. (See the different kinds of support you can offer on page 415.)

You can also ask them open-ended questions such as "*How can I help you?*", "*What do you need from me?*" or "*What are you struggling with the most?*" to explore the support that would benefit them the most and that you can give.

But what if your friend or loved one says they do not want your help? Respect their wishes but **keep checking in on them**. Even if they avoid the subject, you can still support them by being there. For instance, you could ask them if they want to go for a walk, watch a movie, join a class together, etc. If you feel they are more open to discussing their struggles, you can ask questions like, "*How are you? Anything you want to share?*" or "*I won't nag you. Just let me know if you need anything, okay?*"

Here are some other messages your friend or loved one might appreciate hearing from you.

I'm here to listen.
You're not alone.
Your feelings are valid.
It's not just about willpower.
Your health and well-being matter.
I don't understand it, but I'll be here anyway.
Do what makes you happy.
You're stronger than you think.
You can do this!
You don't have to do this alone.

It is admirable that you want to help someone recovering from emotional eating, but please keep the following in mind.

Support does not mean taking over. When you support someone, you offer guidance, encouragement, and assistance—that is it. Empowering them to make their own decisions and taking ownership of their journey is crucial. Taking over completely can inadvertently undermine their sense of autonomy, self-efficacy, and personal growth.

In contrast, by allowing them to navigate their challenges and make their own choices, you are enabling them to develop problem-solving skills, resilience, and independence. It also shows respect for their abilities and acknowledges their capacity to handle their affairs.

Practice self-care. Supporting someone trying to unlearn a maladaptive behavior can be draining and affect your mental, emotional, and physical well-being. As such, be sure to take care of yourself by practicing self-care activities that you find effective, such as meditating, exercising, getting enough sleep, etc. This also means taking a break from your friend or loved one when needed. However, please do not ghost them. Instead, say something like, "*I need some time off, so I won't be available for a while. However, know I support you, so you'll hear from me when I return.*"

Review Request

If you enjoyed this book or found it useful…

I'd like to ask you for a quick favor:

Please share your thoughts and leave a quick REVIEW. Your feedback matters and helps me make improvements to provide the best books possible.

Reviews are so helpful to both readers and authors, so any help would be greatly appreciated! You can leave a review here:

https://tinyurl.com/complete-dbt-review

Or by scanning the QR code below:

Also, please join my ARC team to get early access to my releases.

https://barretthuang.com/arc-team/

THANK YOU!

Further Reading

Be sure to check out my other bestselling DBT books in the Mental Health Therapy series. Here are some of the titles you can find:

- DBT Workbook for Adults
- DBT Workbook for Kids
- DBT Workbook for Teens
- The DBT Anger Management Workbook
- DBT Workbook for PTSD
- DBT Workbook for BPD
- DBT Workbook for Depression

You can get them here:

https://tinyurl.com/mental-health-therapy

About the Author

Barrett Huang is an author and businessman. Barrett spent years discovering the best ways to manage his OCD, overcoming his anxiety, and learning to embrace life. Through his writing, he hopes to share his knowledge with readers, empowering people of all backgrounds with the tools and strategies they need to improve their mental wellbeing and be happy and healthy.

When not writing or running his business, Barrett loves to spend his time studying. He has majored in psychology and completed the DBT skills certificate course by Dr. Marsha Linehan. Barrett's idol is Bruce Lee, who said, "The key to immortality is first living a life worth remembering."

Learn more about Barrett's books here:
https://barretthuang.com/

Index

Acceptance, 51, 192, 194, 195, 196, 198, 200, 202, 212, 217, 238, 239, 240, 242, 243, 293
Acceptance + Change, 339, 427
Acceptance and Change, 44, 56, 115, 143, 293, 332, 333, 435
Aggravated, 29, 30
Amygdala, 26, 38, 39, 147, 186
Anterior cingulate cortex, 38, 39
Anxiety, 16, 17, 33, 36, 39, 47, 57, 68, 74, 131, 141, 319, 325, 328, 332, 356, 376, 381, 407, 414, 434
Avoidance, 178, 182, 185, 239
Avoidance Coping, 182, 239, 261
Awareness, 21, 57, 100, 151
Behavioral avoidance, 239
Binge eating disorder, 322
Binge-eating, 322
Bipolar disorder, 193
Bipolar Disorder, 31
Borderline, 25, 43, 149, 453
Borderline Personality Disorder, 17, 19, 25, 31, 37, 89, 143, 144, 146, 329, 332
Boredom, 316, 328, 357, 363, 368, 376, 384, 390, 412
Boundaries, 392, 394, 396, 420, 428
BPD, 19, 20, 21, 22, 25, 26, 27, 28, 29, 30, 31, 32, 33, 34, 35, 36, 37, 38, 39, 40, 41, 42, 43, 44, 45, 66, 89, 90, 91, 101, 106, 115, 125, 128, 131, 136, 137, 139, 143, 144, 145, 146, 147, 149, 329, 332, 333, 453
BPD Self-Assessment, 144
CBT, 33, 34, 43, 192, 319, 332
Change, 192, 193, 194
Check the Facts, 270
Chronic diseases, 331
Clean Your Plate, 328, 379, 441
Cognitive Behavior Therapy, 319
Cognitive Behavioral Therapy, 33, 181, 192
Comorbid PTSD, 180
Complex PTSD, 180
Compulsions, 16, 17

Content Warning, 17, 22, 45, 66, 89, 136, 139, 163, 167, 170, 174, 176, 185, 188, 216
c-PTSD, 180
Criticism or judgment triggers, 41
CYP, 441, 442
DBT, 17, 22, 24, 33, 35, 43, 44, 45, 46, 48, 51, 56, 57, 72, 73, 83, 89, 90, 94, 101, 115, 129, 131, 143, 151, 162, 163, 164, 166, 167, 169, 176, 181, 183, 189, 192, 193, 194, 196, 197, 202, 203, 212, 217, 222, 233, 238, 239, 243, 244, 252, 276, 288, 291, 293, 319, 320, 332, 333, 334, 339, 340, 392, 405, 427, 435, 436, 453
DBT Exercise
  ACCEPTS, 105
  Box Breathing, 99
DEARMAN, 85, 131, 397
Decision fatigue, 408, 414
Depression, 16, 19, 22, 31, 36, 37, 47, 57, 65, 72, 76, 131, 162, 164, 170, 172, 180, 183, 189, 190, 196, 233, 239, 252, 318, 319, 325, 328, 329, 332, 381, 407
Depressive, 29, 30, 32
Desire to change, 336, 338
Desire to Change, 48, 51
Diagnostic and Statistical Manual for Mental Disorders, 25
Diagnostic and Statistical Manual of Mental Disorders, 27, 139
Dialectical Behavior Therapy, 17, 22, 33, 35, 43, 89, 162, 181, 183, 319, 320, 327, 332, 435
Dialectics, 43
Dieting history, 328
Dissociative PTSD, 180
Distress, 339, 340, 356, 357, 384, 396, 418, 427, 435
Distress tolerance, 356, 357
Distress Tolerance, 56, 65, 67, 73, 82, 101, 115, 129, 141, 143, 152, 202, 211, 212, 220, 238, 252, 266, 276, 293
Dr. Linehan, 24, 43, 44

Dr. Marsha Linehan, 24, 43, 143, 169
DSM-5, 27, 139
DSM-III, 25
Electroconvulsive therapy, 43
Emotion regulation, 339, 340, 368, 417, 418, 427, 435, 436
Emotion Regulation, 56, 72, 73, 115, 143, 202, 215, 217, 238, 266, 275, 293
Emotional abuse, 22
Emotional avoidance, 239
Emotional eater, 322, 329, 339, 341, 353, 368, 369, 394, 445
Emotional eating, 316, 317, 319, 320, 321, 322, 324, 325, 326, 327, 328, 329, 330, 331, 333, 335, 336, 341, 348, 353, 356, 357, 358, 368, 369, 370, 372, 376, 377, 378, 379, 381, 384, 389, 390, 391, 392, 393, 394, 402, 404, 405, 406, 407, 408, 409, 411, 413, 414, 416, 417,419, 421, 424, 425, 426, 427, 428, 429, 431, 435, 436, 437, 440, 441, 445, 446
Emotional hunger, 323, 324, 363, 367
Emotional instability, 28
Emotional invalidation, 22, 26
Emotional Mind, 61, 62, 248, 249, 266, 354
Emotional support, 392, 419
Emotional urge, 113, 114
Emotionally Unstable Personality Disorder, 26
Emptiness, 19, 28, 30
EUPD, 26
Eye Movement Desensitization and Reprocessing Therapy, 182
FAST, 402
Fatigue, 330
Food journal, 377, 378, 408
GAD, 16, 20, 32, 33, 38, 47, 76, 90, 162, 181, 190, 252, 317, 318, 319, 329
General Anxiety Disorder, 16, 162, 252, 317, 329
Genetics, 328
GIVE, 400
Gochisosama, 346
Gratitude, 346, 381, 393, 415, 431, 432, 434, 441
Grounding, 68

Grounding Grid, 361
Happy eating, 357
Healing Statement, 51
Hippocampus, 187
Hyper-Reactivity, 178
Immune system, 331
Impulsive, 28, 29, 31
Inflammation, 325, 330, 331
Insomnia, 330
Intellectual support, 419
Interpersonal effectiveness, 339, 340, 391, 392, 393, 427, 435, 436
Interpersonal Effectiveness, 56, 83, 131, 143, 202, 232, 233, 238, 275, 293
Interpersonal relationships, 26
Intrusive Symptoms, 177
Invalidation, 276
Itadakimasu, 346
Learned behavior, 320, 326, 391
Learned Optimism, 76
Lethargic, 29, 30
Loneliness, 316, 317, 357, 376, 381, 390, 393
Low self-esteem, 327
Mammalian Dive Response, 253
Marsha M. Linehan, 332, 333, 339, 356, 435
MBT, 35
Meal planning, 389, 408, 409, 418, 425, 428, 430, 436
Meal prepping, 389, 408, 409, 410, 411, 425, 428, 430, 436
Mental health, 329
Mentalization-based Therapy, 35
Mindful eating, 339, 345, 346, 347, 348, 405, 413, 422, 425, 427, 428, 435, 445
Mindfulness, 56, 57, 58, 63, 75, 86, 94, 115, 129, 141, 143, 202, 205, 207, 209, 210, 238, 243, 252, 266, 277, 279, 293, 339, 340, 341, 347, 398, 413, 418, 422, 427, 435
Mindless eating, 330
Moral support, 418
Negative Changes in Mood and Thoughts, 178
Non-judgmental, 346, 445
Nutrient deficiencies, 331

Obsessions, 16
Obsessive-Compulsive Disorder, 16, 32, 317
OCD, 16, 20, 32, 33, 38, 47, 76, 90, 131, 162, 181, 190, 252, 317, 318, 319
Opposite Action, 384, 385
Paired muscle relaxation, 367
Physical health, 328, 329
Physical hunger, 321, 323, 324, 328, 352, 407, 435, 437
Physical support, 419
Poor digestion, 330
Post-Traumatic Stress Disorder, 329
Prefrontal cortex, 26, 38, 39
Prefrontal Cortex, 187
Prolonged Exposure Therapy, 182
Psychotherapy, 319
PTSD, 162, 163, 164, 166, 167, 170, 171, 172, 173, 174, 175, 176, 177, 179, 180, 181, 182, 183, 185, 186, 187, 188, 189, 190, 211, 215, 216, 238, 239, 243, 252, 253, 266, 273, 275, 276, 290, 291, 293, 296, 299, 303, 329
PTSD Self-Evaluation, 296
Radical acceptance, 333, 334, 335, 336, 338, 424
Radical Acceptance, 44, 46, 47, 49, 63, 91, 194
Reasonable Mind, 61, 62, 354
Reasoning Mind, 248, 249, 266
Re-Experiencing, 177, 182
Reflection, 415, 431, 432, 434
Relapses, 421, 425, 426, 428
Relationship triggers, 41
Re-parenting, 34
Resource support, 419
Risky behavior, 28
Safe Space, 23
Safety, 167, 238
Schema-focused therapy, 34, 35
Schizophrenia, 43, 193
Self-awareness, 378, 429
Self-care, 393, 417, 425, 441, 447
Self-compassion, 369, 371, 375, 393, 407, 416, 417, 424
Self-destructive, 29
Self-esteem, 393
Self-forgiveness, 369, 373, 424
Self-harm, 22, 28, 30, 31, 41, 139, 140, 141
Self-sabotage, 416, 417
Self-validation, 369, 370, 375
Setbacks, 320, 421, 424, 426, 428, 436
Skin problems, 330
Sleep, 227, 228
Sleep routine, 390, 413, 443
Sleep Routine, 229, 300, 301
Stigma, 149
STOP, 363, 422
Stress, 177, 322, 327, 356, 413
Stress eating, 322
Substance abuse, 27
Suicidal ideation, 28
Support circle, 418
Support system, 420, 428, 436
Take 5, 349, 361, 367, 396, 414, 441
TASTE, 352
The Happiness Advantage, 381
TIPP, 366, 413
Trauma, 22, 41, 327
Trauma Resiliency, 294
Trauma triggers, 41
Trigger Journal, 42, 128, 151
Triggering Event, 128
Turning the Mind, 53, 92
Uncomplicated PTSD, 180
Weight gain, 329
Willpower, 326, 327, 374, 446
Wise Mind, 61, 62, 70, 129, 141, 248, 249, 250, 257, 266, 353, 355
Worksheet
  Trigger Journal, 151
Worksheet: 1:2 Breathing, 246
Worksheet: 4-7-8 Breathing, 100, 344
Worksheet: 5-4-3-2-1 Grounding Technique, 213
Worksheet: A Mindfulness Habit, 207
Worksheet: ABCDE, 81
Worksheet: Acceptance + Change, 200
Worksheet: ACCEPTS, 105, 258
Worksheet: Accumulate, Build, Cope (ABC), 218
Worksheet: Belly Breathing, 60, 342
Worksheet: Better Sleep Using Your 5 Senses, 303

Worksheet: Box Breathing, 59, 206
Worksheet: Check the Facts, 116, 267
Worksheet: Communicating Boundaries, 394
Worksheet: COPE AHEAD, 128
Worksheet: DEARMAN, 85, 234, 277, 397
Worksheet: Desire to Change, 50, 93, 199, 337
Worksheet: FAST, 136, 284, 402
Worksheet: GIVE, 132, 281, 400
Worksheet: Grounding Activities, 102
Worksheet: Identifying Your Emotional Triggers, 377
Worksheet: IMPROVE, 109
Worksheet: Into the Cold, 253
Worksheet: Mindful Body Scan (Self-Observation), 99
Worksheet: Mindful Body Scanning, 251
Worksheet: Mindful Eating, 349
Worksheet: Mindfulness Using Your Five Senses, 97
Worksheet: Nadi Shodhana (Alternate Nostril Breathing), 247
Worksheet: One-Mindfully, 95
Worksheet: Opposite Action, 119, 384
Worksheet: Opposite to Emotion, 271
Worksheet: PASS Kit (Panic Anxiety Stress Support Kit), 263
Worksheet: PLEASE, 122, 222, 389
Worksheet: Problem Solving, 273
Worksheet: PROs and CONs, 113
Worksheet: Radical Acceptance, 49, 198, 335
Worksheet: Radical Acceptance and Desire to Change, 51, 338
Worksheet: Radical Acceptance of Trauma, 242
Worksheet: Radical Acceptance of Triggers, 91
Worksheet: Reflection and Gratitude, 432
Worksheet: Self-Compassion, 371
Worksheet: Self-Forgiveness, 372
Worksheet: Self-Soothe Using Your Five Senses, 68, 359
Worksheet: Self-Validation, 374
Worksheet: STOP, 70, 255, 363
Worksheet: Take 5, 343
Worksheet: TASTE, 352
Worksheet: The Grounding Grid, 361
Worksheet: The Grounding Wheel, 214
Worksheet: The Happiness Habit, 74, 381
Worksheet: TIPP, 103, 264, 366
Worksheet: Turning the Mind, 53
Worksheet: Wise Mind, 62, 248, 353

References

1 Linehan, M. M. (2015). *DBT Skills Training Manual*. The Guilford Press.

2 Friedel, R. O. (2004). *Borderline personality disorder demystified: An essential guide to understanding and living with BPD*. Marlowe & Co.

3 Skoglund, C., Tiger, A., Rück, C., Petrovic, P., Asherson, P., Hellner, C., Mataix-Cols, D., & Kuja-Halkola, R. (2019). Familial risk and heritability of diagnosed borderline personality disorder: A register study of the Swedish population. *Molecular Psychiatry*, 26(3), 999–1008. https://doi.org/10.1038/s41380-019-0442-0

4 U.S. Department of Health and Human Services. (n.d.). *Borderline personality disorder*. National Institute of Mental Health. Retrieved February 1, 2023, from https://www.nimh.nih.gov/health/topics/borderline-personality-disorder

5 Lee, S. S., Keng, S.-L., Yeo, G. C., & Hong, R. Y. (2022). Parental invalidation and its associations with borderline personality disorder symptoms: A multivariate meta-analysis. *Personality Disorders: Theory, Research, and Treatment*, 13(6), 572–582. https://doi.org/10.1037/per0000523

6 Group, T. M. P. (n.d.). *About dr. Theodore Millon*. The Millon Personality Group. Retrieved February 1, 2023, from https://www.millonpersonality.com/dr-millon/

7 Ding, J. B., & Hu, K. (2021). Structural MRI brain alterations in borderline personality disorder and bipolar disorder. *Cureus*. https://doi.org/10.7759/cureus.16425

8 Fornaro, M., Orsolini, L., Marini, S., De Berardis, D., Perna, G., Valchera, A., Ganança, L., Solmi, M., Veronese, N., & Stubbs, B. (2016). The prevalence and predictors of bipolar and borderline personality disorders comorbidity: Systematic Review and meta-analysis. *Journal of Affective Disorders*, 195, 105–118. https://doi.org/10.1016/j.jad.2016.01.040

9 Jordanova, V., & Rossin, P. (2010). Borderline personality disorder often goes undetected. The Practitioner, 254(1729), 23–3.

10 Lynch, P. J., & Jaffe, C. C. (2020). *Ptsd brain*. Wikimedia. Retrieved November 3, 2022, from https://commons.wikimedia.org/wiki/File:PTSD_brain.svg. Original version licensed under Creative Commons Attribution 2.5 License 2006

11 Donegan, N. H., Sanislow, C. A., Blumberg, H. P., Fulbright, R. K., Lacadie, C., Skudlarski, P., Gore, J. C., Olson, I. R., McGlashan, T. H., & Wexler, B. E. (2003). Amygdala hyperreactivity in borderline personality disorder: Implications for

emotional dysregulation. *Biological Psychiatry*, *54*(11), 1284–1293. https://doi.org/10.1016/s0006-3223(03)00636-x

12 Hazlett, E. A., Zhang, J., New, A. S., Zelmanova, Y., Goldstein, K. E., Haznedar, M. M., Meyerson, D., Goodman, M., Siever, L. J., & Chu, K.-W. (2012). Potentiated amygdala response to repeated emotional pictures in borderline personality disorder. *Biological Psychiatry*, *72*(6), 448–456. https://doi.org/10.1016/j.biopsych.2012.03.027

13 Herpertz, S. C., Dietrich, T. M., Wenning, B., Krings, T., Erberich, S. G., Willmes, K., Thron, A., & Sass, H. (2001). Evidence of abnormal amygdala functioning in borderline personality disorder: A functional MRI study. *Biological Psychiatry*, *50*(4), 292–298. https://doi.org/10.1016/s0006-3223(01)01075-7

14 Whittle, S., Chanen, A. M., Fornito, A., McGorry, P. D., Pantelis, C., & Yücel, M. (2009). Anterior cingulate volume in adolescents with first-presentation borderline personality disorder. *Psychiatry Research: Neuroimaging*, *172*(2), 155–160. https://doi.org/10.1016/j.pscychresns.2008.12.004

15 Lei, X., Zhong, M., Zhang, B., Yang, H., Peng, W., Liu, Q., Zhang, Y., Yao, S., Tan, C., & Yi, J. (2019). Structural and functional connectivity of the anterior cingulate cortex in patients with borderline personality disorder. *Frontiers in Neuroscience*, *13*. https://doi.org/10.3389/fnins.2019.00971

16 Koenigsberg, H. W., Siever, L. J., Lee, H., Pizzarello, S., New, A. S., Goodman, M., Cheng, H., Flory, J., & Prohovnik, I. (2009). Neural correlates of emotion processing in borderline personality disorder. *Psychiatry Research: Neuroimaging*, *172*(3), 192–199. https://doi.org/10.1016/j.pscychresns.2008.07.010

17 Schulze, L., Schmahl, C., & Niedtfeld, I. (2016). Neural correlates of disturbed emotion processing in borderline personality disorder: A multimodal meta-analysis. *Biological Psychiatry*, *79*(2), 97–106. https://doi.org/10.1016/j.biopsych.2015.03.027

18 Linehan, M. (2015). *DBT Skills Training Manual*. The Guilford Press.

19 Carey, B. (2011, June 23). *Expert on mental illness reveals her own fight*. The New York Times. Retrieved August 1, 2022, from https://www.nytimes.com/2011/06/23/health/23lives.html

20 Lee, A. (2020, April 7). *Why change is hard . . . and good*. Ideas & Insights. Retrieved February 1, 2023, from https://www8.gsb.columbia.edu/articles/ideas-work/why-change-hard-and-good

21 Keng, S.-L., Smoski, M. J., & Robins, C. J. (2011). Effects of mindfulness on psychological health: A review of empirical studies. *Clinical Psychology Review*, *31*(6), 1041–1056. https://doi.org/10.1016/j.cpr.2011.04.006

22 Gu, J., Strauss, C., Bond, R., & Cavanagh, K. (2015). How do mindfulness-based cognitive therapy and mindfulness-based Stress Reduction Improve Mental Health and wellbeing? A systematic review and meta-analysis of Mediation Studies. *Clinical Psychology Review, 37*, 1–12. https://doi.org/10.1016/j.cpr.2015.01.006

23 Goldberg, S. B., Tucker, R. P., Greene, P. A., Davidson, R. J., Wampold, B. E., Kearney, D. J., & Simpson, T. L. (2018). Mindfulness-based interventions for psychiatric disorders: A systematic review and meta-analysis. *Clinical Psychology Review, 59*, 52–60. https://doi.org/10.1016/j.cpr.2017.10.011

24 Khoury, B., Sharma, M., Rush, S. E., & Fournier, C. (2015). Mindfulness-based stress reduction for healthy individuals: A meta-analysis. *Journal of Psychosomatic Research, 78*(6), 519–528. https://doi.org/10.1016/j.jpsychores.2015.03.009

25 Garland, E. L., Farb, N. A., R. Goldin, P., & Fredrickson, B. L. (2015). Mindfulness broadens awareness and builds eudaimonic meaning: A process model of mindful positive emotion regulation. *Psychological Inquiry, 26*(4), 293–314. https://doi.org/10.1080/1047840x.2015.1064294

26 Jung, N., Wranke, C., Hamburger, K., & Knauff, M. (2014). How emotions affect logical reasoning: Evidence from experiments with mood-manipulated participants, Spider Phobics, and people with exam anxiety. *Frontiers in Psychology, 5*. https://doi.org/10.3389/fpsyg.2014.00570

27 Achor, S. (2018). *The happiness advantage: How a positive brain fuels success in work and life*. Currency.

28 P., S. M. E. (2006). *Learned optimism how to change your mind and your life; with a new preface*. Vintage Books.

29 Mineo, L. (2018, November 26). *Good genes are nice, but joy is better*. Harvard Gazette. Retrieved February 1, 2023, from https://news.harvard.edu/gazette/story/2017/04/over-nearly-80-years-harvard-study-has-been-showing-how-to-live-a-healthy-and-happy-life/

30 Linehan, M. M. (1993). Naturalistic follow-up of a behavioral treatment for chronically parasuicidal borderline patients. *Archives of General Psychiatry, 50*(12), 971. https://doi.org/10.1001/archpsyc.1993.01820240055007

31 Koons, C. R., Robins, C. J., Lindsey Tweed, J., Lynch, T. R., Gonzalez, A. M., Morse, J. Q., Bishop, G. K., Butterfield, M. I., & Bastian, L. A. (2001). Efficacy of dialectical behavior therapy in women veterans with borderline personality disorder. *Behavior Therapy, 32*(2), 371–390. https://doi.org/10.1016/s0005-7894(01)80009-5

32 Verheul, R., Van Den Bosch, L. M., Koeter, M. W., De Ridder, M. A., Stijnen, T., & Van Den Brink, W. (2003). Dialectical behaviour therapy for women with borderline

personality disorder. *British Journal of Psychiatry, 182*(2), 135–140. https://doi.org/10.1192/bjp.182.2.135

33 Stiglmayr, C., Stecher-Mohr, J., Wagner, T., Meißner, J., Spretz, D., Steffens, C., Roepke, S., Fydrich, T., Salbach-Andrae, H., Schulze, J., & Renneberg, B. (2014). Effectiveness of dialectic behavioral therapy in routine outpatient care: The Berlin Borderline Study. *Borderline Personality Disorder and Emotion Dysregulation, 1*(1), 20. https://doi.org/10.1186/2051-6673-1-20

34 Weir, K. (2011, December). *The exercise effect.* Monitor on Psychology. Retrieved February 1, 2023, from https://www.apa.org/monitor/2011/12/exercise

35 Moll, J., Krueger, F., Zahn, R., Pardini, M., de Oliveira-Souza, R., & Grafman, J. (2006). Human fronto–mesolimbic networks guide decisions about charitable donation. *Proceedings of the National Academy of Sciences, 103*(42), 15623–15628. https://doi.org/10.1073/pnas.0604475103

36 Pally, R., & Olds, D. (2018). Emotional processing: The mind-body connection. *The Mind-Brain Relationship,* 73–104. https://doi.org/10.4324/9780429482465-4

37 *Healthy Eating Plate.* The Nutrition Source. (2023, January 31). Retrieved February 1, 2023, from https://www.hsph.harvard.edu/nutritionsource/healthy-eating-plate/

38 Watson, N. F., Badr, M. S., Belenky, G., Bliwise, D. L., Buxton, O. M., Buysse, D., Dinges, D. F., Gangwisch, J., Grandner, M. A., Kushida, C., Malhotra, R. K., Martin, J. L., Patel, S. R., Quan, S., & Tasali, E. (2015). Recommended amount of sleep for a healthy adult: A joint consensus statement of the American Academy of Sleep Medicine and Sleep Research Society. *SLEEP.* https://doi.org/10.5665/sleep.4716

39 Motomura, Y., & Mishima, K. (2014). *Brain and nerve = Shinkei kenkyu no shinpo, 66*(1), 15–23.

40 Palmer, C. A., & Alfano, C. A. (2017). Sleep and emotion regulation: An organizing, Integrative Review. Sleep Medicine Reviews, 31, 6–16. https://doi.org/10.1016/j.smrv.2015.12.006

41 Chen, K. C., Yang, C. H., Li, T. T., Zouboulis, C. C., & Huang, Y. C. (2019). Suppression of *propionibacterium acnes* -stimulated proinflammatory cytokines by Chinese bayberry extracts and its active constituent myricetin in human sebocytes *in vitro.* *Phytotherapy Research, 33*(4), 1104–1113. https://doi.org/10.1002/ptr.6304

42 Salanitro, M., Wrigley, T., Ghabra, H., de Haan, E., Hill, C. M., Solmi, M., & Cortese, S. (2022). Efficacy on sleep parameters and tolerability of melatonin in individuals with sleep or mental disorders: A systematic review and meta-analysis. *Neuroscience & Biobehavioral Reviews, 139,* 104723. https://doi.org/10.1016/j.neubiorev.2022.104723

43 Wang, K., Yang, Y., Zhang, T., Ouyang, Y., Liu, B., & Luo, J. (2020). The relationship between physical activity and emotional intelligence in college students: The mediating role of self-efficacy. *Frontiers in Psychology, 11*. https://doi.org/10.3389/fpsyg.2020.00967

44 Li, J., Huang, Z., Si, W., & Shao, T. (2022). The effects of physical activity on positive emotions in children and adolescents: A systematic review and meta-analysis. *International Journal of Environmental Research and Public Health, 19*(21), 14185. https://doi.org/10.3390/ijerph192114185

45 Jeannerod, M., & Frak, V. (1999). Mental imaging of motor activity in humans. *Current Opinion in Neurobiology, 9*(6), 735–739. https://doi.org/10.1016/s0959-4388(99)00038-0

46 Lee, M.-sun, Lee, J., Park, B.-J., & Miyazaki, Y. (2015). Interaction with indoor plants may reduce psychological and physiological stress by suppressing autonomic nervous system activity in young adults: A randomized crossover study. *Journal of Physiological Anthropology, 34*(1). https://doi.org/10.1186/s40101-015-0060-8

47 Shibata, S., & Suzuki, S. (2001). Effects of indoor foliage plants on subjects' recovery from mental fatigue. *North American Journal of Psychology, 3*(3), 385–396.

48 Carnegie, D. (2021). *How to Win Friends and Influence People*. Farsight Publishers and Distributors.

49 Colle, L., Hilviu, D., Rossi, R., Garbarini, F., & Fossataro, C. (2020). Self-harming and sense of agency in patients with borderline personality disorder. *Frontiers in Psychiatry, 11*. https://doi.org/10.3389/fpsyt.2020.00449

50 Oumaya, M., Friedman, S., Pham, A., Abou Abdallah, T., Guelfi, J.-D., & Rouillon, F. (2008). Personnalité Borderline, Automutilations et suicide : Revue de la Littérature. *L'Encéphale, 34*(5), 452–458. https://doi.org/10.1016/j.encep.2007.10.007 English: https://pubmed.ncbi.nlm.nih.gov/19068333/

51 Zanarini, M. C., Vujanovic, A. A., Parachini, E. A., Boulanger, J. L., Frankenburg, F. R., & Hennen, J. (2003). A screening measure for BPD: The McLean Screening Instrument for borderline personality disorder (MSI-BPD). *Journal of Personality Disorders, 17*(6), 568–573. https://doi.org/10.1521/pedi.17.6.568.25355

52 Zimmerman, M., & Balling, C. (2021). Screening for borderline personality disorder with the McLean Screening Instrument: A review and critique of the literature. *Journal of Personality Disorders, 35*(2), 288–298. https://doi.org/10.1521/pedi_2019_33_451

53 Newson , J. J., Pastukh , V., Sukhoi , O., Taylor , J., & Thiagarajan , T. C. (2021, May 18). Mental Health Has Bigger Challenges Than Stigma. Sapien Labs. Download: https://sapienlabs.org/wp-content/uploads/2021/06/Rapid-Report-2021-Help-Seeking.pdf

54 Wikimedia Foundation. (2022, October 31). *September 11 attacks*. Wikipedia. Retrieved November 1, 2022, from https://en.wikipedia.org/wiki/September_11_attacks

55 Peterson, S. (2018, October 22). *Secondary traumatic stress*. The National Child Traumatic Stress Network. Retrieved November 1, 2022, from https://www.nctsn.org/trauma-informed-care/secondary-traumatic-stress

56 Schlenger, W. E., Caddell, J. M., Ebert, L., Jordan, B. K., Rourke, K. M., Wilson, D., Thalji, L., Dennis, J. M., Fairbank, J. A., & Kulka, R. A. (2002). Psychological reactions to terrorist attacks. *JAMA, 288*(5), 581. https://doi.org/10.1001/jama.288.5.581

57 Jiang, T., Webster, J. L., Robinson, A., Kassam-Adams, N., & Richmond, T. S. (2018). Emotional responses to unintentional and intentional traumatic injuries among urban black men: A qualitative study. *Injury, 49*(5), 983–989. https://doi.org/10.1016/j.injury.2017.12.002

58 Roer, G. E., Solbakken, H. H., Abebe, D. S., Aaseth, J. O., Bolstad, I., & Lien, L. (2021). Inpatients experiences about the impact of traumatic stress on eating behaviors: An exploratory focus group study. *Journal of Eating Disorders, 9*(1). https://doi.org/10.1186/s40337-021-00480-y

59 Maher, M. J., Rego, S. A., & Asnis, G. M. (2006). Sleep disturbances in patients with post-traumatic stress disorder. *CNS Drugs, 20*(7), 567–590. https://doi.org/10.2165/00023210-200620070-00003

60 Babson, K. A., & Feldner, M. T. (2010). Temporal relations between sleep problems and both traumatic event exposure and PTSD: A critical review of the empirical literature. *Journal of Anxiety Disorders, 24*(1), 1–15. https://doi.org/10.1016/j.janxdis.2009.08.002

61 Lien, C., Rosen, T., Bloemen, E. M., Abrams, R. C., Pavlou, M., & Lachs, M. S. (2016). Narratives of self-neglect: Patterns of traumatic personal experiences and maladaptive behaviors in cognitively intact older adults. *Journal of the American Geriatrics Society, 64*(11). https://doi.org/10.1111/jgs.14524

62 Dijkstra, M. T., & Homan, A. C. (2016). Engaging in rather than disengaging from stress: Effective coping and perceived control. *Frontiers in Psychology, 7*. https://doi.org/10.3389/fpsyg.2016.01415

63 American Psychological Association. (n.d.). *Cognitive behavioral therapy (CBT) for treatment of PTSD*. American Psychological Association. Retrieved November 1, 2022, from https://www.apa.org/ptsd-guideline/treatments/cognitive-behavioral-therapy

64 Shapiro, F., & Laliotis, D. (2010). EMDR and the Adaptive Information Processing Model: Integrative Treatment and Case Conceptualization. *Clinical Social Work Journal, 39*(2), 191–200. https://doi.org/10.1007/s10615-010-0300-7

65 *Va.gov: Veterans Affairs*. How Common is PTSD in Adults? (2018, September 13). Retrieved November 3, 2022, from https://www.ptsd.va.gov/understand/common/common_adults.asp

66 *Worldwide prevalence of PTSD*. NeuRA Library. (2021, October 27). Retrieved November 3, 2022, from https://library.neura.edu.au/ptsd-library/epidemiology-ptsd-library/prevalence-epidemiology-ptsd-library/worldwide-prevalence/

67 Grasso, D., Boonsiri, J., Lipschitz, D., Guyer, A., Houshyar, S., Douglas-Palumberi, H., Massey, J., & Kaufman, J. (2009). Posttraumatic stress disorder: the missed diagnosis. *Child welfare, 88*(4), 157–176.

68 Riddle, J. (2018, November 25). *PTSD symptoms in women: Unnoticed and undiagnosed - psycom*. PSYCOM. Retrieved November 3, 2022, from https://www.psycom.net/PTSD-symptoms-women

69 Gagnon-Sanschagrin, P., Schein, J., Urganus, A., Serra, E., Liang, Y., Musingarimi, P., Cloutier, M., Guérin, A., & Davis, L. L. (2022). Identifying individuals with undiagnosed post-traumatic stress disorder in a large United States civilian population – A machine learning approach. *BMC Psychiatry, 22*(1). https://doi.org/10.1186/s12888-022-04267-6

70 Sherin, J. E., & Nemeroff, C. B. (2011). Post-traumatic stress disorder: The neurobiological impact of psychological trauma. *Dialogues in Clinical Neuroscience, 13*(3), 263–278. https://doi.org/10.31887/dcns.2011.13.2/jsherin

71 Lynch, P. J., & Jaffe, C. C. (2020). *Ptsd brain*. Wikimedia. Retrieved November 3, 2022, from https://commons.wikimedia.org/wiki/File:PTSD_brain.svg. Original version licensed under Creative Commons Attribution 2.5 License 2006

72 Zotev, V., Phillips, R., Misaki, M., Wong, C. K., Wurfel, B. E., Krueger, F., Feldner, M., & Bodurka, J. (2018). Real-time fmri neurofeedback training of the amygdala activity with simultaneous EEG in veterans with combat-related PTSD. *NeuroImage: Clinical, 19*, 106–121. https://doi.org/10.1016/j.nicl.2018.04.010

73 Akiki, T. J., Averill, C. L., Wrocklage, K. M., Schweinsburg, B., Scott, J. C., Martini, B., Averill, L. A., Southwick, S. M., Krystal, J. H., & Abdallah, C. G. (2017). The

Association of PTSD symptom severity with localized hippocampus and amygdala abnormalities. *Chronic Stress, 1*, 247054701772406. https://doi.org/10.1177/2470547017724069

74 Arnsten, A. F. T., Raskind, M. A., Taylor, F. B., & Connor, D. F. (2015). The effects of stress exposure on prefrontal cortex: Translating basic research into successful treatments for post-traumatic stress disorder. *Neurobiology of Stress, 1*, 89–99. https://doi.org/10.1016/j.ynstr.2014.10.002

75 MediLexicon International. (n.d.). *Gaslighting: What it is, long-term effects, and what to do*. Medical News Today. Retrieved November 3, 2022, from https://www.medicalnewstoday.com/articles/long-term-effects-of-gaslighting

76 Bontempo, A. C. (2022). The effect of personalized invalidation of symptoms by healthcare providers on patient depression: The mediating role of self-esteem. *Patient Education and Counseling, 105*(6), 1598–1605. https://doi.org/10.1016/j.pec.2021.09.034

77 Mushtaq, R. (2014). Relationship between loneliness, psychiatric disorders and physical health ? A review on the psychological aspects of loneliness. *JOURNAL OF CLINICAL AND DIAGNOSTIC RESEARCH*. https://doi.org/10.7860/jcdr/2014/10077.4828

78 Lee, S. L., Pearce, E., Ajnakina, O., Johnson, S., Lewis, G., Mann, F., Pitman, A., Solmi, F., Sommerlad, A., Steptoe, A., Tymoszuk, U., & Lewis, G. (2021). The association between loneliness and depressive symptoms among adults aged 50 years and older: A 12-year population-based Cohort Study. *The Lancet Psychiatry, 8*(1), 48–57. https://doi.org/10.1016/s2215-0366(20)30383-7

79 Steen, O. D., Ori, A. P., Wardenaar, K. J., & van Loo, H. M. (2022). Loneliness Associates strongly with anxiety and depression during the COVID pandemic, especially in men and younger adults. *Scientific Reports, 12*(1). https://doi.org/10.1038/s41598-022-13049-9

80 Sareen, J. (2014). Posttraumatic stress disorder in adults: Impact, comorbidity, risk factors, and treatment. *The Canadian Journal of Psychiatry, 59*(9), 460–467. https://doi.org/10.1177/070674371405900902

81 Fox, V., Dalman, C., Dal, H., Hollander, A.-C., Kirkbride, J. B., & Pitman, A. (2021). Suicide risk in people with post-traumatic stress disorder: A cohort study of 3.1 million people in Sweden. *Journal of Affective Disorders, 279*, 609–616. https://doi.org/10.1016/j.jad.2020.10.009

82 Hori, H., & Kim, Y. (2019). Inflammation and post-traumatic stress disorder. *Psychiatry and Clinical Neurosciences, 73*(4), 143–153. https://doi.org/10.1111/pcn.12820

83 Linehan, M. (2015). *DBT skills training manual*. The Guilford Press.

84 Carey, B. (2011, June 23). *Expert on mental illness reveals her own fight*. The New York Times. Retrieved August 1, 2022, from https://www.nytimes.com/2011/06/23/health/23lives.html

85 Linehan, M. M. (2015). *DBT Skills Training Manual*. The Guilford Press.

86 Maddux, W. W., Adam, H., & Galinsky, A. D. (2010). When in Rome … learn why the Romans do what they do: How multicultural learning experiences facilitate creativity. *Personality and Social Psychology Bulletin, 36*(6), 731–741. https://doi.org/10.1177/0146167210367786

87 Ratner, P. (2022, April 19). *Want happiness? Buy experiences, not things, says a Cornell psychologist*. Big Think. Retrieved November 3, 2022, from https://bigthink.com/neuropsych/want-happiness-buy-experiences-not-more-stuff/

88 Franke, H. (2014). Toxic stress: Effects, prevention and treatment. *Children, 1*(3), 390–402. https://doi.org/10.3390/children1030390

89 Wiebe, J. (2021, May 3). *The good stress: How eustress helps you grow*. Talkspace. Retrieved November 3, 2022, from https://www.talkspace.com/blog/eustress-definition-good-stress/

90 American Psychological Association. (n.d.). *APA Dictionary of Psychology*. American Psychological Association. Retrieved November 2, 2022, from https://dictionary.apa.org/emotion

91 Levine, G. N., Cohen, B. E., Commodore-Mensah, Y., Fleury, J., Huffman, J. C., Khalid, U., Labarthe, D. R., Lavretsky, H., Michos, E. D., Spatz, E. S., & Kubzansky, L. D. (2021). Psychological health, well-being, and the mind-heart-body connection: A scientific statement from the American Heart Association. *Circulation, 143*(10). https://doi.org/10.1161/cir.0000000000000947

92 Sawhney, V. (2021, August 6). *Weirdly true: We are what we eat*. Harvard Business Review. Retrieved November 3, 2022, from https://hbr.org/2021/08/weirdly-true-we-are-what-we-eat

93 Fox, N. (2022, February 1). *The many health risks of Processed Foods*. LHSFNA. Retrieved November 3, 2022, from https://www.lhsfna.org/the-many-health-risks-of-processed-foods

94 Hecht, E. M., Rabil, A., Martinez Steele, E., Abrams, G. A., Ware, D., Landy, D. C., & Hennekens, C. H. (2022). Cross-sectional examination of ultra-processed food consumption and adverse mental health symptoms. *Public Health Nutrition, 25*(11), 3225–3234. https://doi.org/10.1017/s1368980022001586

95 Zinczenko, D. (2019). *Eat This Not That!: The best (& the worst) foods in America*. Ballantine Books.

96 Maltz, M. (1960). *Psycho-Cybernetics* (First). Simon & Schuster.

97 Watson, N. F., Badr, M. S., Belenky, G., Bliwise, D. L., Buxton, O. M., Buysse, D., Dinges, D. F., Gangwisch, J., Grandner, M. A., Kushida, C., Malhotra, R. K., Martin, J. L., Patel, S. R., Quan, S., & Tasali, E. (2015). Recommended amount of sleep for a healthy adult: A joint consensus statement of the American Academy of Sleep Medicine and Sleep Research Society. *SLEEP*. https://doi.org/10.5665/sleep.4716

98 Almondes, K. M., Marín Agudelo, H. A., & Jiménez-Correa, U. (2021). Impact of sleep deprivation on emotional regulation and the immune system of healthcare workers as a risk factor for covid 19: Practical recommendations from a task force of the Latin American Association of Sleep Psychology. *Frontiers in Psychology, 12*. https://doi.org/10.3389/fpsyg.2021.564227

99 World Health Organization. (n.d.). *Physical activity*. World Health Organization. Retrieved November 18, 2022, from https://www.who.int/news-room/fact-sheets/detail/physical-activity

100 Umberson, D., & Karas Montez, J. (2010). Social Relationships and Health: A flashpoint for health policy. *Journal of Health and Social Behavior, 51*(1_suppl). https://doi.org/10.1177/0022146510383501

101 Tough, H., Siegrist, J., & Fekete, C. (2017). Social Relationships, mental health and wellbeing in physical disability: A systematic review. *BMC Public Health, 17*(1). https://doi.org/10.1186/s12889-017-4308-6

102 Pagura, J., Stein, M. B., Bolton, J. M., Cox, B. J., Grant, B., & Sareen, J. (2010). Comorbidity of borderline personality disorder and posttraumatic stress disorder in

the U.S. population. *Journal of Psychiatric Research, 44*(16), 1190–1198. https://doi.org/10.1016/j.jpsychires.2010.04.016

103 Frías, Á., & Palma, C. (2014). Comorbidity between post-traumatic stress disorder and borderline personality disorder: A Review. *Psychopathology, 48*(1), 1–10. https://doi.org/10.1159/000363145

104 Steil, R., Dyer, A., Priebe, K., Kleindienst, N., & Bohus, M. (2011). Dialectical behavior therapy for posttraumatic stress disorder related to childhood sexual abuse: A pilot study of an intensive residential treatment program. *Journal of Traumatic Stress, 24*(1), 102–106. https://doi.org/10.1002/jts.20617

105 Bohus, M., Dyer, A. S., Priebe, K., Krüger, A., Kleindienst, N., Schmahl, C., Niedtfeld, I., & Steil, R. (2013). Dialectical behaviour therapy for post-traumatic stress disorder after childhood sexual abuse in patients with and without borderline personality disorder: A randomised controlled trial. *Psychotherapy and Psychosomatics, 82*(4), 221–233. https://doi.org/10.1159/000348451

106 Harned, M. S., Korslund, K. E., & Linehan, M. M. (2014). A pilot randomized controlled trial of dialectical behavior therapy with and without the dialectical behavior therapy prolonged exposure protocol for suicidal and self-injuring women with borderline personality disorder and PTSD. *Behaviour Research and Therapy, 55*, 7–17. https://doi.org/10.1016/j.brat.2014.01.008

107 Bohus, M., Kleindienst, N., Hahn, C., Müller-Engelmann, M., Ludäscher, P., Steil, R., Fydrich, T., Kuehner, C., Resick, P. A., Stiglmayr, C., Schmahl, C., & Priebe, K. (2020). Dialectical behavior therapy for posttraumatic stress disorder (DBT-PTSD) compared with Cognitive Processing Therapy (CPT) in complex presentations of PTSD in women survivors of childhood abuse. *JAMA Psychiatry, 77*(12), 1235. https://doi.org/10.1001/jamapsychiatry.2020.2148

108 Cronkite, R. C., Moos, R. H., Beckman, E. E., & Leber, W. R. (1995). Handbook of depression.

109 Grant, D. M. M., Wingate, L. R. R., Rasmussen, K. A., Davidson, C. L., Slish, M. L., Rhoades-Kerswill, S., Mills, A. C., & Judah, M. R. (2013). An examination of the reciprocal relationship between avoidance coping and symptoms of anxiety and depression. *Journal of Social and Clinical Psychology, 32*(8), 878–896. https://doi.org/10.1521/jscp.2013.32.8.878

110 Elliot, A. J., Thrash, T. M., & Murayama, K. (2011). A longitudinal analysis of self-regulation and well-being: Avoidance personal goals, avoidance coping, stress generation, and subjective well-being. *Journal of Personality, 79*(3), 643–674. https://doi.org/10.1111/j.1467-6494.2011.00694.x

111 Penley, J. A., Tomaka, J., & Wiebe, J. S. (2002). *Journal of Behavioral Medicine, 25*(6), 551–603. https://doi.org/10.1023/a:1020641400589

112 Jung, N., Wranke, C., Hamburger, K., & Knauff, M. (2014). How emotions affect logical reasoning: Evidence from experiments with mood-manipulated participants, Spider Phobics, and people with exam anxiety. *Frontiers in Psychology, 5*. https://doi.org/10.3389/fpsyg.2014.00570

113 Kyriakoulis, P., Kyrios, M., Nardi, A. E., Freire, R. C., & Schier, M. (2021). The implications of the diving response in reducing panic symptoms. *Frontiers in Psychiatry, 12*. https://doi.org/10.3389/fpsyt.2021.784884

114 Dossey, L. (2018). The Helper's High. *EXPLORE, 14*(6), 393–399. https://doi.org/10.1016/j.explore.2018.10.003

115 Pally, R., & Olds, D. (2018). Emotional processing: The mind-body connection. *The Mind-Brain Relationship*, 73–104. https://doi.org/10.4324/9780429482465-4

116 Brooks, H. L., Rushton, K., Lovell, K., Bee, P., Walker, L., Grant, L., & Rogers, A. (2018). The power of support from companion animals for people living with mental health problems: A systematic review and narrative synthesis of the evidence. *BMC Psychiatry, 18*(1). https://doi.org/10.1186/s12888-018-1613-2

117 Grajfoner, D., Ke, G. N., & Wong, R. M. (2021). The effect of pets on human mental health and wellbeing during COVID-19 lockdown in Malaysia. *Animals, 11*(9), 2689. https://doi.org/10.3390/ani11092689

118 Lunsford-Avery, J. R., Engelhard, M. M., Navar, A. M., & Kollins, S. H. (2018). Validation of the sleep regularity index in older adults and associations with cardiometabolic risk. *Scientific Reports, 8*(1). https://doi.org/10.1038/s41598-018-32402-5

119 *Blue Light has a dark side*. Harvard Health. (2020, July 7). Retrieved November 3, 2022, from https://www.health.harvard.edu/staying-healthy/blue-light-has-a-dark-side

120 Matsakis, A. (1994). *Post-traumatic stress disorder: A complete treatment guide.* (L. Tilley, Ed.). New Harbinger.

121 Lillehei, A. S., Halcón, L. L., Savik, K., & Reis, R. (2015). Effect of inhaled lavender and sleep hygiene on self-reported sleep issues: A randomized controlled trial. *The Journal of Alternative and Complementary Medicine, 21*(7), 430–438. https://doi.org/10.1089/acm.2014.0327

122 American Psychiatric Association Publishing. (2022). *Diagnostic and statistical manual of mental disorders, fifth edition text revision: Dsm-5-Tr.*

123 Firth, J., Gangwisch, J. E., Borsini, A., Wootton, R. E., & Mayer, E. A. (2020). Food and mood: How do diet and nutrition affect mental wellbeing? *BMJ*, m2382. https://doi.org/10.1136/bmj.m2382

124 ElBarazi, A., & Tikamdas, R. (2023). Association between university student junk food consumption and mental health. *Nutrition and Health*, 026010602311514. https://doi.org/10.1177/02601060231151480

125 Wang, Q.-P., Lin, Y. Q., Zhang, L., Wilson, Y. A., Oyston, L. J., Cotterell, J., Qi, Y., Khuong, T. M., Bakhshi, N., Planchenault, Y., Browman, D. T., Lau, M. T., Cole, T. A., Wong, A. C. N., Simpson, S. J., Cole, A. R., Penninger, J. M., Herzog, H., & Neely, G. G. (2016). Sucralose promotes food intake through NPY and a neuronal fasting response. *Cell Metabolism, 24*(1), 75–90. https://doi.org/10.1016/j.cmet.2016.06.010

126 Herle, M., Fildes, A., & Llewellyn, C. H. (2018). Emotional eating is learned not inherited in children, regardless of obesity risk. *Pediatric Obesity, 13*(10), 628–631. https://doi.org/10.1111/ijpo.12428

127 Edwin Thanarajah, S., DiFeliceantonio, A. G., Albus, K., Kuzmanovic, B., Rigoux, L., Iglesias, S., Hanßen, R., Schlamann, M., Cornely, O. A., Brüning, J. C., Tittgemeyer, M., & Small, D. M. (2023). Habitual daily intake of a sweet and fatty snack modulates reward processing in humans. *Cell Metabolism, 35*(4). https://doi.org/10.1016/j.cmet.2023.02.015

128 Schnepper, R., Georgii, C., Eichin, K., Arend, A.-K., Wilhelm, F. H., Vögele, C., Lutz, A. P., van Dyck, Z., & Blechert, J. (2020). Fight, flight, – or grab a bite! trait emotional and restrained eating style predicts food cue responding under negative emotions. *Frontiers in Behavioral Neuroscience, 14*. https://doi.org/10.3389/fnbeh.2020.00091

129 Yin, H. H., & Knowlton, B. J. (2006). The role of the basal ganglia in habit formation. *Nature Reviews Neuroscience, 7*(6), 464–476. https://doi.org/10.1038/nrn1919

130 Carpio-Arias, T. V., Solís Manzano, A. M., Sandoval, V., Vinueza-Veloz, A. F., Rodríguez Betancourt, A., Betancourt Ortíz, S. L., & Vinueza-Veloz, M. F. (2022). Relationship

between perceived stress and emotional eating. A Cross Sectional Study. *Clinical Nutrition ESPEN*, *49*, 314–318. https://doi.org/10.1016/j.clnesp.2022.03.030

131 Shehata, W. M., & Abdeldaim, D. E. (2023). Emotional eating in relation to psychological stress during COVID-19 pandemic: A cross-sectional study in Faculty of Medicine, Tanta University, Egypt. *BMC Public Health*, *23*(1). https://doi.org/10.1186/s12889-023-15177-x

132 Zellner, D. A., Loaiza, S., Gonzalez, Z., Pita, J., Morales, J., Pecora, D., & Wolf, A. (2006). Food selection changes under stress. *Physiology & Behavior*, *87*(4), 789–793. https://doi.org/10.1016/j.physbeh.2006.01.014

133 Talbot, L. S., Maguen, S., Epel, E. S., Metzler, T. J., & Neylan, T. C. (2013). Posttraumatic stress disorder is associated with emotional eating. *Journal of Traumatic Stress*, *26*(4), 521–525. https://doi.org/10.1002/jts.21824

134 Schroeder, K., Schuler, B. R., Kobulsky, J. M., & Sarwer, D. B. (2021). The association between adverse childhood experiences and childhood obesity: A systematic review. *Obesity Reviews*, *22*(7). https://doi.org/10.1111/obr.13204

135 Hoare, P., & Cosgrove, L. (1998). Eating habits, body-esteem and self-esteem in Scottish children and adolescents. *Journal of Psychosomatic Research*, *45*(5), 425–431. https://doi.org/10.1016/s0022-3999(98)00025-7

136 Izydorczyk, B., Sitnik-Warchulska, K., Lizińczyk, S., & Lipiarz, A. (2019). Psychological predictors of unhealthy eating attitudes in young adults. *Frontiers in Psychology*, *10*. https://doi.org/10.3389/fpsyg.2019.00590

137 Werneck, G. de, & De Oliveira, D. R. (2021). Autoestima e Estereótipos do Comer Emocional. *Revista Psicologia e Saúde*, 117–130. https://doi.org/10.20435/pssa.v13i3.1157

138 Goossens, L., Braet, C., Van Vlierberghe, L., & Mels, S. (2009). Loss of control over eating in overweight youngsters: The role of anxiety, depression and emotional eating. *European Eating Disorders Review*, *17*(1), 68–78. https://doi.org/10.1002/erv.892

139 Konttinen, H., van Strien, T., Männistö, S., Jousilahti, P., & Haukkala, A. (2019). Depression, emotional eating and long-term weight changes: A population-based prospective study. *International Journal of Behavioral Nutrition and Physical Activity*, *16*(1). https://doi.org/10.1186/s12966-019-0791-8

140 Burnatowska, E., Surma, S., & Olszanecka-Glinianowicz, M. (2022). Relationship between mental health and emotional eating during the covid-19 pandemic: A systematic review. *Nutrients*, *14*(19), 3989. https://doi.org/10.3390/nu14193989

141 Moynihan, A. B., Tilburg, W. A., Igou, E. R., Wisman, A., Donnelly, A. E., & Mulcaire, J. B. (2015). Eaten up by boredom: Consuming food to escape awareness of the bored self. *Frontiers in Psychology, 6*. https://doi.org/10.3389/fpsyg.2015.00369

142 Ahlich, E., & Rancourt, D. (2022). Boredom proneness, interoception, and emotional eating. *Appetite, 178*, 106167. https://doi.org/10.1016/j.appet.2022.106167

143 Higgs, S., & Thomas, J. (2016). Social influences on eating. *Current Opinion in Behavioral Sciences, 9*, 1–6. https://doi.org/10.1016/j.cobeha.2015.10.005

144 Nilsson, F. (2022, June 20). *Emotional eating: How culture, generation and Emotion Drive Food Purchase Decisions, 91% of Aussies have more intense food category view post-covid, big opportunities for FMCG brands: Mi3*. Welcome to Mi3. Retrieved April 1, 2023, from https://www.mi-3.com.au/20-06-2022/emotional-eating-how-culture-generation-and-emotion-drive-food-purchase-decisions-91

145 Ilyuk, V., Block, L., & Haws, K. L. (2019). Justifying by "healthifying": When expected satisfaction from consumption closure increases the desire to eat more and biases health perceptions of unhealthy leftovers. *Appetite, 133*, 138–146. https://doi.org/10.1016/j.appet.2018.10.030

146 Bresch, A., Rullmann, M., Luthardt, J., Becker, G. A., Patt, M., Ding, Y.-S., Hilbert, A., Sabri, O., & Hesse, S. (2017). Hunger and disinhibition but not cognitive restraint are associated with central norepinephrine transporter availability. *Appetite, 117*, 270–274. https://doi.org/10.1016/j.appet.2017.06.020

147 Betancourt-Núñez, A., Torres-Castillo, N., Martínez-López, E., De Loera-Rodríguez, C. O., Durán-Barajas, E., Márquez-Sandoval, F., Bernal-Orozco, M. F., Garaulet, M., & Vizmanos, B. (2022). Emotional eating and dietary patterns: Reflecting food choices in people with and without abdominal obesity. *Nutrients, 14*(7), 1371. https://doi.org/10.3390/nu14071371

148 Javaras, K. N., Laird, N. M., Reichborn-Kjennerud, T., Bulik, C. M., Pope, H. G., & Hudson, J. I. (2008). Familiality and heritability of binge eating disorder: Results of a case-control family study and a twin study. *International Journal of Eating Disorders, 41*(2), 174–179. https://doi.org/10.1002/eat.20484

149 van Strien, T., Snoek, H. M., van der Zwaluw, C. S., & Engels, R. C. M. E. (2010). Parental control and the dopamine D2 receptor gene (DRD2) interaction on emotional eating in adolescence. *Appetite, 54*(2), 255–261. https://doi.org/10.1016/j.appet.2009.11.006

150 Kinney, J. W., Bemiller, S. M., Murtishaw, A. S., Leisgang, A. M., Salazar, A. M., & Lamb, B. T. (2018). Inflammation as a central mechanism in alzheimer's disease. *Alzheimer's & Dementia: Translational Research & Clinical Interventions, 4*(1), 575–590. https://doi.org/10.1016/j.trci.2018.06.014

151 Linehan, M. (2021). *Building a Life Worth Living: A Memoir*. Random House.

152 Roosen, M. A., Safer, D., Adler, S. N., Cebolla, A., & Strien, T. van. (2012, November 21). *Group dialectical behavior therapy adapted for obese emotional eaters; a pilot study*. Vrije Universiteit Amsterdam. Retrieved April 1, 2023, from https://research.vu.nl/en/publications/group-dialectical-behavior-therapy-adapted-for-obese-emotional-ea

153 Rahmani, M., Omidi, A., Asemi, Z., & Akbari, H. (2018). The effect of dialectical behaviour therapy on binge eating, difficulties in emotion regulation and BMI in overweight patients with binge-eating disorder: A randomized controlled trial. *Mental Health & Prevention, 9*, 13–18. https://doi.org/10.1016/j.mhp.2017.11.002

154 Brown, T. A., Wisniewski, L., & Anderson, L. K. (2020). Dialectical behavior therapy for eating disorders: State of the research and New Directions. *Eating Disorders, 28*(2), 97–100. https://doi.org/10.1080/10640266.2020.1728204

155 Lee, A. (2020, April 7). *Why change is hard ... and good*. Ideas & Insights. Retrieved February 1, 2023, from https://www8.gsb.columbia.edu/articles/ideas-work/why-change-hard-and-good

156 Olson, K. L. L., & Emery, C. F. (2015). Mindfulness and weight loss. *Psychosomatic Medicine, 77*(1), 59–67. https://doi.org/10.1097/psy.0000000000000127

157 Arch, J. J., Brown, K. W., Goodman, R. J., Della Porta, M. D., Kiken, L. G., & Tillman, S. (2016). Enjoying food without caloric cost: The impact of brief mindfulness on laboratory eating outcomes. *Behaviour Research and Therapy, 79*, 23–34. https://doi.org/10.1016/j.brat.2016.02.002

158 Zuraikat, F. M., Makarem, N., Liao, M., St-Onge, M. P., & Aggarwal, B. (2020). Measures of poor sleep quality are associated with higher energy intake and poor diet quality in a diverse sample of women from the Go Red for Women Strategically Focused Research Network. *Journal of the American Heart Association, 9*(4). https://doi.org/10.1161/jaha.119.014587

159 Järvelä-Reijonen, E., Järvinen, S., Karhunen, L., Föhr, T., Myllymäki, T., Sairanen, E., Lindroos, S., Peuhkuri, K., Hallikainen, M., Pihlajamäki, J., Puttonen, S., Korpela, R., Ermes, M., Lappalainen, R., Kujala, U. M., Kolehmainen, M., & Laitinen, J. (2021). Sleep-time physiological recovery is associated with eating habits in distressed working-age Finns with overweight: Secondary analysis of a randomised controlled trial. *Journal of Occupational Medicine and Toxicology, 16*(1). https://doi.org/10.1186/s12995-021-00310-6

160 Moore, S. (2021, December 7). Adapted from *What is 'mindful eating'?* NC Cooperative Extension News. Retrieved April 1, 2023, from https://stokes.ces.ncsu.edu/2021/12/what-is-mindful-eating/

161 Carpio-Arias, T. V., Solís Manzano, A. M., Sandoval, V., Vinueza-Veloz, A. F., Rodríguez Betancourt, A., Betancourt Ortíz, S. L., & Vinueza-Veloz, M. F. (2022). Relationship between perceived stress and emotional eating. A Cross Sectional Study. *Clinical Nutrition ESPEN, 49*, 314–318. https://doi.org/10.1016/j.clnesp.2022.03.030

162 Shehata, W. M., & Abdeldaim, D. E. (2023). Emotional eating in relation to psychological stress during COVID-19 pandemic: A cross-sectional study in Faculty of Medicine, Tanta University, Egypt. *BMC Public Health, 23*(1). https://doi.org/10.1186/s12889-023-15177-x

163 Bongers, P., Jansen, A., Havermans, R., Roefs, A., & Nederkoorn, C. (2013). Happy eating. the underestimated role of overeating in a positive mood. *Appetite, 67*, 74–80. https://doi.org/10.1016/j.appet.2013.03.017

164 Hamilton, D. (2021, July 26). *Use your body to change how you feel.* David R Hamilton PHD. Retrieved April 1, 2023, from https://drdavidhamilton.com/use-your-body-to-change-how-you-feel/ s

165 Oliver, G., Wardle, J., & Gibson, E. L. (2000). Stress and food choice: A laboratory study. *Psychosomatic Medicine, 62*(6), 853–865. https://doi.org/10.1097/00006842-200011000-00016

166 van Strien, T., Cebolla, A., Etchemendy, E., Gutiérrez-Maldonado, J., Ferrer-García, M., Botella, C., & Baños, R. (2013). Emotional eating and food intake after sadness and joy. *Appetite, 66*, 20–25. https://doi.org/10.1016/j.appet.2013.02.016

167 Achor, S. (2018). *The happiness advantage: How a positive brain fuels success in work and life.* Currency.

168 Pally, R., & Olds, D. (2018). Emotional processing: The mind-body connection. *The Mind-Brain Relationship*, 73–104. https://doi.org/10.4324/9780429482465-4

169 *Healthy Eating Plate.* The Nutrition Source. (2023, January 31). Retrieved February 1, 2023, from https://www.hsph.harvard.edu/nutritionsource/healthy-eating-plate/

170 López-Cepero, A., Frisard, C., Mabry, G., Spruill, T., Mattei, J., Austin, S. B., Lemon, S. C., & Rosal, M. C. (2022). Association between poor sleep quality and emotional eating in US latinx adults and the mediating role of negative emotions. *Behavioral Sleep Medicine, 21*(2), 162–171. https://doi.org/10.1080/15402002.2022.2060227

171 St-Onge, M.-P., Wolfe, S., Sy, M., Shechter, A., & Hirsch, J. (2013). Sleep restriction increases the neuronal response to unhealthy food in normal-weight individuals. *International Journal of Obesity, 38*(3), 411–416. https://doi.org/10.1038/ijo.2013.114

172 Greer, S. M., Goldstein, A. N., & Walker, M. P. (2013). The impact of sleep deprivation on food desire in the human brain. *Nature Communications, 4*(1). https://doi.org/10.1038/ncomms3259

173 Watson, N. F., Badr, M. S., Belenky, G., Bliwise, D. L., Buxton, O. M., Buysse, D., Dinges, D. F., Gangwisch, J., Grandner, M. A., Kushida, C., Malhotra, R. K., Martin, J. L., Patel, S. R., Quan, S., & Tasali, E. (2015). Recommended amount of sleep for a healthy adult: A joint consensus statement of the American Academy of Sleep Medicine and Sleep Research Society. *SLEEP*. https://doi.org/10.5665/sleep.4716

174 Christakis, N. A., & Fowler, J. H. (2007). The spread of obesity in a large social network over 32 years. *New England Journal of Medicine, 357*(4), 370–379. https://doi.org/10.1056/nejmsa066082

175 Armstrong, L. E., Ganio, M. S., Casa, D. J., Lee, E. C., McDermott, B. P., Klau, J. F., Jimenez, L., Le Bellego, L., Chevillotte, E., & Lieberman, H. R. (2012). Mild dehydration affects mood in healthy young women,. *The Journal of Nutrition, 142*(2), 382–388. https://doi.org/10.3945/jn.111.142000

176 Pross, N., Demazières, A., Girard, N., Barnouin, R., Metzger, D., Klein, A., Perrier, E., & Guelinckx, I. (2014). Effects of changes in water intake on mood of high and low drinkers. *PLoS ONE, 9*(4). https://doi.org/10.1371/journal.pone.0094754

177 *Dietary reference intakes for water, potassium, sodium, chloride, and sulfate dri*. (2005). National Academies Press.

178 Li, Y., Zhang, C., Li, S., & Zhang, D. (2020). Association between dietary protein intake and the risk of depressive symptoms in adults. *British Journal of Nutrition, 123*(11), 1290–1301. https://doi.org/10.1017/s0007114520000562

179 Gerber, M., Jakowski, S., Kellmann, M., Cody, R., Gygax, B., Ludyga, S., Müller, C., Ramseyer, S., & Beckmann, J. (2023). Macronutrient intake as a prospective predictor of depressive symptom severity: An exploratory study with Adolescent Elite Athletes. *Psychology of Sport and Exercise, 66*, 102387. https://doi.org/10.1016/j.psychsport.2023.102387

180 Jaret, P. (2022, November 22). *Daily Protein Requirements: Are You Getting Enough?*. WebMD. https://www.webmd.com/food-recipes/protein

181 Annesi, J. J., & Mareno, N. (2015). Indirect effects of exercise on emotional eating through psychological predictors of weight loss in women. *Appetite, 95*, 219–227. https://doi.org/10.1016/j.appet.2015.07.012

182 Smith, K. E., O'Connor, S. M., Mason, T. B., Wang, S., Dzubur, E., Crosby, R. D., Wonderlich, S. A., Salvy, S., Feda, D. M., & Roemmich, J. N. (2020). Associations between objective physical activity and emotional eating among adiposity-discordant

siblings using ecological momentary assessment and accelerometers. *Pediatric Obesity*, *16*(3). https://doi.org/10.1111/ijpo.12720

183 Okoye, A. (2023, March 10). *Benefits of working out before bed*. The Sleep Doctor. https://thesleepdoctor.com/exercise/benefits-of-exercise-for-sleep/

184 Raghunathan, R., & Chandrasekaran, D. (2020). The association between the attitude of food-waste-aversion and BMI: An exploration in India and the United States. *Journal of Consumer Psychology*, *31*(1), 81–90. https://doi.org/10.1002/jcpy.1168